3/8

14-
Ⓐ

The Music

Other Books by AMIRI BARAKA

The Autobiography of LeRoi Jones/Amiri Baraka
Black Music
Blues People: Negro Music in White America
Daggers and Javelins: Essays
Dutchman and the Slave: Two Plays
Home: Social Essays
The Motion of History and Other Plays
Selected Plays and Prose of Amiri Baraka/LeRoi Jones
Selected Poetry of Amiri Baraka/LeRoi Jones

by AMIRI BARAKA and
AMINA BARAKA

Confirmation: An Anthology of African-American Women

The
Music
Reflections on Jazz and Blues

AMIRI BARAKA (LeRoi Jones)
and AMINA BARAKA

WILLIAM MORROW and COMPANY, INC.
New York

Grateful acknowledgment is made for permission to use material as specified below:

From India Navigation Company, the right to reprint liner notes from the following albums: *Aboriginal Affairs* by Craig Harris; *Mystic Winds* and *Solo Album* by Jay Hoggard; *Flying Out* by Cecil McBee; *Circle of Destiny* by Dennis Moorman; *Pretty Music* by Bob Neloms; *The Outside Within* by Chico Freeman; all reprinted by kind permission of India Navigation Company, 177 Franklin Street, New York, New York 10013.

From the Berlin Jazz Festival magazine, which commissioned and first printed "The Phenomenon of Soul in African-American Music" in 1983, the article is reprinted by kind permission of JazzFest Berlin, Budapester Strasse 50, D-1000 Berlin 30, West Germany.

From Muse Records, the right to reprint liner notes from *Future's Gold* by Ricky Ford through the kind permission of Muse Records, 160 West 71st Street, New York, New York 10023.

The essay "Miles Davis: One of the Great MFer's" first appeared in a different version in *The New York Times,* Volume 134, Number 46442, on June 16, 1985, under the title "Miles Davis," registered in the United States Copyright Office under Number TX 1-598-992, and is used by permission of The New York Times Company.

The poem "reggae or not!" is reprinted from the edition by Contact II Publications, Box 451, Bowling Green, New York, New York 10004.

From Columbia Records, the right to reprint liner notes from *Woody Three!* by Woody Shaw granted by kind permission of Columbia Records.

From *The Village Voice,* the right to reprint the essay "Jazz Writing: Survival in the Eighties."

Library of Congress Cataloging-in-Publication Data

Baraka, Imamu Amiri, 1934–
    The music: reflections on jazz & blues.

    1. Afro-Americans—Music.   2. Afro-American
musicians.   3. Jazz music.   4. Blues (Songs, etc.)—
United States.   I. Baraka, Amina.   II. Title.
ML3556.B17   1987   781.7'296073   86-18164
ISBN 0-688-04388-7

Printed in the United States of America

First Edition

1 2 3 4 5 6 7 8 9 10

BOOK DESIGN BY ELLEN LOGUIDICE

*For Blues People
and for Kimako Baraka*

Contents

GRAPHICS
    Illustrations—Vincent D. Smith
    Photographs—Stephanie Myers

Introduction

This is a collection of recent work relating to African, mainly African-American, music. The poetry, essays, jazz drama included here enclose fairly recent observations and analyses as well as reflect and *exist as* feeling forms of that music.

Langston Hughes said, "I want to capture the form and content of Negro Music." Profundity rides profundity and our access, he instructed, is our most naturally extended and essential lives.

Amina's poetry is itself child of the music, as Jazz is Blues'. Image, rhythm, improvising, creating, verb-formed, content as that of the music, hers and ours, particularly the African-American, the Black woman, the working person and political revolutionary, wife and mother, the singer and poet's life.

The work wants, in its multi form, to be as polyregistering as the rhythm, which is livings' Black heart.

We say *The Music,* as do the players and people closest to it. We know what we mean; here in America that identification provides much of what little light there is.

Dubois *Souls* is the classic of structural diversity on a focused theme. In it are found the substance the scholarly classic analysis of the music as well:

Little of beauty has America given the world save the rude grandeur God himself stamped on her bosom; the human spirit in this new world has expressed itself in vigor and ingenuity rather than in beauty. And so by fateful chance the Negro folk-song—the rhythmic cry of the slave—stands to-day not simply as the sole American music, but as the most beautiful expression of human experience born this side the seas. It has been neglected, it has been, and is, half despised, and above all it has been persistently mistaken and misunderstood; but notwithstanding, it still remains as the singular spiritual heritage of the nation and the greatest gift of the Negro people.

The child sang it to his children and they to their children's children, and so two hundred years it has travelled down to us and we sing it to our children, knowing as little as our fathers what its words may mean, but knowing well the meaning of its music.

13

This was primitive African music; it may be seen in larger form in the strange chant which heralds "The Coming of John":

"You may bury me in the East,
You may bury me in the West,
But I'll hear the trumpet sound in that morning,"

—the voice of exile.

Ten master songs, more or less, one may pluck from this forest of melody—songs of undoubted Negro origin and wide popular currency, and songs peculiarly characteristic of the slave. One of these I have just mentioned. Another whose strains begin this book is "Nobody knows the trouble I've seen." When, struck with a sudden poverty, the United States refused to fulfill its promises of land to the freedmen, a brigadier-general went down to the Sea Islands to carry the news. An old woman on the outskirts of the throng began singing this song; all the mass joined with her, swaying. And the soldier wept.

The third song is the cradle-song of death which all men know,— "Swing low, sweet chariot,"—whose bars begin the life story of "Alexander Crummell." Then there is the song of many waters, "Roll, Jordon roll," a mighty chorus with minor cadences. There were many songs of the fugitive like that which opens "The Wings of Atalanta," and the more familiar "Been a-listening." The seventh is the song of the End and the Beginning—"My Lord, what a mourning! when the stars begin to fall"; a strain of this is placed before "The Dawn of Freedom." The song of groping—"My way's cloudy"—begins "The Meaning of Progress"; the ninth is the song of this chapter—"Wrestlin' Jacob, the day is a-breaking,"—a pæan of hopeful strife. The last master song is the song of songs—"Steal away,"—sprung from "The Faith of the Fathers."

There are many others of the Negro folk-songs as striking and characteristic as these, as, for instance, the three strains in the third, eighth, and ninth chapters; and others I am sure could easily make a selection on more scientific principles. There are, too, songs that seem to be a step removed from the more primitive types: there is the maze-like medley, "Bright sparkles," one phrase of which heads "The Black Belt"; the Easter carol, "Dust, dust and ashes"; the dirge, "My mother's took her flight and gone home"; and that burst of melody hovering over "The Passing of the First-Born"—"I hope my mother will be there in that beautiful world on high."

These represent a third step in the development of the slave song, of which "You may bury me in the East" is the first, and songs like "March on" (chapter six) and "Steal away" are the second. The first is African music, the second Afro-American, while the third is a blending of Negro music with the music heard in the foster land. The result is still distinctively Negro and the method of blending original, but the elements are both Negro and Caucasian. One might go further and find a fourth step in this development, where the songs of white America have been distinctively influenced by the slave songs or have incorporated whole phrases of Negro melody, as "Swanee River" and "Old Black Joe." Side by side, too, with the growth has gone the debasements and imitations—the Negro "minstrel" songs, many of the "gospel" hymns, and some of the contemporary "coon" songs,—a mass of music in which the novice may easily lose himself and never find the real Negro melodies.

In these songs, as I have said, the slave spoke to the world. Such a message is naturally veiled and half articulate. Words and music have lost each other and new and cant phrases of a dimly understood theology have displaced the older sentiment. Once in a while we catch a strange word of an unknown tongue, as the "Mighty Myo," which figures as a river of death; more often slight words or mere doggerel are joined to music of singular sweetness. Purely secular songs are few in number, partly because many of them were turned into hymns by a change of words, partly because the frolics were seldom heard by the stranger, and the music less often caught. Of nearly all the songs, however, the music is distinctly sorrowful. The ten master songs I have mentioned tell in word and music of trouble and exile, of strife and hiding; they grope toward some unseen power and sigh for rest in the End.

W.E.B. DuBois
"Of the Sorrow Songs"
The Souls of Black Folk (1903)

Fred Douglass a half century earlier laid his feelings, perception, and rationale, which can still instruct us as deeply as any sound:

The slaves selected to go to the Great House Farm, for the monthly allowance for themselves and their fellow-slaves, were peculiarly enthusiastic. While on their way, they would make the dense old woods, for miles around, reverberate with their wild songs, revealing at once the highest joy and the deepest sadness. They would compose and sing as they went along, consulting neither time nor tune. The thought that came up, came out—if not in the word, in the sound;—and as frequently in the one as in the other. They would sometimes sing the most pathetic sentiment in the most rapturous tone, and the most rapturous sentiment in the most pathetic tone. Into all of their songs they would manage to weave something of the Great House Farm. Especially would they do this, when leaving home. They would then sing most exultingly the following words:—

> "I am going away to the Great House Farm!
> O, yea! Oh, yea! O!"

This they would sing, as a chorus, to words which to many would seem unmeaning jargon, but which, nevertheless, were full of meaning to themselves. I have sometimes thought that the mere hearing of those songs would do more to impress some minds with the horrible character of slavery, than the reading of whole volumes of philosophy on the subject could do.

I did not, when a slave, understand the deep meaning of those rude and apparently incoherent songs. I was myself within the circle; so that I neither saw nor heard as those without might see and hear. They told a tale of woe which was then altogether beyond my feeble comprehension; they were tones loud, long, and deep; they breathed the prayer and complaint of souls boiling over with the bitterest anguish. Every tone was a testimony against slavery, and a prayer to God for deliverance from chains. The hearing of those wild notes always depressed my spirit, and filled me with ineffable sadness. I have frequently found myself in tears while hearing them. The mere recurrence to those songs, even now, afflicts me; and while I am writing these lines, an expression of feeling has already found its way down my cheek. To those songs I trace my first glimmering conception of the dehumanizing character of slavery. I can never get rid of that conception. Those songs still follow me, to deepen my hatred of slavery, and quicken my sympathies for my brethren in bonds. If any one wishes to be impressed with the soul-killing effects of slavery, let him go to Colonel Lloyd's plantation, and, on allowance-day, place himself in the deep pine woods, and there let him, in silence, analyze the sounds that shall pass through the chambers of his soul,—and if he is not thus impressed, it will only be because "there is no flesh in his obdurate heart."

I have often been utterly astonished, since I came to the north, to find persons who could speak of the singing, among slaves, as evidence of their contentment and happiness. It is impossible to conceive of a greater mistake. Slaves sing most when they are most unhappy. The songs of the slave represent the sorrows of his heart; and he is relieved by them, only as an aching heart is relieved by its tears. At least, such is my experience. I have often sung to drown my sorrow, but seldom to express my happiness. Crying for joy, and singing for joy, were alike uncommon to me while in the jaws of slavery. The singing of a man cast away upon a desolate island might be as appropriately considered as evidence of contentment and happiness, as the singing of a slave; the songs of the one and of the other are prompted by the same emotion.

FREDERICK DOUGLASS
Narrative of the Life of Frederick Douglass (1845)

Poetry

by *AMINA BARAKA*

Wailing for the Funk Dealer, oil by Vincent D. Smith   Collection: Mr. and Mrs. Leslie Stewart

Lover Man, monoprint by Vincent D. Smith   *Alex King, Jr.*

22

Miles Ahead, monoprint by Vincent D. Smith   *Alex King, Jr.*

Fly Me to the Moon, monoprint by Vincent D. Smith   *Alex King, Jr.*

The Things I Love

i love a full moon
i love a summer at midnight
i love a Duke Ellington Song
i love a Sarah Vaughan Melody
i love a Billie Holiday Phrase
i love a Monk Tune
i love John Coltranes changes
i love African Art
i love a Vincent Smith Painting
i love a Toni Morrison Book
i love a Romare Bearden Collage
i love Zora Neale Hurstons People
i love Albert Aylers Ghost
i love an Amiri Baraka Reading
i love the way Larry Neal Dressed
i love a Smokey Robinson Poem
i love a B. B. King Blues
i love a Bob Marley Reggae
i love Lenins analysis of imperialism
i love a Stevie Wonder Lyric
i love Maos Cultural Revolution
i love Henry Fonda in Grapes of Wrath
i love Paul Robeson in Proud Valley
i love a Peoples War
i love the Working Class of all Nationalities
i love Revolution
i love Freedom
& i love to write a poem
i love Clifford Brown & the Strings
i love Collard Greens & CornBread
i love Burritos
i love Fried Dumplings
I love Sushi
i love a Rare Steak
i love to do the Mambo
i love to Dance
& i love to have my way

25

THE MUSIC

i love a warm shower
i love my Children
i love antique rocking chairs
i love sweet potato pie
i love Charlie Parker
& i looooooove to fly————

No Name Poem

pain hides, behind windows
i close my eyes a lot these days
i seem frail . . . in comparison . . . to others
though i'm fat from abuse
there is no-one left to tell
no shoulders to cry on
they demand what the blues wont allow
me to give
they need march songs, & drum rolls for war
they need fighting slogans
& precise sum-ups of a bright future

    & i ain't got nothin
    but the blues

Birth Right

i don't care
if my children carry the blues in their throat
i hope they do—
i hope a feelin sleeps in their stomach
 it will keep them close to their people
i wanna gospel note to live on their breath
& speak black music in their voice
i don't care if my children
come from my womb
into the world of black
beautiful people
like a hundred Duke Ellington songs
sung by a million city blues singers
cause—
perhaps thats how they will survive racism

High Society

very dry
  cold
dust settles in throat
        tongue slowly
  grows brittle

        cracks

                words fall
"broken Arrow"

  scrambled sounds

nothing lives
i did not want to die
                gone.

        do not bury me
                let my ashes fly
                    and kiss the ground
                    on green dolphin street

Blues

blue songs come
more than they go
  tunes live in your soul
  & take your life for granted
lyrics control your thoughts
& lines come like midnight
   hanging around your eyes
blues is your dues
  its what you pay
  for a certain kinda
  livin.

For Tom White

if i wrote at sixteen
i learned from a place called "World Wide"
you'd think it was a hip metaphor
for a girl who would later become a Communist
even if i told you
you could get East Indian sandals there
African earrings
jewelry from Asian & Latin America
books on Black cowboys & Slaves
handbags from all over the world
& a history on each item you bought
Chianti was always kept around for hipsters
who wanted to know,
about Birdland or who was playing what & where
& directions how to get to Greenwich Village
before SoHo
you might think it is another metaphor
for becoming an early Bohemian
& if i tell you
he has had two heart attacks
& was run out of business
you would know it was not a metaphor
but America
& if i tell you he is still around struggling
you might say "So what"
but if you do,
Please play Miles Dewey Davis's version
recorded at Carnegie Hall on May 19, 1961,
with: Miles on Trumpet, Hank Mobley, Tenor Sax, Wynton Kelly, Piano,
Paul Chambers, Bass, Jimmy Cobb, Drums,
with Gil Evans & his 21 piece Orchestra
& then hum

For The Lady in Color

it is the blue part of
billies flame
that enchants me
something in common
w/the Lady
the man i love
you've changed
on me
was a high Lady
the needle brought down
did they bury the flower
in her hair too
is that where flowers have gone
naked courage strolled
the streets
searching for love
looking for dignity
in a song
music was the vehicle
the carpet
that carried her
the story was
important to the Lady
she staged it in
High Drama
on the road
in a one woman show
the woman sang
and even when
her lyrics smiled
water laid in her eyes
waiting to overflow
in phrase and a crying note
it was not magic
that we heard
it is the oppression
this country can lay on you
black & oppressed
poor & aint got nowhere
to go
love dont stay

when it comes
it takes off
looking for softer pillows
to lay on
the darker you are
the harder you fall
did the Lady
sing the blues
or not
yeah
i tell you
its the blue part
of billies flame
that enchants me
cause its the
hottest

Hip Songs
(For Larry Neal)

did you ask me
who was the hippist singer
in the world
well, i'd go so far
as to say
it was the first slave
that gave a field holler
& a shout in the field
i mean thats
what i would say
i'd say the hippist singer
must have been
the local gospel group over yonder there
down the country road while pickin cotton
& they tell me little willie james father
was the hippist blues singer in town
& they say his mama got her freedom once
the master heard her screaming a crying song
but you know
the hippist singer i heard
wassa dude in new orleans
playing a piano & singing a kinda different tune
although . . .
in chicago there was this fast singing woman
w/a blues bottom & a lotta rhythms behind her
she was hip
now i've heard some hip singers
i know a hip song
when i hear one
you know w/hip lyrics & all
but, let me say this
one of the hippest singers
i ever heard
was a poet
singing
"Don't Say Good-bye to the PorkPie Hat"

For Pharaoh Sanders

blue southern flower
purple shirt man
wrapped in ancient color
spinning gold
 instrument of history
  pygmy son
   bring the low-down high

black saxophone man
carrying freedom in your mouth

     the wind turns Red
    in the middle east
         Israeli Imperialists have invaded Lebanon!
i hear the lyrics in your voice
Trane-ing on

     we must fight!

All Is One for Monk

caught me sittin
on a stoop in the 50s
in love w/dark glasses
& berets
off chords, & split notes
black stockings
& no bra
breakin Free
me make-up
straight,
chasin Monk
to watch the piano player
dance
slides, runs, turns &
quick steps
over-there/some-where
arms holdin up the sound
"Off Minor"
tunes riffin
"Jackie-ing"
Sets w/Monk
dealin
& you
you couldn't be there
if you couldn't Be-Bop

For Abbey Lincoln

when Aminata sings . . .

Malindy dances—
the "Golden Lady"

got magic in her eyes
a song in her throat
a drum on tongue
when Aminata sings . . .
ancient sound sashay out her mouth
     mind me of drum/in a cotton field
     mind me of sugar/in lemonade
     mind me of watermelon/in the desert
     mind me of history rising

when Aminata sings . . .

For John Hicks

like—
  the Baptist
  John is got the fire
  and the holy ghost
  in his hands
  can make you
  wanna shout!
  it could save
  you

For Jazz
(For Mel, Phyllis, Ralph, Edward, Allison, Horst, Joe, Carol)

my grandma
believed in magic carpets

but i dont
  now,

here come—
Arthur Blythe, Bobbie Battle, Reggie Workman & John Hicks

with the all seein eye
& all
right in Sweet Basils
with all them other
hot spices
    Flyin High

THE MUSIC

For Jerry Butler

nothing spoiled
the ice man done come
& gone
everything is
Fresh

No-Mo Blues

your metaphor done got out of control
you dont like me
no mo
what you have to think about
when you think about me
makes you dont want me
no mo
what you think of
when you think of me
makes you dont want to stay here
no mo
your image of me
makes me be what i cant be
no mo
so, i guess you just up and left
cause you just cant love me
no mo

Poetry

by AMIRI BARAKA

Obalaji as Drummer, Ras as Poet

if ever rain sing beats flashes like mellow life remembered
we will be standing singing in unison
like the world
writing half written books all the way
jumbled between the flashes like communication
from far away
ourselves talking
the notes of the bigfisted scholars
caught crazed in the jungle
by the deadly missionary piranhas
who sailed with buddy rich
that fateful day in 1492 when benny goodman
discovered a jackson in his house
and transcribed it into warsongs.
We are afro-american wizards, but secular wizards
we like the magic of toasters and computers
the finality of a good machine gun
Donaldduck incoherence we understand
we were patted on the back by it
as "boys" even when elderly
but now john bull backed against the wall
protests against the cowboys' insanity
the brands on my ass and the endless cotton
marched in with that message long before jeff davis
started eating the "peanuts" out of his shit, daring bastard!
So you can pat your foot, how totally intelligent
though if the flying saucer in your kitchen belches
friendly life, we'd have to get back to the drawing board
of the assassination research & development team, tho thats crude
but blues you know yourself
suffers from such
blunt categories
of emotional focus.
Oh yes, we went to college for awhile
and were kicked out for cursing education
by our winedrinking oathfulness. You want a
portrait of us from that time, go to your local

45

autofactory, or coal mine, sit on the loading dock
of the postoffice, or get them dishes off that mf'ng
table rat away. (You rat, a chicago winter talking!)
We were never any good, which is why we is so bad.
That's what Michael Jackson says as he spins, and I imagine
Arthur Blythe biting that reed to make those high sounds
and when the music go through me I swear I imagine all kinds
of things. A world without pain, a world of beauty, for
instance. You dont believe it, you dont believe
old rich ass, that we
could do without you.
Then why does Duke Ellington
keep saying
that?!

I Love Music

"I want to be a force for real good.
In other words, I know that there are bad forces,
forces that bring suffering to others and misery to the world,
but I want to be the opposite
force. I want to be the force which is truly
for good."

Trane

Trane

Trane sd,

A force for real good, Trane. in other words. Feb '67
By july he was dead.
By july. He said in other words
he wanted to be the opposite
but by July he was dead, but he is, offering
expression a love supreme, afroblue in me singing
it all because of him
can be
screaming beauty
can be
afroblue can be
you leave me breathless
can be
      alabama
             I want to talk to you
                      my favorite things
                              like sonny
can be
life itself, fire can be, heart explosion, soul explosion, brain explosion.
can be. can be. can be. aggeeewheeeuheageeeee. aeeegeheooouaaaa
deep deep deep
expression deep, can be
capitalism dying, can be
all, see, aggggeeeeoooo. aggrggrrgeeeoouuuu. full full full can be
empty too.
nightfall by water
round moon over slums
shit in a dropper
soft face under fingertips trembling
can be

47

THE MUSIC

can be
can be, trane, can be, trane, because of trane, because
world world world world
can be
sean ocasey in ireland
can be, lu hsun in china
can be,
     brecht wailing
          gorky   riffing
               langston hughes steaming
                        can be
                        trane
                        bird's main man
                        can be
          big maybelle can be
        workout workout workout
               expression
               orgunde
               afroblue can be
all of it meaning, essence revelation, everything together, wailing in unison
               a terrible
wholeness

Bang/Bang Outishly
(For Monk)

Tinkle
as ifs
ands
three toed musical afternoon dreams
            midnight visions
these are caped players cooking
blueglassed cookers funking
edgewise questions inside the answers
chunks
there
edgewise bluedom near boil
funk tree landscape tinkle brewed—as answered questions
cardboard piano orchestras singing as if the hit parade was interplanetary
we see, he say
lurks, notes on shoeshine boxes
sideways dudes with big musical fingers
quiet screaming hooded holyrollers
preacher-space
rocket church
nutty logic/
            straight
            no chaser

The Speed

The speed
The speed
we dis
appearing
is appearing
The speed
The speed
raise it raise it from 4s to 8s to 16s to 32nds
From Pres to Bird to Trane
the speed
the speed
we di
sappearing
higher life higher
making sense at faster
and faster
speeds
from feet to horse to car to plane
the speed
the speed
its dis
appearing
onward and upward
the constant raising
spiral
the speed
the speed
we
dis
appear
ing
faster faster faster, the change
    ancient communism
  to slavery
  to feudal
   ism capital
   ism
    the speed the speed
    social
    ism
    capitalism is the age of steam
    socialism of electricity

and past that
the speed
the speed
to communi
sm
atomic
life
the speed
the speed
collects life in its raging whirl
submerge emerge, change change
the speed
we dis
appear
from George to Coyt to Amiri to Ras
the speed
the speed
faster and higher and upward and finer
wider and more of it, extract light from the dark
places
the speed
the speed
past all endings
all beginnings
to goals not yet
conceived
the speed
the speed
endless revolutions
endless explosions
from one end to another end to another end
and begin somewhere out there
in here
through the ground
through the clouds
atom and giant flying monsters
in your breath and hair
the speed
the speed
war pestilence peace adventure
jungle drums ride the water
to New Jersey gospel symbol
the savoy sultans ready their
funk
Trane is in the shadow

of his coming and going in the light
and blast of it
the speed
the speed
washington's in flames
new york rebellions
britain long fallen
france in commie hands
the third world for years building socialism
the speed
the speed
the good ship jesus
sails out the disco caves
nixon and hitler rumble near stonehenge
attila and andy young
negotiate with Lancelot
cowboys shoot pterodactyls
and Duke Ellington composes
Robin Hoods hip forest
ode
the speed
light
the speed
faster faster
the speed
we are alive this moment taste it, look at everything
and smile
toward the future lives of all the species
rising and being
more advanced
than they
were
the speed
hail progress
hail life
hail revolutionary/ motion

In Walked Bud

Summer evening ghetto style
sidewalks collect us
up under radio lies
pregnant babies crowned queen
of no where
to go
Young boys bop into madness
& death
We laugh
We scream
We fuck a lot
We dance a lot
We drink a lot
Get high
high   high
       high we get high—eyeiiii
   What?
   Who?
   Where?
   No! No! Bang (ahhhhhhhhhh!)
What is life
but a whiskey
dream
Yeh, we cry
alot
the machine
wont let us
alone
die
alot
so much bitter black bottomless anger
& frustration
characterize
our nation
rage
wont get on any
page
if I—What?
   You What?
Think What?
Say What?

53

                        so much rage
                    black anger
                yet beneath the pavement
                of our faces
                there is real love & touching
                tenderness
        We sing "Close the door
                Let me give you
                what you've
                been waiting
                for"
                & rise off the
                ground
                when we see beautiful we
                comin down
                dressed in some musical
                Extravaganza
                dope slide
                ugliness hide
                sweet piano bass
                talking warm
                mornings
                In walked
                Who?
                you know
                we say
                you know
                rhythm
                our
                business
            the African
            in the west
            with European harmonies
            but the beat, man,
            World, Black
                Hey, Black

        In Walked
        us

Caution: A Disco Near You Wails Death Funk

Substance of the dead is alive in the middle of the living
who are killed by them
at worst at nights they steal they lie and hate
truth

Substance of dead is moving toward death trying to convince
life to follow it without living
without revolution
Substance of death smokes a pipe and wears an eyepatch
has a big natural and travels with Martov's
colored mammy
who was the same woman whose shadow is seen on DW Griffiths
biographical fragment long suppressed
in which he is seen kneeling at the altar
of black womanhood
Substance of death laughs at him and you and me and the water near
the gate
Jimmy Carter wears a tee shirt marked substance of death
with a skull but no cross bones
this known as reform

Your sequins: The substance of death
the shadows in the men's room, and JEdgar Hoover's slouch towards it
sweating. The bullet holes in Malcolm again. Substance of death
these compradors like W. saying he is a patriot
he wears a tee shirt that says fool written in dumb-ink. A bean pie
will not erase dumb-ink. A handout from the govt will not. Nor Bundini Brown
in all his wisdom, finally play the guitar and sing them night time
bighead notes, Disco lady, born again christian, miss colored american
everything you know is swirling away. Speak the unknown tongue lost
twilight strutters into midnight.
At night bats fly out the white house
it looks creepy like that allright, I swear to you
its true, I saw a man on the balcony, open up his red
silk cape, and turn into a bat.
I dont remember the sponsor
but the bloody bird came down near me
I felt important to be in a commercial as important
as that one
I called that bat by name, bela, bela, the bat hovered
sucking bloodybucked teeth, bela, bela, the bat
refused to heel, or acknowledge my call. (And I had a book,

some instructions on how to act. The root that Sandy gave
Douglass, I carried on my side. Some ground up peanut shells
I threw around his surge. You may think it wild but
I refused to carry a cross. The real shit was heat in my
pocket, and the shadows in which I stood, checking but unobserved.
The bat, wove his circle ignoring me, but he was not alone. A smoky
twist of early night-shading hid the colony of blood suckers with him.
A squadron of ghouls, spinning slowly 360 degrees to see on all sides
whatever threatened their liege. Calling Bela did no good, why didnt
the head bat answer acknowledge me and cool out and return to the
rose room where possibly they were still serving alcohol? But no
the bastard maintained his motionless hover the cry of BELAAAAAAA
went up. Go get back in your tuxedo you're fucking up our evening!
A wise guy with us, sd Jimmy. He called out, in the dark, like a
hissed whisper, Jimmy. He called Jimmy, Jimmy. The bat turned like very
very slowly so you cd see that odd color of something drinking blood
and having a stomach full of it. But he turned now, to face us.
Jimmy, more of us called Jimmy—the bad mens got youse? Huh? Huh?
The bat sd, "I is a bad mens . . . dont you understand that . . . I is a
bad mens, but I dont need money for my personal self. I got a farm.
Commuting makes this a home too. I have the bulletproof DracSuit
on." (His brother has died in a heap of beercans.) The bat had curly
hair, and spoke American with a southern accent
Aggghhh, agggghhh eee ahee aghhee agghhee
Whip step
Agghhh eee agggghh ee ooeeoo aggg uhhh eeeggg egggg
in america the ingenue searches for a lover
in america
agggheeee aggeeeeaggee oooee
in the streets and
Lollipop lounges
in low cut blouse and high boots
aggghheee
baldhead lover in red silk cape
hovers in midair typing
squadron of droning bunnies playboying
night air sweats like dracula
agggghee america, agggheee america
whip step hipper than the freak
freak step whip step teeth step death
flying bunnies sucking agggeee agggeee parrot fever
death of nixon door
nixon odor rises in swamp america geeeagghhooo
the naked centerfolds have *Now* buttons pinned

\

& tattooed to their parts aggeeehuuuooo gnawing
babies' skulls agggggeeee poison silver playboys
sucking aggeeehuuuh uhhh uhhh eeeee bloody swamp
nixon odor
rising
dogface hoovers try to suck the air out the world
america aghheee slum odor war sucking agggeeee madonna
in the garbage can
run the murder game
ageeee ohuuu aggeee uhhoooo eeugggeee map of hatred
stares. Crawling S's/D face down in the shit
our dreams scratch their ankles bloody, our dreams are junkies
finally, trying to read philosophy ahhheeegggeee ageee ooohhheee uhhh
agggheee ooooussss impotent bastard dying,
hitler's behind poked out a phone booth
Professor stupids party you going to
the indians are in the other direction
the nation is in jeopardy. Bats and wolves
and Agnews and Sons of Sam and Dave are busted
Mars in his helmet squats on 42nd street waiting
for the newspaper strike to end.
Why is terror so contrived and orderly?
Why lies now from lovers, and the backs of heads
disappearing instead of warm lips and open legs.
Dont blame this shit on jesus, just smack Rev Ike
and rob him, don't blame this shit on Mjinga Mjinga
just expose his backward ass. aerials on fire night time
and the stars advertise thousands of years
of night
aheeeeeggg agggheeee ahee ahhggeeeee you taking this all this down
aghheeeee (whistle) aggggheee (whistle) remember for me
what time it happened
the dates and days
and the months of the years
who won the pennant in the american
league
and who was tonto
for then
you see me hear me crying
you hear with me all alone
no you not here no more are you, you gone too
you gone toooo
you gone toooo
you gone tooooo

you gone toooooo
you gone tooooooo
Uhhhss
Uhhsssaaa
Uhhhssssaaaa
Uhhhssssssaaaaa
Uhhhssssaaaaaaaaa
no love poem tonight
no you neither
uhhhhsssss
american tragedy
uhhhh sssaaaa
I was born here lady
and I left the singer hanging on the
phone
over 40 years ago lady
what can you do any way
you are looking for your own hot bone
I was born here lady
you see they were whispering while this
hopeless dialog was going
you see
in cupped hands over brandies
this is not governors island
its rikers
yeh
rikers
the fuckin
yeh
prison

Caution, death funk
Caution, death funk, death funk
Caution, death funk, america
hideous aromas airplane through senor jeemys buks/teeth
caution, death funk. Boodsie in the u.n. purple bloomers flaming funk-
dumb boodsie wail yr tired tail of white ladies spreading money in the sack
funk dum, gino hotdog scream, come on, do do, they come boodsie wail
funk dum, disco lady, whirl. talk petty life of heartred, dog face lover
reality, cause. hurt. tired. cry. love. be yr self. hurt. love. hurt. die.
caution, death funk. wail stink blow. hurt. cry. love. hurt. cry.
caution, hunger hear. death. chauvinism. africa rise. soul rise. people rise.
socialism rise. tomorrow rise. all rise. caution
battlefield drops. from the skies of america and russian rise. tonk players

get up. die. hurt. love is draining away. music gone. night. night caution
silent streets. caution. death funk.

caution
death funk
caution
death funk

agg agg agg agg agg agg agg agg agg
bumpty bump bumpty bump agg bumpty agg bumpty agg bumpty
duh dump duh dump duh dump duh dump duh dump duh dhupt

caution
listen
down the
caution
glistening
quiet
caution death death funk funk funk funk funk assassin night funk funk

At Roseland

in the daily news, they sd
dancers danced till they dropped.
Featured in deathless sets like the Harvest Moon
Ball. They danced. The Lindy. The Jitterbug. The
Mambo. All them dances of the 40s & 50s. By 1976
the science fiction future, my son won a "robot" contest
at Madison Elementary. And now there's Carter and Brezhnev,
the two superpowers, the third world's crushing in imperialism's
skull, and discos dot the streetwaves. The Music is Stevie Wonder,
and The Floaters ("Float On"), and David Murray's *Flowers,* kids doin
The Cadillac and Spanish Hustle. Day, Day, Day, Day, Day, and the nights
in between. I actually remember Larry Darnell. "Why you fool, you poor sad worthless
foolish fool," nightpoet of the blues, shouterpoet, hair tight as Hawaii
the spiraling world zig zags upwards dancing onward and upward, Pearl Harbor,
Korea, Jordan, Vietnam, footprints of losers and winners, rushing in and out
of our songs.

The Wayfarers
(From the ancient Bebop)

All hear.
The mouth of day is working. Silences
& music, portraits of the dead economy dying.
Politicians
Lying. The people
too often crying.
—This city is iron top leather inside
blues bootie. With pizza, sausage drawl
& a puerto rican chicaw chicaw salsa shake
sunglasses & umbrella
—Contemporary gargoyles
still garring
and goyling
they want you to be amos
but not really
the goddam europeans are suggesting
that american foreign policy
is gibberish
"incoherent" is what the english voice
declared, they accuse an aging johnny weissmuller
who they've made put on his
clothes, of not even understanding
other white
people—he is yet so
wild
& the masked man has been ordered by the courts
to wear
sunglasses, is that sterility, addiction
or cool?

Choruses

Abstraction
& Formality—avoid life avoid life
       my
    dear.

    The stylized fixation
    & there is also what is the source
    of all
    life
    The Beat!

The Beat
    is the dialectic
    Contract & Expand
    Ying & Yang
    What is
        Sound

    That there is developed
    life.

I Felt Sad When I Looked At You & Thought One Day We'll Both Be Dead
(June 25, 1979, 12:40 A.M.)

Uuudah—ee blew day—reports coming in thru cloud bluedom
    Ooshee doo shee doo repeeohh beebop . . . falling
        like a sheath of cold days drowning in dead unopened dreams
                    uuuudeeeelyah uudeeelyall
            yaboom rabbabababa
    ydada
      like opened up could come
      straightness, talking oooo
     like calm it
     it could come
     too
       anything,
          battering
          crazy rhythm slopes in air
out yo mouth erupts new music
Zoot suit o rootie, marchers stalk europes madness
drafted to play tenor saxophone between jail stints
buda'll ya doooo ya doooo (hymn to the orient
                starring john wayne
                and metro
                    bloomidido rising
                    mars ascendant, plus
                    a recording ban
                    a deck'a luckies
                    in his mitt
whats the flag of yr country
look like
sitting in a slum
with niggers so frustrated and mean
they throw little white girls
in front of oncoming trains
cutoff left hands twitching
on the track. Madplace. Cocaine in club 54, chortling
"Mama, mama," screaming as the train rests
over her, "I gotta go . . . I gotta go
to . . . to college" . . . conflict of conflicting
dreams.

THE MUSIC

Our lives designed
by money freaks   cataa ooo
        oilies, redaaaa   blee foo
        cd tell you the saga   doo roo
    of dee oilies
          robber bebop
          turn you to
                dirt
          you to
             dirt
               to garbage
                    shit
                       before
                          your
   turn you to
   murdering for gasoline   turn you to
   screaming neurotics
   shivering catatonics
   pornography consumers
                  waste, asdooocan see the fleas
        inside yr
   bebop
     knees,   babeeee
            here in the center of the target
            the red center pulse of terror
            magicless reality

cd turn you to
  one splits into two
          cd burn you through
          purple white laser hot
          bathe yr purpose
   from behop glasses and berets
   to steven daedalus of the south side
   to barney googles sabu sidekick snorting cocaine & skinpopping
   for the sake of the economy
   to the man who wd be king(kong-nights in tunisia
   kukamop, whose head was a diamond big as the ritz
   who discovered layers of idealism and mistook them for
plantation revelation
whoo lost, it, feet pointing,
footprints. bootless sage returned in a shitty idea by
a designer whose name you wear under yr eyelids

who broke out to broke in, broken like a sick lost bird

i heard a you during those years—you was yul brynner
and refused to celebrate christmas.

and the hosts of ghosts and liars for the cause collected
make it clear you felt oppressed and used. Fucked with by the world
by the runners and rulers. By white people, and some niggers too.
Inside a horn player runs it, bleee doooya dooobleee roooo ddeedeee wa
hada   wahada . . . wahadaaaaaaaa

                    scramble
                like an airplanedriver
             asleep at the switch
         like
          a   censored
          censored
               censored
                censored

like kneeling compromisers
in love with people
they know
are not perfect
can you live with that, even tho
you both cd rise up higher and hold yr head up
struggling to change yrself
and the world.

Grows inside and outside self
thoughts cut off from reality
subjectivism-selfishness, from
the same root.

Life is defined in the world. What you do
is real and exact. Yo description

like the slice of music smoking through
yr
brain
we'll see the world erupt and happiness
wrung
from
blood!

Early Cool

Miles
Blues
Who's
little boy with a trumpet bag on High street bopping
day of promises in blue transparent stone shining inside you low & cool
glissando
the runs of notes
each one speaks a path beyond the ghetto sun
blue bop speak to us as a guiding laughter heating our hip young walk
So *Venus de Milo*
was beauty
after
all,
   black marble hey blow muted slickness jaunty one
   African things . . .
   Black Venus in us blue light soft like earth's immemorial
laughter
Hey Miles
Master of blue light
and the turn
hand on hip
the horn hung ready
Hey Miles, my man, blue light
and the whirring metal groove

A Snide Aside

A Motherfucker
who think he went "past
Coltrane" need to check out
Peetie Wheatstraw
& see if he caught up/with
him
yet.

Keep Right on Playin
Right Thru the Mirror
and Out Over the Water
Be Ever
Out

These were messages
from AIR
A banquet concerto
for fingers hands
& mouth.

And so the feeling. (Anyone hear?)
     Staggered feeling
       arrest search outside rhythms
      slide as if
     then they
      without seeing the others
     in a stark statement of the days
     affairs
The peace we want is lasting rocks music
ground verse, vision walls, personal flight.
    There they'd go
   as if out a blue cloud
    seacaptain bloody snuffer monied from corpses
Electricity is so much a part of the sea!
The Heavens Are Real! Investigate the complexity
of the real.

New Music

grreesssa uu garble eekcrull there
staring, staring, it come at us grinning blood
dripping in a whee whee whee whee whee whee whee
dirty stare,
dead folks stare without pennies cooling them out
thing in the water stare, uncle sams eyes blow bad breath on us
collect in our heads ugly
white garrrr white garrrr white garrrr eeee gruuuulll gruu
roaming in his head queen elizabeth
roaming in her hair farrah fawcett major
sir mantan kingfish the tonto
lady toothy bloodletter
all ro-morgue orgiastic ar roach dye groo-ave-oom balls
buster dead person ugly
ugly sucks at us confident as television
there
crumb dumb. jefferson slave sucking
georg georg georg, the name of a television poison
i inside sliding in fist screech metal fighting
eyes bulge from choking the naacp snake wrapped around
Macy-satan's neck undercover cop necklace
wisdom hip
sharp,
shadows in the park crumbling under death blows
rumgroo-eeee ek-ek doo doo doo doo doo doooo doo doo doo doo doo doo
doooo, thin beauty lady waving curled rasta waving, witch waving night
waving, eyes under cab leaving lateness waving, motion yes its real
real for touching feeling touching feeling (the same) touching feeling
touching
feeling.

The Aesthetic

If you can understand the
complexity, of an African
mask, the tense ambiguities
of Black Blues
then my work should be clear
to you, what I say
easily understood.

Portrait

His name
cd've been "Blue"
The music
he made
wdve been called
"Blue's," But
he'd never learned
how to play. The
  Dope
  Kept him
  that
  way.

Stomp (Funk World)

Stomp Stomp Stomp Stomp
down
there
stomp stomp stomp stomp
  stomp
  up
  there
  collision
  of stomps
  collision
  of stompers
  eh?
  The roofs
  coming off
  they say
  coming
  off
  The roof's
  coming off
  coming right & left
  on off

Water Music
(For Albert Ayler)

Cry
Cry
Cry Albert
Albert
Cry
Cry
there is
no God
no
There is no
no God Albert
cry
cry Albert
there is
no God
no God
no God
no Devil
no no Devil
& no fucking
God.

   (2)
Laugh
Laugh
Laugh
Laugh
Laugh
Hahahahahaha
Albert
Hahahahahaha
Albert
haha
Albert
haha
Albert
haha
Albert
there is no
God!

(3)
you were dead
& stopped crying
you were dead
& never laughed
again
But we can laugh
the rest of us Albert
because the people are
all there is
Nature the world
is all there
is
Laugh Albert
Laugh workers
Laugh people
Laugh all the giants Albert spawned
Laugh revolutionaries
Laugh struggling nations & people
Hahahahaha laugh Albert
laugh
laugh Albert
laugh

cryings over

cryings over
no more crying
bloody rulers cry now
We rip their lie tongues out
no more crying people
Albert
no Albert no no Albert
No more crying
laugh
hahahahahahahahahahaha
laugh
hahahahahahahahahahaha
a world
a world
a world

(4)
yes world
this world
we can win it brother
Dead weeping beautiful lost singer
no more crying
we can win!

Jazz Notes

After the dark night
of the soul
our father, the Sun,
(Ra) gives us
Lady Day!

Abby and Duke

From our memory of ourselves, we construct
a portrait of the world. We can see all that
must be seen to understand what needs to be
understood. We can sing can even dance can even
walk slow and cool beset with the suns gold which
makes us glistening brown. Sunday is our day naturally
Sun people must have a day. And Sun music would be Duke
say Abby together, a music match for Sunday think about it.
* * * *
Rumbling chords and deep blue arias.
Sunday match would describe our loves and history
wd sew our pain in colors to contemplate inside the real cool
the real image persons the poets of everyday conjure. And when we
do sing, its to recreate and create and hold on to and bring into
the world.

> Are there evil niggers, you say? Of course
> You are most familiar with them aint you
> from how the paper spreads them out inside
> our errors like they were the flag and the race
> and the national genius, cunning betrayal.

But a rumbling piano and a burring blue spoon span lovers reach
where you actually live inside this stunning beautiful body
yall got. The rumbling piano the softness hey sun, browned us up
for centuries. So the brown people the black ones, who have withstood
and made do, when the smoke cleared was still there standing a little apart
and humming you could hear if you were close enough, humming, something.
A rumbling deep blue thing. You'd see the pain, the life, the staggering
gorgeousness of us, in this woman's lips and fantastic eyes.

> Sun music it wd be, for the Sun people.
> Hot and blue black in you on you stay away
> unless you dig being colored, deep colored
> mind body soul, deep colored, black brown
> & beige, from the beautiful woman's lips
> conjured from silence to sound by common royalty
> Dangerous shit, sunday music, dangerous, and powerful
> this sun, from our memory of ourselves, we construct
> a portrait of the world. Black, Blue, Gold and Brown.
> Red and Green. Life green & still growing

RhythmBlues

I am the boogie man
    the woogie man
    catch as catch can
    The rabbit
    The monkey
    Blue hard
    Blue slick
    Blue slow
    Blue quick
    Blue cool
    Blue hot
    Everything I am
    Everything I'm not

Slave boy, leroy, from Newark Hill
If capitalism dont kill me, racism will!

Shazam Doowah

be there with us, back through time
oh wah wah
back through years age, & old wars clime
oh wah wah
be there with us, our primitive ways
oh wah wah
when witch doctors was presidents and
the people was slaves
oh wah wah

when work, health, education was mysteries
and filth was on the tube
oh wah wah
and racists was in power
and a minority ruled
oh wah wah
oh wah wah
oh wah wah
oh wah wah wah
dont blame you for not goin
i aint happy with it neither
dont blame you for stayin
off there in the future
oh wah wah
our primitive age
oh wah wah
oh wah wah
wanna stand tho, we wanna stand on up
we wanna stand tho, we wanna stand on up
oh wah wah, off all fours, oh wah wah
oh wah wah
this is called the deep red blues oh wah oh wah owah wah wah

The Rare Birds
(For Ted Berrigan)

   brook no obscurity, merely plunging deeper
for light. Hear them, watch the blurred windows tail
the woman alone turning and listening to another time
when music brushed against her ankles and held a low light
near the table's edge. These birds, like Yard and
Bean, or Langston grinning at you. Can't remember the shadow
pulled tight around the door, music about to enter. We hum
to anticipate, more history, every day. These birds, angular
like sculpture. Brancusian, and yet, more tangible like Jake's
colored colorful colorado colormore colorcolor, ahhh, it's about
these birds and their grimaces. Jake's colors, and lines. You
remember the eyes of that guy Pablo, and his perfect trace of
life's austere overflowings.

              Williams writes to us
of the smallness of this American century, that it splinters into
worlds it cannot live in. And having given birth to the mystery
splits unfolds like gold shattered in daylight's beautiful hurricane.
(praying Sambos blown apart) out of which a rainbow of anything you need.
I heard these guys. These lovely ladies, on the road to Timbuctoo
waiting for TuFu to register on the Richter scale. It was called
Impressions, and it was a message, from like a very rare bird.

The Real Construction

New ways to swing,
               dont put down
               New ways, dont, betty boop, dont
               yr shit aint so fly you can talk down the
               new
          New Ways To Swing
          Chicago Art
          Albert's burnt message
          from the roof of Lincoln Center
          Sterling Brown's old funk note amidst DC nigger socialites
Amidst these social heavies who oppress the entire fucking world
  New ways to swing
  New truths to bring
  New songs to sing
  dont put that down, Betty Bop, halfhip kittycat scatter
  carrying one half of sassy's terrible arsenal
  the other half was, after all, a motherfuckin beautiful
  Voice!
          New ways to swing
          uncover to see the sun
          bust out dust flung speed
          the corporations heap us in slowness
          run up the skull and crossbones it says CBS, WRVR,
          trying to suck out our lives
          to get us in their bag, they throw it over our head
          and try to suffocate our
          dreams, and fuck up
          our reality. Make it something a balding executive can lose
          in his vest pocket.
          New ways to swing, we wanna know new ways to swing
new songs to sing,
  new truths, new truths,
  to bring. New challenges to
  fling. New hurts to
  sting.
          Calling sense, consciousness, breakout bootsies brainfever jail
          Out run Roots' rags to riches stale tale of
          the jivier parts of the nigger middle class

THE MUSIC

New ways to swing.
Calling sense   dadadadadadadadadadadada..........
                calling consciousness.......ssssssssssssssss
                    break out raghead george jefferson white blues
                    the jockey with the ring in his nose is rev. young
                    we need a new song a song that needta be sung
                        no betty beblip dont put down the new
                        the tired shit you run is halfhip
                            because it was once all new
                            except the ties with all
                            beginnings
                                    (as we stand up
                                    in the dark
                                    & screw a light
                                    bulb at the
                                    mouth
                                    of the cave.
a tired mimmy jimmy put that down. light is evil they sd, in they darkness.
and cars is too. Dracula slobbering on our artbooks, and even recording music
for us to dig. Jimmy Carter had a bunch of hiplights dimmed by his
                                    corn & murder
Saltpeanuts on the whitehouse lawn is the end of that era
    and the errormen and wimmens who walked with it faded into the past
    & even some new dudes only got missed cause they just didn't
                            need em or know em
    but they time will come to prove whether they in the past or the
    future. (The present is always in contention.)

New ways to swing. Say it. sing it. Blooomdido baby sunday
                            morning cool.
    Bloomdido, among the murderers, and klaktoveedesteen too.
                        Bird. Monk. Diz.
    then were the sun rising, on the horizon. Heat to come baby,
                            heat and heat
    smoke sizzling blues to come. the tradition of the new, the new
                            consciousness
        unable to be beat back. And when the bodysnatchers came and
        tried to tell us our fire was cool, then Max and Clifford, Horace
        & Art Blakey told them they ass was loose and Sonny
                            Rollins buried
            them under a ton of honked calypsos.
                        New ways to swing
                    New eyes to see. Yeh pres!
                New things

to be. No bopbetty, dont put down the rest of
life yet to come, cause you to three notes you can hit
with some halfway swinging shit. New truths to tell, New understanding and direction to jell, new tyrants to quell, no betty bebop
dont put down what is coming into existence, otherwise you will be going
out of existence. New ways to swing. New songs to sing. New eyes to see.
New life(s) to be.
So Ornette and Cecil and Trane's majestic wings, hatched
new funky suns rising in our world. Where Pharaoh returned to dance us into
tomorrow & SunRa plugged us into the new energy electricity (dont stand in
the dark and praise blindness deal with the new, its hard, yeh, frankenstein
running shit for dracula trying to turn even the new into vomit rocks of dumbness
its hard, the world's an open blast of changing energy, but we need
new ways to see
new constructs to raise us all
new life new heart new strength new direction
dont kill us with tired competence and repeats and covers and replays
of stuff what *was* hip and new we need what is *now* hip and *now* new which
could be old if it sung right
could be ancient if it is flung bright and people tough
against the dangerous bloody knives of the dying rulers

no betty blam against the stirring thrusts of what am
dont put down the life blood of us all
the creativity of the world
we look at everything dialectically, break it in two,
look for the bad, search for the good
discard one, use the other,
but dont put down the new

More Trane Than Art

as if sun itself was day
alone
world
itself on fire
with dreams

—

he shd not say rhythms are absent they are our
life
our memory
carrying houses
& faces, and lovely women
and spread out landscapes of whispered
revenge.
But that heaviest rhythms packed on top and bottom driving
that cry of names and dates and acts inside our description
of ourselves

there is buhainia
dont make no mistake
buhainia and max and steve and roy and elvin
milford sonny dennis michael carvin rumbling with us
in us
is us
sun in pieces thrown down
down
inside our beings
freeing
color geography tender
ness
as if the bashing a soul calendar
      a touching opening
      the crashing
      a fixed evidence of our beating hearts
      our hearts are art
      beating
      playing
      the basic love and existing thing
      we is
      & beeeeeeeeeeeeeeeeeeeeeeeeeeeeeeeeeeeeeeeeeeeeeeeeeee
But the blown thing the hope neon-eyed daylighting darkness

the whole cry with headshattered beats, whips, stirring stirring uproaring
inside as it goes and comes rises, erupts, the whole voice of love
Colormantic
Dawnsudden
crown of light life/breath our being
               as beating
               love poetry of the creators
               love workers
               real magicians of the
               actual
               the felt
               the seen
               the vibrating material self
is
trane
is blown
is
self
is
all
and beating
and loving
and revolutionary leaping
leaping
leaping
enthralled by its life in reflection of it and all of what life
expresses
is
like a blowing
art art art too beat the fast role
       is such a swift
       and swifter
       turning invisible, and so
      is the one
       and the other
        and the every
         look
          there is yr self, finger foot head
          patting
          singing
that's how we're born
and death transforms this
yet it is abeating then,

THE MUSIC

another rhythm
another beating
another level, stage, progression,
does not dis
appear

reggae
or
not!

by
amiri baraka

Reggae or Not!
A piece to be read with Reggae accompaniment

Inside beyond our craziness is reality. People rushing through life
dripping with
funk. Inside beyond our craziness and the lies of philistines
who never wanted to be anything
but Bootsie
w/golden curls
and a dress tho they black as tar
beyond our inside, beyond wvo, beyond craziness
dripping with
reality
is the funk
the real fusion of life and life
heart and history
color and motion grim what have you's
beat us eat us send us into flight
on the bottom-ism on the bottom
up under-ism, up under
way down-ism way down under-ville
feet bottoms, everybody put us down
we down
how we got down
how we got, hot, how we got so black
& blue
how we cd blow
how we cd know
how we cd, and did, and is, and bees, how
how how, and how how how, and how and why and why why
like big eye nigger motion
heavywt champ
white hope party
populists in hoods
the real jesse jackson
our history
our pain
our flight
our fright

our terror . . . AHEEESSSSHHHHHHHHEEEEEEEEEEEEEEEEEE
our women watched when the crackers cut off our balls
in the grass, they made the little girls watch

stuffed them in our mouths
(this was before they complained about
OPEC, before they complained about baraka being rude
before malcolm set kenneth clark on fire
(and after too . . .
                    but history
                        the development of the afroamerican nation
                        in the black belt south.

from blue slaves
from green africa
from drum past and pyramid hipness
from colors colors all the time, everyday, bright—bright—brightness
    red green yellow purple orange wearing niggerssssss AAAAAAHHHHHH
    violet violent shiny head shiny shoe knife carryin niggersssssss
                        AAAAAAAAA
                        dust, cripples staggering
                        white hats, blood, blood in the cotton
                        wear the fuck out it
                    love you baby
                    drunk motherfucker
            preachin in the twilight madness and jesus fuckem
            hell all around
            white face hell
                inside beyond the madness history
            beyond the scag, history
        beyond the oppression and exploitation
                                    Aheeeeeeeeeee—balls
                                        in the sand

            preach!!
            baldhead rip off
                        teach!!
            chicken eatin metaphysical
                loud talkin chained up motherfuckas
        anykinda nigger jet plane flyin ishmael reed lyin nigger
andy young hung like a sign announcing the new policy
    get a paycheck pay the madness pay the blood pay the history
            beyond the sickness and racism
                history
            today's combustion
                for the revolutionary future
                beyond the madness and cocaine
                beyond the male chauvinism and baby actin niggers
                who want disco to substitute for their humanity & struggle

And the alligators clappin they hands Garvey, man
                    yeh, Nat man, alligators in the sunlight
                    in the daytime now
                        sittin beside us groundin
            man, I see it
                it no fool I
            I no be fool dem tink
                no fool I
            alligators Marcus
                    Nat man, they come right up to us
                and explain scientific why our shit aint right
            why we need to be under dem,
        why we need to bend and sway like
dead boy wilkie, downtown with them
        no fool I, I no for fool, bee, bee crazy sometime
            sometime be out, be way out,
        like crazy mother fucka
    purple language come out I mouth
    ya know,
                    but Nat man,
                    Marcus,
                        alligator
                    they organize to love us
                    take us out ourselves
                got whip mout whip eye whip talk
                all for fool I but I no be no fool for they
            I no go for ghost, like dig, pig, I fuck you up for fun

        like a dance
        like pussy russo in the joint
    want to control the pills
instead the blood drove a shank in his titty
    ya punk he scream they take him into solitary
        an alligator
            he say why you want to separate bozo
                ((that he inside name for I

        bozo, like H. Box Brown say, the muthafucka
        upsidedown
    he bozo
        I—I
                    all eyes, a we eye, us, like raging black purpleness
                    as music, as rhythmic sun screams our color lay for them

The nation, he said,
he had been cut,
the nation
does not, he said,
>
> and before he cd get it out
> I drove the blade deep down thru
> the adam's apple, severing the jugular
>
> and man, hey, instead a blood
> ya know, the racist punk,
> all words spill out
> > all words run on ground like bleach waterbug
> > all words say no, like lula, say no, say, like lula, no
> > say, hey, say, no, like lula, trying to kill i i no like clay
> > say he, words spill out where blood shd be, abstract shit all out
> > say hey, why you gonna split

> 1979 a calm time compared
> 1979 cool compared to what will be
> 1979 fire in me banked compared
> up against what will be

all I's, this cant go on
this cant go on, all this
this craziness, beyond it is us
> is history, our lives, and
> the future. Beyond this
> beyond craziness, beyond capitalism
> beyond national oppression and racism
> beyond the subjugation of women
> disco bandit style beyond
> lies of the disco bandit
> beyond lies of the mozart freaks
> beyond joe papap and papap joe
> beyond brezhnev, and all the little multi-colored brezhnev clones
> masquerading as radicals telling persons they revolutionaries
> beyond all the little latest generation of human failure pettybourgeois
> explainers of the bullshit, beyond everything but what will last what is
real, what the people will make and demand, what they are and have been,
there is Self Determination and Revolution
There is Revolution and Self Determination
there is the fire so broad a rainbow of fire, a world full of fire
there is all bullshit for now exploding
so ready all busshit for next be explode
all fire so flame rise so for fire be heavy and everywhere now

THE MUSIC

Self Determination
& Revolution } (sing)
Revolution
& Self Determination
World, to be, for I and that person
and every person, for all I's all we's all they's all all's together be
cool now compared to explosion life future
when every minute is blow up of everything stupid always
is cool now compared to all exploded jack the ripper rich ass
to people smashed powerful garbage dead forever by our hand
to destroyed dumb systems of exploited pain corrected by annihilation only
forever till the next shit
be in the struggle conscious comrade
be in the struggle righteous friend
its cool now, the nation, the workers mad but shit aint rose
beyond the calmness history and pain
beyond the torture history and future fill each other with flame
its cool now, the alligators talking to us like we cant see whats on they mind
jimmy carter cant talk to you
jesse jackson cant talk to you
bootsie and the funkadelic cant talk to you
Who can talk to you—who can still bullshit you
                who can set you up with lies you aint heard
                    with unscientific science and metaphysical analysis
                alligators in the disguise of the hiptime
            alligators from the old alligator pad,
            fake communists, sham revolutionaries
            they can and do and will till broke head screams
            talk to you they can shorenuff anyway busshit the besta
you, but a alligator got bad breaff smell like a alligator
a alligator eyes is white and bloodshot, full of alligator
images, a alligator brain is fulla alligator thoughts teethy
and slimy and fulla dead half ate animals. a alligator bite
when they talk and they tryin to con you they be bitin and it
        hurt so you bash them and they look at you weird you say stop
        bitin muthafucka and talk if you goin to i dont eat no alligator
        but they make hip pouches to carry my goddam papers in
It's a higher level of bullshit goin down
a much higher level of bullshit
goin down, aint even bullshit, it's alligator shit
some sophisticated amphibian feces goin down
up under they bumps and tears, up under they alligator eyes
mostly up under they alligator
lies. a much higher level of bullshit goin down

do you really think Henry Winston was hipper than Rochester and if so why
do you really think Andy Young was hipper than Andy Old
or that "comrade" A was hipper than Beulah or Poncho be with Cisco
or that Alligators got sidekicks hipper than Gabby was with Roy & Dale
Some sidekick muthafuckers some sidekicks, want us to call the nation
                                                    sidekickania
got sidekick inside they eyes eat and breathe love bein sidekicks and
                                                    got sidekickitis
so much gray stuff hang out they ears droolin eye tears into dirt
come out the closet sidekicks
it's calm now & cool, 1979 a calm time, sidekicks can still get over
ride alligators upriver to trade, the jungle is smokin but coolin
and the sidekick deals get made. Come out the closet sidekick
Roy Rogers retired, Cisco doin reruns
Mantan been canonized by the Sidekick society
And Booker T. been made an official militant on the lower east side

cant tell multinational unity
from side kick-ism-itis might even fight us
but all folk got to dig it for be real
for be hot
for be us
for be life thrown into future
too much pain go down
too much hate
too many people like we, no go for alligator
                                ghost
      we is nation in suffering
      we is nation in chains
      the latest spears will not even be spears
      tho the warcries sound the same
      reach out for the comrades reach out for true comrades
      reach out for allies reach out for real allies
      no fool I this alligator, all I's look for light
      we no be fool for alligator, nor the alligator big time friend
      We be for heat & fire
      We be for genuine war
      No be fool for alligator
      Self Determination }
      Revolution   } (sing)
      We know our friend for fighting
      We know our comrade for struggle
      no be bullshit only for word noise
      no be dry dull stuff but war war war war war

fuck a bourgeois alligator
lyin he tryin to be help
we know our friend for fighting
we see our comrade they struggle
no be fool for alligator
with some new time chauvinistic lie, by, by, by, no fool I
                                         by, no fool all I

dead folks dead pass away
rich shit dead pass away
liars imitating revolution die
pass away
beyond bullshit is history
beyond deadshit is history & pain
niggers riding alligators will get blown away when the alligator do
even in the calmest of times
Self Determination Revolution } (sing)
Revolution Self Determination
We no be fool
for alligator
our comrade hear and understand
To liberate we got kill
To liberate blood must flow
To liberate imperialism gotta go
we for kill racism, we for kill our oppression and every other person
too
alligator bullshit for big time rich folks
he bite yr militance off like sleepy monkey with tail
in the wrong place
its calm now, jojo, story teller, compared to other future time hotting
hotting be back be back be black be black and all other color too
we for win anyway
we for all us win
we in people laughing our victory song
our victory
song go like this

Self Determination
Revolution
Self Determination
Revolution
Self Determination   (sing)
Revolution
Self Determination
Revolution

94

Socialism Socialism Socialism
DEATH TO ALLIGATOR EATING CAPITALISM
DEATH TO BIG TEETH BLOOD DRIPPING IMPERIALISM
I be black angry communist
I be part of rising black nation
I be together with all fighters who fight imperialism
I be together in a party with warmakers for the people
I be black and african and still contemporary marxist warrior
I be connected to people by blood and history and pain and struggle
We be together as party as one fist and voice
We be I be We, We We, the whole fist and invincible flame
We be a party soon, we know our comrade for struggle
We be war to come we bring war we no go for alligator
we kill his trainer too

Self Determination ⎫
Revolution   ⎪
Self Determination ⎬   (sing)
Revolution   ⎭
Socialism Socialism Socialism   Only Socialism will save
the Black Nation
Only Socialism
will save the Black Nation
Only Socialism will save
America
Only Socialism will save
the world!

Class Struggle in Music (1)

What is the emotion?
    What is the
      Feeling?
Who are it feeling
    are it a "humming"?
Flashes like Flags waving
(Reagan raving)
Day flashes like trees waving
(Dr. Faustus' craving)

What is the emotion, What is its
opposite?
Who are it,
          it feeling
          it under
          standing
          it a (k) nave
          a savant of the
          un real
          it reaching
          it un teaching
          it equivocating
like distant enemy marchers, but yrself
like like (liking as)
like distant national marchers, but yrself
like yrself
        it
        & it again, it

What is the emotion?
    A trembling
    A drugstore
    A scholarship in Snow
    Snow
    a bird
    16th notes
    alterations
    of the negative—(we are thinking)
    bandaids
    brain damage
          commerce
          inner openings

                    trance—
                    lights
                ((Cockney killing echoes
                ((Racist drag queens
                ((electric training
                ((crashes
& it
a wither of jungle
a dance
a ocean & an ocean
        bilingual disputes
                it
                it
        What is the
        emotion?
                it
        Niggerfrankensteins
        Niggerkillerscum
                it
        & the rest of us, somehow, anyway

        What is the emotion
          overpowering
        general
        of all
            all
            it/all
            it/over
that yr voice cd make alone atop the others
gentle lyric wafting morning song
        not it
          you
        not any other

        What is
    the emotion
    not the colonized mercedes in heat
            briefcases
            ties
            words arranged
            by picture window rote

        Our emotion, not
        its
        not the witch training

                not the denials of self and family
                not the isolated dead corpse negro
        accepting the hating cup
        of Cortez' asshole-hat wearers

        But the us emotion
            the love
                emotion
            the love
            heat,
            snowball,
            heat,
            move-
            ment
            life
            yeah, vitality
          beat beat beat beat beat
        boom buppa doompa doom
        boom buppa doompa doom
        boom buppa doompa doom
        boom buppa doompa doom
                yeh,
                that and
        boom buppa doompa doom
        boom buppa doompa doom
        boom buppa doompa doom
                That is the emotion
                the us emotion
                the love emotion
                the heat emotion
        boom buppa doompa doom
        boom buppa doompa doom
        boom buppa doompa doom
        boom buppa doompa doom
        boom buppa doompa doom
                yeh, that one
        boom buppa doompa doom
        boom buppa doompa doom
        boom buppa doompa doom
        boom buppa doompa doom
                we/us—eye
                we/us—eye
            a blues emotion
            a black country nigger emotion

a steel blue blues city thing
a factory girder reflection emotion
an assembly line thing
a love heat
in we/us—eye
a love beat
in we/us—eye
   eyes
   sees
   Blue us
   Blue we's   (Blue *ooos)*
a boom boopa doompa doom
a boom boopa doompa doom
a boom boopa doompa doom
a boom boopa doompa doom

   That one

a boom boopa doompa doom
a boom boopa doompa doom
a boom boopa doompa doom
a boom boops doompa doom

Class Struggle in Music (2)

Black
Music.
By George, we were
talk
ing
he was
say
ing
"I was with them until they made me ride in this broken down bus . . ."
By
George,
we
were
talk
ing
(cd see eyes roll/ing a cackle
    laugh, tongue slip/ping out the lip)
                            Music
          Black   Music
                    Drums
          at one   point
          & Drums
          & Drums, rhythm, rhythm, a
          beat, funk, rhythm, smoke,
cook, jam, work, smoke, steam, wail,
cook, jam, work, smoke, steam, wail,
get it, get down, hit it, get up, do it
get it, get down, hit it, get up, do it
cook
cook
jam
jam
work
work
smoke
smoke
steam
steam
wail

Opposed
two
apposites
two
beings
seeings
we split tings
we and us cut in half by
life,
social
life,
crazy nigger at juilliard giggling
blues built up in me all the time
cant love nothing for crying cant cry
for lying
cant love I'm
dying
and you wants to know
what the blues is
the blues is we us
split in half by sorrow
we wee wee wee wee wee wee weee
ussssssss

then here come
chamber
lurkers
heard berg, and cd not dig monk dug bird dug duke dug
thought stravinsky was hip and he was
but what to do with
Transbluesency
balue
sense
eeeee
cd not step, hey, step, hey
cd not twist and turn, hey, turn, hey
cd not, get down, yeh, get down, yeh
without a crystal glass reflect vibration
endless melodies over one taptap
endless dragging violins singing death to niggers anyway—

a ping against the silence
when alla michael jackson waits a dropout from dust universe
city

THE MUSIC

of the wall & all
hack step hop jump funk, and then
yeh, bump, jump, hey, and then
wham, each, reach, teach, wail, yeh
"dum dum dum," say, look, touch, blue suit
homburg
tails
bare feet
nails
conk
fonk
honk

       "this is not bebop,"
     he sd
          (& he were
            right, far
            right)

         this aint even
         excuse me
         certainly this is not
         what is known, as, aruuum,
         blues.
         a colored object.
And we fell down in his head weeping and kneeling and feeling sorry
tragic, small and samboish, like something Ralph Ellison despised.
We felt like that, amidst the violins & twinkle twinkle dots and dashes
of snowman jism they shat out of their fingertips like dollar confetti.
Ahhaaa. Here he come. Balaue. Balueee. Baloo. Shreeks and Screeks,
                    on his heels
turning the corner of the bar on two wheels, "Gimme a double bourbon."
Then sat and came in on the flat five like our flat speech, full of
death and laughter and lynch screech. "*Rootie Tootie,* motherfuckers," he
began, "And *Straight, No Chaser,*" he went on. *"Nutty,"* he called looking at
the colorless negro piano player from No Heaven.
Then shit, they got mean, from the back room, a nigger with a twotoned
beard. And distance rolling out his nose. "It aint about you!" he said,
eyeing the dead things who were making dusty quartets with outofshape philoso
                    phers.
and the suicidal solipsists threw down their violins hiding their alienation
under white women. *"Ghosts! Ghosts!"* He screamed. Eeery blew
              down. Low shit.
Spooky
niggers scared of everything. *"Ghosts!"* A Honk. A mean low scream like

102

rich people dying in front of their offices with nigger janitors grinning
and susycueing into jeeps with mounted bazookas. Weird march music
for weird marches. We rose from our paralyzed stuttering and ran to
meet them—

       "Albert!
       Monk!" We called
       "Where's . . . ? (and before we got it out
       John Coltrane
       came down thru the roof blowing *Impressions* faster than
       light
(or was it Pharaoh, Chico, Ricky, Tyrone, David, Arthur, Julius,
Hamiett, Oliver,

Joseph . . .)
& the dismal pinkerton niggers sued for peace. Which meant they cd
only produce their albums with a disclaimer that said, "This music
will turn you into rich peoples' underwear."
       & they went out in the snow of
       their own
       creation
       humming the fanon, efranklin frazier
       black anglosaxon unblues
       & what did we do
       we did what we needed
       to do

       we blew
       & blew
     & blew blue
     blue blue blue blue

& even reached you . . .

   & even reached you

      & even reached you

   & even reached you

     & even reached you

     reached you

       reached you

         you

          you

In the Tradition
(For Black Arthur Blythe)

"Not a White Shadow
But Black People
Will be Victorious . . ."

Blues walk weeps ragtime
Painting slavery
women laid around
working feverishly for slavemaster romeos
as if in ragtime they spill
their origins like chillers   (lost chillen
in the streets to be
telephoned to by Huggie
Bear from channel 7, for the White Shadow
gives advice on how to hold our homes
together, tambien tu, Chicago Hermano)

    genius bennygoodman headmaster
    philanthropist
    romeos—
    but must coach
    cannot shoot—

    hey coah-ch
    hey coah-ch
    trembling fate wrapped in flags
    hey coah-ch
    you can hug this
    while you at it
    coah-ch

Women become
goils gals grinning in the face of his
no light
Men become
boys & slimy roosters crowing negros
in love with dressed up pimp stupidity death
hey coah-ch
wanna outlaw the dunk, cannot deal with skyman darrell
or double dippin hip doctors deadly in flight
cannot deal with Magic or Kareem . . . hey coah-ch coah-ch
bench yrself in the garbagecan of history o new imperial dog

105

THE MUSIC

denying with lying images
our strength & African
funky beauty

nomatter the three networks idiot chatter

Arthur Blythe
Says
it!
in the
tradition

2

Tradition
of Douglass
of David Walker
Garnett
Turner
Tubman
of ragers yeh
ragers
(of Kings, & Counts, & Dukes
of Satchelmouths & SunRa's
of Bessies & Billies & Sassys
& Mas
Musical screaming
Niggers
yeh
tradition
of Brown Welles
& Brown Sterling
& Brown Clifford
of H Rap & H Box
Black baltimore sister blues antislavery singers
countless funky blind folks
& oneleg country beboppers
bottleneck in the guitarneck dudes
whispering thrashing cakewalking raging
ladies
& gents
getdown folks, elegant as
skywriting
tradition
of DuBois
Baby Dodds & Lovie

106

Austin, Sojourner
I thought I heard Buddy Bolden

       say, you're terrible
      you're awful, Lester
     why do you want to be
    the president of all this
   of the blues and slow sideways
  horn. tradition of blue presidents
 locked up in the brig for wearing zoot suit
army pants. tradition of monks & outside dudes
of marylous and notes hung vibrating blue just beyond just after
just before just faster just slowly twilight crazier than europe or its
racist children

       bee-doo dee doop bee-doo dee dooo doop (Arthur
       tradition
       of shooters
       & silver fast dribblers
       of real fancy motherfuckers
       fancy as birds flight, sunward/high
              highhigh
              sunward
              arcs/swoops/spirals
      in the tradition
¼ notes
eighth notes
16th notes
32nds, 64ths, 128ths, silver blue
presidents
      of Langston & Langston Manifestos
      Tell us again about the negro artist
      & the racial mountain so we will not
      be negro artists, Mckay Banjoes and
      Homes In Harlem, Blue Black Boys &
      Little Richard Wrights, Tradition of
For My People Margaret Walker & David Walker & Jr Walker
& Walker Smith Sweet Ray Leonard Rockin in Rhythm w/ Musical Dukes,
What is this tradition Basied on, we Blue Black Wards strugglin
against a Big White Fog, Africa people, our fingerprints are everywhere
on you america, our fingerprints are everywhere, Cesaire told you
that, our family strewn around the world has made more parts of that world
blue and funky, cooler, flashier, hotter, afro-cuban james brownier
      a wide panafrican
      world

THE MUSIC

Tho we are afro-americans, african americans
let the geographic history of our flaming hatchet motion
hot ax motion
hammer & hatchet

our cotton history
our rum & indigo
sugar cane
history

Yet, in a casual gesture, if its talk you want, we can say
Cesaire, Damas, Depestre, Romain, Guillen
You want Shaka, Askia, (& Roland Snellings too)
Mandingo, Nzinga, you want us to drop
Cleopatra on you or Hannibal
What are you masochists
paper iron chemistry
& smelting
I aint even mentioned
Troussaint or Dessaline
or Robeson or Ngugi

Hah, you bloody & dazed, screaming at me to stop yet,
NO, hah, you think its over, tradition song, tradition
poem, poem for us together, poem for arthur blythe
who told us again, in the tradition
in the
tradition of

life & dying
in the tradition of those klanned & chained
& lynched and shockleyed and naacped and ralph bunched

hah, you rise a little I mention we also the tradition of amos and andy
hypnotized selling us out vernons and hooks and other nigger crooks of
gibsons and crouches and other assorted louses of niggers that turn from
gold to shit proving dialectics muhammad ali style
But just as you rise up to gloat I scream COLTRANE! STEVIE WONDER!
MALCOLM X!
ALBERT AYLER
THE BLACK ARTS!

Shit & whistling out of my nkrumah, cabral, fanon, sweep—I cry Fletcher
Henderson, Cane, What Did I Do To Be So Black & Blue, the most perfect
couplet in the language, I scream Moon Indigo, Black Bolshevik, KoKo,
Now's the Time, Ark of Bones, Lonely Woman, Ghosts, A Love Supreme,
Walkin, Straight No Chaser, In the Tradition

of life
& dying
centuries of beautiful
women
crying
In the tradition
of screamed
ape music
coon hollers
shouts
even more profound
than its gorgeous
sound
In the tradition of
all of us, in an unending everywhere at the same time
line
in motion forever
like the hip chicago poet Amus Mor
like the Art Ensemble
like Miles's Venus DeMilo
& Horace Silver reminding us
& Art Blakey sending us messages
Black Brown & Beige people
& Pharaoh old and new, Blood Brotherhoods
all over the planet, land songs land poems
land sculptures and paintings, land niggers want still want
will get land
in the tradition of all of us in the positive aspect
all of our positive selves, cut zora neale & me & a buncha other
folks in half. My brothers and sisters in the tradition. Vincent
Smith & Biggers, Color mad dudes, Catlett & White Chas & Wm, BT,
Overstreet
& the 60s muralists. Jake Lawrence & Aaron Douglass & Ademola
Babatunde Building More Stately Mansions
We are the composers, racists, & gunbearers
We are the artists
Dont tell me shit about a tradition of deadness & capitulation

of slavemasters sipping tea in the parlor
while we bleed to death in fields
tradition of cc rider
see what you done done
dont tell me shit about the tradition of slavemasters
& henry james I know about it up to my asshole in it

dont tell me shit about bach mozart or even ½ nigger
beethoven
get out of europe
come out of europe if you can
cancel on the english depts this is america
north, this is america
where's yr american music
gwashington won the war
where's yr american culture southernagrarians
                    academic aryans
                    penwarrens & wilburs

          say something american if you dare
             if you
                can
                    where's yr american
                    music
                       Nigger music?

(Like englishmen talking about *great* britain stop with tongues
    lapped on their cravats you put the irish on em. Say shit
man, you mean irish irish Literature . . . when they say about they
you say nay you mean irish irish literature you mean, for the
last century you mean, when you scream say nay, you mean yeats,
synge, shaw, wilde, joyce, ocasey, beckett, them is, nay, them is
irish, they's irish, irish as the ira)

you mean nigger music? dont hide in europe—"oh thats classical!"
    come to this country
          nigger music?

You better go up in appalachia
and get some mountain some coal mining
songs, you better go down south in our land
& talk to the angloamerican national minority
they can fetch up a song or two, country & western
could save you from looking like saps before the world
otherwise
                    Palante!
                    Latino, Native American
                    Bomba, Plena, Salsa, Rain dance War dance
                    Magical invective
                    The Latin Tinge
                    Cherokee, Sonny Rollins w/Clifford Brown
                    Diz & Machito, or Mongo SantaMaria

        Comin Comin World Saxophone Quartet you cannot stand up
against, Hell No I Aint Goin To Afghanistan, Leon Thomas million year
old pygmies you cannot stand up against, nor Black Arthur tellin you
like Blue Turhan Bey, Odessa, Romance can Bloom even here in White Racist
Land It can Bloom as Beautiful, though flawed by our oppression it can
bloom bloom, in the tradition
                        of revolution
                            Renaissance
                            Negritude
                            Blackness
                            Negrissmo
                            Indigisme
                    sounding niggers
                swahili speaking niggers niggers in turbans
    rna & app & aprp & cap black blacks
& assembly line, turpentine, mighty fine female
        blacks, and cooks, truck drivers, coal miners
            small farmers, iron steel and hospital workers
                in the tradition of us
                the reality not us the narrow fantasy
    in the tradition of african american black people/america

nigger music's almost all
you got, and you find it
much too hot

            in the tradition thank you arthur for playing & saying
            reminding us how deep how old how black how sweet how
we is and bees
when we remember
when we are our memory as the projection
of what it is evolving
in struggle
in passion and pain
we become our sweet black
selves

once again,
    in the tradition
        in the african american
            tradition
                    open us
                    yet bind us
                    let all that is positive
                    find
                    us

we go into the future
carrying a world
of blackness
yet we have been in the world
and we have gained all of what there
is and was, since the highest expression
of the world, is its total

& the universal
is the entire collection
of particulars

ours is one particular
one tradition
of love and suffering truth over lies
and now we find ourselves in chains
   the tradition says plainly to us fight plainly to us
   fight, that's in it, clearly, we are not meant to be slaves
it is a detour we have gone through and about to come out
in the tradition of gorgeous africa blackness
says to us fight, it's all right, you beautiful
   as night, the tradition
thank you langstron/arthur
says sing
says fight
in the tradition, always clarifying, always new and centuries old
says
   Sing!
   Fight!
         Sing!
         Fight!
               Sing!
               Fight! &c. &c.
                        Boosheee dooooo doo doooo dee doooo
                        dooooooooooo!
                        DEATH TO THE KLAN!

For Sylvia or Amina
Ballad Air&Fire

There is music
sometimes
in lonely
shadows
blue music
sometimes
purple music
black music
red music
but these are left from crowds
of people
listening and singing
from generation
to generation

All the civilizations humans have built
(speed us up we look like ants)
our whole lives lived in an inch
or two. And those few seconds
that we breathe

in that incredible speed
blurs of sight and sound
the wind's theories

So for us to have been together, even
for this moment
profound like a leaf
blown in the wind

to have been together
and known you, and despite our pain
to have grasped much of what joy exists
accompanied by the ring and peal of your
romantic laughter

is what it was about, really. Life.
Loving someone, and struggling

Wailers
(For Larry Neal and Bob Marley)

Wailers are we
We are Wailers. Dont get scared.
Nothing happening but out and way out.
Nothing happening but the positive. (Unless you the
negative.) Wailers. We wailers. Yeh, Wailers.
We wail, we wail.
>   We could dig Melville on his ship
>   confronting the huge white mad beast
>   speeding death cross the sea to we.
>   But we whalers. We can kill whales.
>   We could get on top of a whale
>   and wail. Wailers. Undersea defense hot folk
Blues babies humming when we arrive. Boogie ladies strumming our
black violet souls. Rag daddies come from the land of never say die.
Reggae workers bringing the funk to the people of I. We wailers all right.

Hail to you Bob, man! We will ask your question all our lives.
Could You Be Loved? I and I understand. We see the world
Eyes and eyes say Yes to transformation. Wailers. Aye, Wailers.
Subterranean night color Magis, working inside the soul of the world.
Wailers. Eyes seeing the world's being

Hey, Bob, Wail on rock on Jah come into us as real vision and action
Hey, Larry, Wail on, with Lester and the Porkpie, wailing us energy
for truth. We Wailers is all, and on past that to say, wailing for all
we worth. Rhythm folks obssessed with stroking what is with our
sound purchase.

Call he Thelonius, in my crowded Wail Vessel, I hold the keys to the
funk kingdom. Lie on me if you want to, tell folks its yours
But for real wailing not tale telling, the sensitive know who the Wailers
Be We. Be We. We Wailers. Blue Blowers. The Real Rhythm Kings.
We sing philosophy. Hambone precise findings. Image Masters of the
syncopated. Wailers & Drummers.
>   Wailers & Trumpet stars.
>   Wailers & Box cookers.
>   Wailers & Sax flyers.
>   Wailers & Bass thumpers.
>   Wailers and Hey, wail, wail. We Wailers!
>   Trombone benders. Magic singers.
>   Ellingtonians.

The only Tranes faster than rocket ships. Shit.
Cut a rocket in our pocket and put a chord on the wall of the wind.
Wailers. Can you dig Wailing?

Call Me Bud Powell. You wanna imitate this?
Listen. Spree dee deet sprree deee whee spredeee whee deee

My calling card. The dialectic of silence.
The Sound approach.
Life one day will be filled even further with we numbers we song
But primitive place now, we wailing be kept underground.

But keep it in mind. Call me something Dukish. Something Sassy.
Call me by my real name. When the world change
We wailing be in it, help make it, for real time.

Call Me. I call you. We call We.
Say, Hey Wailers.   Hey, Wailers.
Hey hey hey, Wailers. Wail On!

Reflections

When I was a child, and then a young
man, Ronald Reagan was an actor
of small reputation. Later, in college,
Clarence Pendleton, a mustachioed hotdog
a comical braggart, who one day disgraced
his family and friends by leaving his fiancée
standing at the altar, in a church packed with
the cream of negro Washington. Youth, like a cave
of the winds, useless pompadoured guys chortling
stupidly in films of no importance about stupid
things. And dudes you knew obliquely, your roommates
buddies, who talked dumb shit in the room souped up
on beer and frat pins and lies nobody (then) could
disprove. But oh, don't you know, in the world, in the
world. It was there all the time, in the cave, and
before, life's frightening pits and contradictions.
The wind in the cave is life's speedy trace, the motion
the motion, of everything. And you then (and now) be awake,
old man, raise your eyelids young girl, in that motion
know it or dont. Where it leaves you, not what you leave
it, as if there were grades as well as graves, but the
meaning, like you say, what everything's about. We know
what we know and what we dont knows us. Now we see Ronnie
& Penny—those stupid guys!! Alas, where it's led us, this
crumbling America! That these stupid guys are now our leaders.
What would you have said had I whispered this in the last minutes
of *Bonzo Goes to College,* and what wd you have sd if I
pointed at Bonzo and said, and that's the Civil Rts Commissioner aint it?
Both our fucking leaders. You'd throw popcorn at me and curse
laughing on your knees, safe in the darkened flick. But now
brother, sister, it aint no movie. Take that slice of wonder bread
and mash it in your hand till it's nasty dough, and then put a monkey
suit on any creep you know, make him dance and dance and slobber on
the flo'. You has the American Dream, goddammit, you has it, you has it.
Why aint you laughin?

116

The Lady

The Lady said of her life here that she 1st
heard part of her own voice, (Bessie & Louie),
in a whore house; but she wasn't the only one
          The Lady said
But also that the whore
house
was the only place where
there was even a semblance
of democracy
People say
no one says the word
"Hunger"
"Love"
    I want to remember

Real Song Is a Dangerous Number
(For Amina, Nina, Grachian, Abdul, and Akida, December 27, 1984)

I am Johnny Ace
accidental suicide
from Russian roulette, maybe my name
is Sam Cooke, dead in a room by an unknown
hand. I could be Otis Redding, airplane sunk
at the dock of the bay. You might know me as
Teddy Pendergrass, smashed ½ flat, they say with
a queen, cripple now, but off the scene.
Marvin Gaye, my old man took me
away. Bob Marley was my name
in jam down, cancer shot up through
my toe. *Redemption Song* to be heard
no more. If I was white, they'd call me
Lennon, blasted flat by a crazy man.
Dont make no deal, you get kill. Yr voice
too strong, yr charisma too long. The rhythm
of yr image, hotter than napalm. But I cd be
a poet name Larry Neal (or Henry Dumas)
for the very same reason I cd also get kill.

Musical

Primitive World: An Anti-Nuclear Jazz Musical

David Murray, composer,
saxophone

Photo © Stephanie Myers

The Money Gods:
Sado (left),
Akbar Ali, violin;
Maso (right),
LeRoy Jenkins, violin;
Ham (center),
John Purcell, reeds

Photo © Stephanie Myers

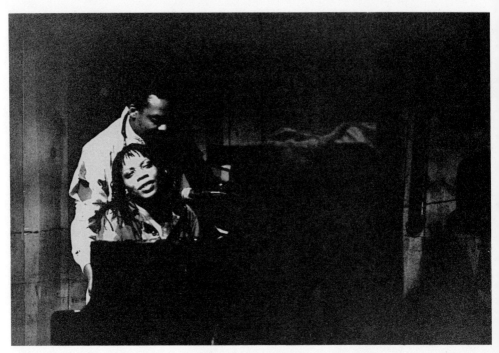

MTU, David Murray (composer, saxophone, vocals); Naima, Amina Myers (piano, vocals)

Photo © Stephanie Myers

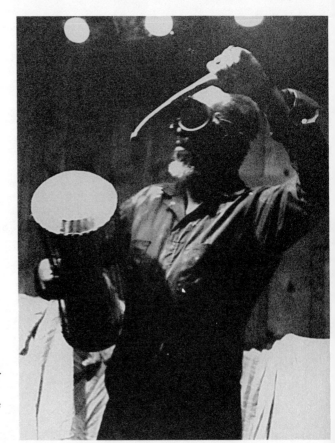

Heart, Steve McCarr (talking drums)

Photo © Stephanie Myers

CAST

Black Musician (MAN)
Black Musician (WOMAN)
Ham (STATESMAN)
Sado (MONEY GOD)
Maso (MONEY GOD)
Heart (DRUMMER)
Black Musician (WOMAN), *Heart's Wife*
White Musician, Latino Musician, *Heart's Companions*

Music composed and performed by David Murray

(A MAN *carrying a tenor saxophone which is in parts comes running into his space. A shack, a mixture of future and primitive beginnings. In the background a kind of wind music, like voices in pain, like people seeing their world blown apart. And across the back of the stage, faded red-and death-colored slides sweep across, sporadically—in some kind of out rhythm. Suddenly—and just swifter than clear identification—an image of horrible suffering blows by—in the rhythm of the music, the sharp broken glass shreds of sound.*

There are lights, like fires, that come up, then fade. Flicker bright.

The MAN *has apparently been bitten by something. Blood is streaming down his arm.* HE *is wearing some kind of metallic jump suit-looking garment, and a helmet that seems to have an oxygen mask fitted into it.*

HE *is wrapping up his arm, and placing the horn on a table where* HE *can look at it and work on it.* HE *works on his arm, sprinkles powder on it.* HE *is concerned about it, but not panicky. But still* HE *tries to fit the horn together; but some of the parts are warped and* HE *is having some trouble making them fit. Occasionally,* HE *will pick up the mouthpiece part of the horn and make some sounds on it. Simple, then more ambitious. But then, this will simply drive him back to trying to fix it.)*

At one point, HE *seems to* SMELL *something, and rises quickly to go to the window and tries to seal it even more tightly.* HE *sniffs at the bottom of the door.* HE *goes back to the horn, and fumbling with it, sings snatches of a song.*

123

THE MUSIC

MAN

in the mountains
in the valley
in the ruins
in the dead blown-up city

Poison death
fire left
Cloud of horror
Silent memory

(Repeat first stanza.
HE *stands and picks up a pile of records and weighs them in his hand.*
HE *shuffles through them. Then looks at a record player that is in parts.*
HE *shuffles them around, singing the song, a blues ballad, quiet and*
precise.)

Where are you
Where are me
Where are life
Where are sun

poison death
fire death
blow up death
murder death

in the mountains
in the valley
even niggers in the alley
all blown up destroyed

Poison death
Fire left
Clouds of horror
Silent tongue, silent memory

(Upstage, from the darkness a spot illuminates a STATESMAN *talking. A*
tall, aging man with spinning eyes. His hair plastered down like
Superman. HE *is in a dark business suit, but has a red cape. There is a*
dollar sign on the cape. HE *is surrounded by garbage cans full of*
money—big bills bulge out of each can so that the tops sit slightly
askew. HE *is making a speech, and every once in a while looking at a*
script HE *has in his inner pocket, trying to memorize. The* MAN's
dialogue must be in rhythmic, musical raltionship to the song the
MUSICIAN *sings, a kind of counterpoint. But, of course,* THEY *are not in*
*the same place—*THEY *are separated by time and understanding.*

The MUSICIAN, when HE is frustrated with his attempted repair job, blows on the mouthpiece, making a hard music. HE sings in many styles—Bluesy old, Bluesy-Stevie, Jazzy like Joe Lee Wilson, cool like Johnny Hartman.)

HAM

Therefore, since we have tried to live with everybody and they didn't want to live with us.
(*HE's memorizing, repeating, missing and coming clear*)
Since we tried to live . . . with everyone . . . and they won't have it. They won't have our peace.
(*HE is reading, but the thought of what HE is saying animates him*)

(The MAN is making wild sounds with the mouthpiece. HE is beating on floor and walls like a drum. It is a weird music, as accompaniment for HAM's speech in the process of being memorized.

There is a banging on the door in the MUSICIAN's space. It is tentative, but it gets harder, as if the person were trying to act forceful. At first we cannot see where the noise comes from, then we see it is a YOUNG WOMAN, slender, dark. SHE is also looking over her shoulder.

The MUSICIAN, hearing the knocking, does not respond. The WOMAN is getting bolder and bolder, knocking.

The STATESMAN, memorizing the speech, postures and speaks, at the same time doing a kind of dance. It is a dance of slow rising murderousness. HE is gesturing and pointing, like a tribesman dancing a bitter challenge, in some anonymous clearing a million years ago. But we see his surroundings are more modern than today in the hard technology. HE is speaking, but also HE gives the speech some rhythm, some music emphasis, drawing out and shortening the lines, so that it is poetic, musical, and frightening.)

HAM

We pleaded with them. We showed them light. We told them we were better than the world. More holy. More red and white more blue. We said Holy mother of profit, make these people, these all these people love us as we are. But today . . . yes today
(*HE repeats, picks out certain words and lines . . .)*

(The MUSICIAN is trying to see who is out there. The WOMAN begins to call softly. Then more loudly.)

WOMAN

Is there anyone in there?
(*Knock knock knock.)*
Is there anyone in there?

125

THE MUSIC

(The MUSICIAN *is frozen, but curious.* HE *hears,* HE *draws closer to the door.* HE *is still fiddling with the horn, but more quietly, obviously looking at the door, but continuing to do something as if nothing was happening.* HE *is still singing quietly, more quietly, his song.*

Now the WOMAN *is knocking, and falling back from the door, looking around, but also, checking out the shack, the windows sealed, the bottom of the door sealed, but* SHE *thinks she detects a light.)*

Is anyone there?

> Is anyone there?
> Is anyone there?
> Don't ask again
> Someone waiting for you
> Is anyone there?
> Is anyone there?
> Alone in the . . .

> *(Suddenly the* MUSICIAN *gets up and pulls the door open.)*

MAN

Shit! Hey. Ain't nothing bad enough to put me out past whatever it is. Yeh? Who is it? A monster? Red smoke? Death on a motorcycle? Ancient shit. New horror? Hey. Dig this.
> *(*HE *holds up his horn, still unable to put it together.)*
This is me!

*(*WOMAN, *her head around the doorway. The* BROTHER *has taken some stance like* HE *is going to defend himself, if necessary, by blowing the horn. The* WOMAN *pokes her head around, still tentative, amazed at the stance of the* BROTHER. HE *has worked himself up, to where* HE *is "going to town," squatting suddenly with the horn in some kind of karate pose extension of himself . . .)*
Yeh . . .
> *(Gesturing with the horn, not even seeing the* WOMAN . . .)*
Yeh, dig *this*—this is me, horrible shit all together—crazy life—this is me!

WOMAN

Well.
> *(*HE *looks, and finally, sees!)*
You all right?

MAN

Oh?
> *(Digs himself, like someone not used to people or other eyes.)*
Oh? OK, hello . . . hello and shit.

WOMAN

You all right?
(SHE *edges forward.* HE *is trying to welcome her, but still not certain of
what and how, etc., edges backward.*)

MAN

All right? What you mean? Who're you? Out there in the dark.
Asking me am I OK, all right? What about you? Shit, you might be a
ghost, some ambitious smoke. I might be dead . . .
(HE *is admitting her to the house and retreating at the same time.*)
Am I all right?

WOMAN

All right?

MAN

Yeh.

WOMAN

Well, are you inviting me in?

MAN

Yeh, I opened the door.
(HE *is gesturing with the horn, now somewhat embarrassed at his
wildness.*)
Am I all right?
(Sings and toots on mouthpiece.)
Am I all right? Am I cool?
Am I all right? Am I well?
Am I all right? Do I have what I need?
Am I all right? Am I still breathing fine?

I'm all right, sure I'm great. It's the world
That's blown, I'm cool. It's the world
That's smashed, I'm in perfect shape.

It's just the world
It's blown apart
It's just the world
I'm doing fine.

WOMAN

(SHE *stands looking at the* MAN *and over her shoulder, etc.*)
He's doing great
It's just the world
He's in perfect shape
It's just the world

Wow, it's so profound
he's cool, he's hip
it's just the world
he's all right, it's just the world

(SHE laughs, and the laughter while ridiculing his unrealistic stance, at the same time relaxes him. HE smiles, half grudging.)

MAN

That does sound out, don't it? I'm all right, it's just the world that's fucked up. Wow! Wow is right!!
(Then focusing on her.)
Well, come on in anyway. You know so much about how we connected with the world, how come you running around in it?

WOMAN
(Relaxing, unzippering the jump suit enough to get some air.)
Hey, you don't want the whole story now, do you?
(Laughs, a mixture of lightness and bad memory.)
I was part of a good thing . . .
(Heavy pause.)
and it got . . . blown . . . wasted . . .

(HAM, the Statesman, with congealed hair, is doing his cave dance surrounded by the garbage cans overloaded with money.)
Cans marked

HAM
(Sings.)
We told them, you read it
We warned them, don't dread it
We were right, you knew it
We were white, we were rich

You poor ones, don't worry
We represent your suffering too
You black and red and brown and
Yellow ones, don't worry, we are
Absolutely in touch with you

Don't do it, we screamed, don't
Try to live. Don't try it, we sung—
We won't allow any life but ours.

Holy Mother of profit, you know
We are always true. Money Lord

128

we are more white, more red
more blue.
(Pause, looking around at the garbage cans as if for response.)

HAM *(continued)*

And now,
what is the pleasure of the
center of the earth, what is
the will of the money gods?

(The light has been raised to show the section of the stage where the
STATESMAN, *like from a past age, a fading nightmare, continues to
perform a life exorcism, a death ritual to bring the dying on.*

*The song is a poem/chant of rising death feeling. A rising strangle on
light and love.*

The STATESMAN, *as* HE SINGS *and* DANCES, *makes motions from time to
time like* HE *is playing a violin.* HE *plays an imaginary violin,
sometimes, uses different parts of his body, arms, legs, head, as an
imaginary violin, and saws away, spitting out the doomlike song.)*

And now? And now? And now?
We've begged and pleaded
Compromised and defended
But now? But now! We'll have no more
of this. But now? But now!

We'll right the world for good.
But now! But now! But now, and now,
and now.

*(His dance turns into a "blowup" mime, his arms and body making
explosion gestures, each larger and larger, and more devastating.)*

So what is the word
From the Money Gods?
What is the word of Boss
Divine? Now, and now and now!!

What is the word
of the Money Gods?
What does eternity
speak? And now and now and now!!

*(Suddenly, the garbage cans begin to move. They wobble like they're
going to fall over, and as they tilt, the* STATESMAN [HAM] *shrieks his
doom chant more intensely, like Ra & Yma Sumac.)*

129

THE MUSIC

Begged and pleaded, pretended to
be mortal, acted humble like humans
but none of that worked, none of it
made them see who we were. And now

And now, Money Gods, answer, Money
Gods, speak to us, now and now the time
is now, we've acted like humans and other
passive things too long, now and now we've
come to another time, it's passed into

another clime. And now, they'll know
we'll show, the depth and breadth
of our power. We wait, only for a sign
let the money gods roar out their pleasure!

*(The cans rocking, and one at a time, but rapidly, the tops of all four of
them pop open—and out of the two of the cans, there are* TWO MEN *with
top hats on who rise up, the money that has covered them, flying
everywhere.*

The STATESMAN [HAM] *is ecstatic,* HE *leaps in the air, for his prayers
have been answered. The* MONEY GODS *have appeared.* HE *leaps, and
saws the imaginary violins crazily. The* MONEY GODS *also have violins,
real ones, and* THEY *play as* THEY *sing and speak and chant.* ONE's *face
is painted into a smile, the* OTHER *into a frown. But* THEY *have no
faces, rather* THEY *are wearing layers and layers of masks. And every so
often, at indicated moments, their singing and chants take on more
significance as* THEY *discard one of the masks only to reveal the mask
under it is the same as the mask the opposite one is wearing. So the*
SMILING GOD *takes off a mask to reveal a frown as the* FROWNING GOD
takes off his mask to reveal a smile.

The MONEY GODS *play the violins like telegraph messages from all over
the world. The* dit dit dit *of world news tonight. To the heightened
razor craziness of their violin playing, their voices in bizarre song,
which seems to combine stock exchange jargon and atmosphere and the
entire range of television, radio, and billboard commercials—one after
another, and intermixed, the national anthem of commercials is their
lyrics.*

*These commercials and violin playing must be delivered in much the
same rhythm as the* telegraph message *violins. As* THEY *emerge from
out the cans it is a ritualized dance, which at the same time reveals their*

130

lives as merchants and controllers of society. It is a power-mime *dance* THEY *do as* THEY *emerge shouting the crazed commercials.)*

(The MUSICIAN *and the* WOMAN *are standing closer in the room, talking quietly about each other's lives.* HE *is still trying to fix the horn, to make it play, and still occasionally playing the mouthpiece blues and rags, singing snatches of* "Am I All Right," *humming it, now scatting it lightly, punctuating with the mouthpiece, or the horn's keys pressed rapidly like subtle percussion runs.)*

WOMAN

You know I can fix that horn?

MAN

Well how come you didn't fix it when you first got in here?

WOMAN

Because I was waiting for you to admit that we'd met before, that you knew my name and that you had known me before, out there with the people of disaster!

MAN

Why would you say that? This is the first time I ever saw you.

WOMAN

The explosions took your memory.

MAN

Why are you saying this?

WOMAN

That I can fix the horn?

MAN

No. That too, but the other stuff.

WOMAN

Then who are you?

MAN

I only tell who I am to people I am in love with.
                    (A pause, an uneasy smile.)
Who're you?

WOMAN

You really don't know me?

MAN

Why are you talking like this?

131

THE MUSIC

WOMAN
(Shrugging, like an unexpected delay.)
What is that pile in the corner over there? Extra wood for the fire?

MAN
(Blowing into the mouthpiece.)
It just might be . . .
(HE goes over and pulls back the tarpaulin.)
It's a piano . . . wasted . . . I can't do nothin' with it anyway. But it's
out past Cage right now. It's been prepared by violent reality!

*(The sound of the STATESMAN/MONEY GODS in their wild dance is
heard from time to time, like sound effects, percussive bits and pieces,
and a spotlight—reminds you of flashing neon signs in which flashes of
the killer statesman ritual dance, with the speaker, HAM, transfixed like
a true believer and worshiper, are seen.)*

*(The WOMAN sits down at the piano on a box, SHE dusts it off, rubs at it
to clean it, removes boxes and bottles from around it, SHE pokes at it, a
few smooth runs, her voice trailing the notes swooning up and down the
keys. SHE does very little, but what SHE does makes the MUSICIAN stop
and look at her.)*

MAN
Uhhuh.
(Acknowledging.)
What you gon' do? You can play that?

WOMAN
(Nodding at the horn.)
About as well as you can play that. And yours is broke!

MAN
You said you can fix it!

WOMAN
Then remember me, lover man!
*(SHE begins to play the piano. It is a sad little ballad, at each break of
the line, SHE almost hums tears, tears, tears.)*

MAN
You can sing too?

WOMAN
(Extending the melodic little piece, sings.)
As it is with the world
so it is with love

132

as it's light or dark
so it is with love

under the stars
is more than astrology
it has some influence
on your psychology

so let's change our lives
for a change let's make our world
beautiful. So let's change our world
for a change let's make our lives
beautiful!

(SHE *finishes the piece with a slowing, brooding introspection, humming
and slipping in and out of the lyrics, the piano poignant, but panging
and banging slightly out of tune.*)

MAN

Hey.
(HE *holds the horn up looking at it.*)
That was nice—some real music for a change.

WOMAN
(SHE *wheels around off the box.*)
You think I wasn't serious about fixing this horn? I can play that horn
too.

(HE *looks at her.*)

But that ain't my specialty. My father and grandfather could play—
they built bridges and played music. They never was on television, but
they swung harder than most of them that were! There was always
horns and instruments, a piano around our house. Not to be looked at,
like a pretty piece of furniture, but to be low down played.

MAN
I don't know why I can't fix it myself. (*Pause.*) Goddam, I can play it.
And can't fix it. But where I was you could send 'em out to be fixed.

(*The* WOMAN *has the horn, looking at it.* SHE *pads it, pushes the keys in
silent rushing scales. Looks at the mouthpiece.*)

(*Now the dit dit dit madness is brought up in the lights. The* MONEY
GODS *are frozen in their maniacal dance posture.* THEY *are trembling
and jerky like* THEY *still must play, play, but* THEY *are fixed and
staring, eyes rolling around.*)

133

THE MUSIC

                    HAM
Ah, masters of reality, creators of the future, you've responded.

                    SADO
              (Smiling face.)
Yes, of course.
       (Loose sing-song, like one of Snow White's dwarfs, Dopey.)
Of course, yes. We're like that. Always generous to a fault.

                    MASO
              (Frowning face.)
We must respond. We know how absolutely powerful we are. How we
run everything.
                    (HE *breaks into a* song.)

    If it's run
    We run it
    If it's fun
    We own it
    If it's valuable
    We define it
    If it's rebellious
    We confine it

                    HAM
Now that you've come, to give me my words. My thoughts for the
year. How to deal with weird events, invasions and such, bombings of
reactors and fundings for bad actors. Overthrowing governments,
assassinating patriots.

   (HE *is taken by his speech, swaying back and forth like a drunk getting
                   ready to have an orgasm.*

   Suddenly MASO *and* SADO *go into wild violin duet.* HAM, *picking up on
   it, starts to pick up his sway, the* TWO VIOLINISTS *are "competing" with
                each other,* one-upping, *snarling, jumping.*)
                    MASO
Uhh, Uhh.

                    SADO
Umm Umm.

       (THEY *jump toward each other, and away like a boxing match.*

       HAM *dances to their playing—*HE *has a smaller violin which* HE
          scratches at, puts in his pocket, spinning, eyes crossing.)

HAM
(Sings.)

Knowledge
and death
everything
and death
jungle lights itch
and death
all of it is life
all of it is death
and death

(MASO and SADO pick up death chant, sawing away at their axes. HAM now begins on flute, accompanying the MONEY GODS, singing and grunting and dancing.

Every so often the TWO exchange masks and change the key THEY sing in or the tempo to show the change.)

MASO

and death
the answer

SADO AND MASO

and death
and question

nothing anywhere resembles
great death, nothing

in or outside
the sun

the bloody
moon

we know, we do know
what's great

immortal
death.

SADO
(Abruptly.)

What . . .

THE MUSIC

MASO

Do you want?

> *(A stock market board bell rings and we hear ticker tape, when* THEY
> *laugh.)*

SADO

Sell!

MASO

Sell? Sell? Sell?

> *(Looks around wildly.)*

SADO

Sell!

> *(The sound of chains being dragged somewhere, slave moans like the
> blood market of king cotton.)*

HAM

> *(Spinning, looking out at audience.)*

You hear that
Sell, Sell, Sell!

> *(The* THREE *like spastic madmen go through the act of* selling—
> *Freeze—)*

HAM *(continued)*

And the prophecy, the future? Today is the day when all that is
settled! When the things worldwide are set. Have they come? Will
they survive? Who will wake? The powerful Gods.

> *(Gestures at the mad* MONEY GODS *grating* Sell. HAM *goes back into
> dance, a trio, with two violins and flute.)*

> *(Lights up on the* MUSICIANS—*the* WOMAN *is still bent over the horn,
> playing it in pantomime, checking her embouchure, etc.)*

MAN

So what's the problem? Thought you had no trouble with such as this.
You played it and repaired it and come in out the night—some black
lady beautiful wizard—gonna fix my horn.

WOMAN

> *(Looking up, wistfully, not saying anything at first.)*

It's fixed!

MAN

> *(Laughing, light disbelief.)*

Ah, yes, fixed. Could you fix the world as easy?

WOMAN

Fix the world?
> *(Half-laugh, then silence.)*
You remember that old song, "If This World Was Mine"? . . .
> *(SHE sings the first stanza of it . . .)*

MAN
> *(HE is listening and not saying a word for a long time.)*
If This World Was Mine . . . If it was either one of ours, if it had ever
been . . .

WOMAN

But it never was . . . and if you think of times ancienter than these last
few decades of destruction. If we go back beyond the scene of this
crime. If we go back to where the black nation dwelt across the seas,
years and years before our slavery . . . you'd see more destruction. A
nation committing suicide . . . kings and queens selling farmers to
merchants . . .

MAN

A world of destruction, now it comes round, there it goes, now it
comes round again, now blood smeared on stone. Now bombs and
bullets, now death flesh ripped.
> *(Straightens up.)*
But we had no say in this last million murders . . . we had no say . . .

WOMAN

No? No way . . .
> *(SHE is looking at the horn . . . SHE slowly holds it up for him . . .)*
You wanted this?

MAN

Oh, it's still fixed?
> *(Laughs.)*
You mean you can really fix . . .

WOMAN

Can you really play?

MAN
> *(Tentatively seizing the horn.)*
Can I play?
> *(Pause.)*
If I can't play—the world will end now!

SADO

What . . .

                              MASO
Do you want?
(Staring stupidly at HAM, *who, bathed in their madness, has drawn up*
as large as THEY—*their stares shrink him.)*

                              HAM
Yes . . . Want?
                        (Lower key.)
The future—

                              SADO
That's it, Bucks, that's it, of course. That's what distinguishes us, the
Money Gods, from the . . . rest!

                              MASO
Our money—of course, dear Dough . . .

                              SADO
Of course—but all the others . . . *want*! They're always wanting—
wanting stuff. Always wanting.

                              MASO
Of course, yes, that's it—always wanting.

                              SADO
Of course, that's why this crazy path—this whining about Mars, this
refusal to see our greatness-power.

                              HAM
                        (Illuminated.)
Want—Of course . . .

                              SADO
                        (Screaming.)
They want food!
                      (Screaming—sawing.)

                              MASO
                        (Screams.)
Why, Why, Why, they want *LIFE*!

                              SADO
SELL!

                              HAM
Yes, yes, that's it. They be talking 'bout . . . all these.
                        (At audience.)

                              MASO
Wanters—out there! Wanting! All The Time Wanting!

SADO

Crazed with Desire. While we are Wholly cool, coolly whole. A buck!

MASO

Hey, wanters!

(ALL THREE take up their instruments and shoot *them at the audience, sawing and screaming!)*

ALL THREE

Hey, WANTERS! WANT ALL YOU WANT! WANT WANT WANT!
(Crazed laughter.)

SADO *(To* HAM.*)*

Now what calls us through your mouth?

MASO

Your teeth—your armpits.

SADO

SELL!

MASO

Trace the faces negative all impinge upon us as our conquests
(Waves.)
These faces!

(Violins.)

SADO

They want stuff, don't they?

HAM

Yes.

(Flutes, flutes, whistles, kazoos, etc.)

MASO *(Accusingly at* HAM.*)*

The future, you wanted.

HAM

Why—Yes—I thought—My job was to—tell these—
(Harshly.)
miserable wanters—what they wanted was wanting!

MASO AND HAM
(Howling.)

HaHaHaHaHaHa.

SADO

Veddy good. What they wanted was—Ha Ha.

MASO
(Grabs them.)
But this is serious, Bread. There are evil forces everywhere. Stronger forces—than these tie-wearing weaklings who also want
(Trancelike.)
who at this very moment conspire to back us against the wall.

SADO

Our rocket

(Breathy rhythm on flute underscoring.)

MASO

Their rocket

SADO

Our triple nuke

MASO

Their triple nuke

SADO

Our dirt killing bleed-more

MASO

Their dirt killing bleed-more

SADO

LASERS

MASO

LASERS

SADO

A million niggers with razors

(MASO and HAM look.)

MASO

What?

HAM

Not that?

SADO

Well, in a manner of speaking.
(A joke.)

HAM

They're called something
else in the Eastern
steppes.

140

MASO

But they're darker
and starker
always wearing
our parka
Our enemies
got niggers
Too!

(Amazed.)

MASO/SADO/HAM

Wow!
The really secret
Weapon

(Song.)

But here with us they're
wanting
throughout this land
like a
haunting

MASO

Always!

SADO

Always!

(Sawing.

HAM *whistles, blowing things, throwing them away.)*

MASO

Buy.

(Reverse motions, clacking of stock board.)

Buy!

(Making buy motions, changing masks.)

SADO

But they can't get nothing. All over there—depths of jungle—dying
folks—you'll never—never

HAM

They'll, You'll, never! That's it—They'll never! Never! That's it, Sirs,
Never

(Sawing and humping up and down.)

uh uh

THE MUSIC

(The SISTER *is handing the horn toward the* BROTHER, *the antics of the* STATESMEN *are quiet in pantomime.)*

WOMAN

So you were saying about the world ending . . .

(The MAN *takes the horn, laughing, begins to play. A solo piece—*
"From the Old to the New"!

Drawing somewhat closer.)

So you can

MAN

I can

WOMAN

That was . . .

MAN

"Out of the Old into the New."

WOMAN
(Turning toward window.)
Out there, in that poison dark. Where the dead rule all that is left of a world.

*(*BROTHER *plays behind her.*
Repeat.)

MAN

All that is left of
a world

*(*SHE *plays behind him.)*

Destroyed
by idiots!

WOMAN

But play some more—Hey, it's dark—
Light up the world.

(The MAN *plays up tempo "The World Destroyed By Idiots Can Yet*
Rise Again"!

Second chorus, SHE *gets in, sharp fertile chords.*

Tableau: The MADMEN—*the* MUSICIANS *in Flashing Lights.*

THEY *take turns singing and accompanying each other.)*

142

MAN

All that I am
All that I own
Nothing it seems
Nothing but dreams

WOMAN

Dreams can be real
Make life what you feel
Be all you need
A blue spirit freed

MAN

Here in the dark
Death kills the spark
You brought light with you
You brought life with you

WOMAN

Dreams can be real
Make life what you feel

MAN

You brought light with you
You brought life with you

(Instrumental duet.

Instrumental and vocal duet, saxophone, piano, vocals.)

MAN AND WOMAN

But we are alive here together
This is no dream, as grim as it is
This is our lives, our broken world
We meet tonight, like lovers in a book
But this is no dream, we are alive
in love, here together, to remake
our world, our lives, together
This is no dream, our hearts know
it's real, remake our world
broken hearts of dreamers
the madness of screamers
But this is no dream, broken
world crying. This is no dream
millions are dying. Remake our
hearts, like lovers, together.

>   This is no dream. Our lives
>   reality. Let life go on
>   Let life go on go on
>   This is no dream!

                                    HAM
So today—News for the Wanters

                              MASO
The Screamers

                              SADO
The Pleaders

> *(The sweep of the* MUSICIANS' *love song comes like a breath of air and
> the* MADMEN *visibly shiver, pull up their coats.)*

                              MASO
Ah . . . what's that?

>   *(Instrumental duet.)*

                              SADO
Crazies protesting the bomb.

                              MASO
Or protesting our beautiful nerve gas.

                                    HAM
PEACE FREAKS.

                              SADO
Or Niggers complaining.

                              MASO
Women exclaiming.

                              SADO
But it does no good—we own the world.

                              MASO
Yes, bux, you got that very right.

                                    HAM
Right! Right!
Far Far Far Right!

                              MASO
WHITE ON!

144

HAM

The News today will be awesome. I've set up an all-Universe
broadcast, a universal fact layout session.

SADO AND MASO
(Duet.)

They think
they can
threaten us

They think
we can
be scared

They think
it's flesh
and blood here

When it's coin,
and legal tender
silver certificates

instead of organic
parts. No feelings

No Souls
No memory
and most of all no hearts

Back us against the wall
These wanters. Whole countries
of them.

(A rock through the window hits HAM.*)*

HAM

The News is why they
Wait. The Big News
The End News. Anchor
of Anchors.

MASO

Tell Them we've tried.

MASO AND SADO
(Duet.)

That cannot be
denied.   But

no one can
back us
against
    the wall
        no one
            not at
                all

These wanters
These taunters
These marchers
Draft Dodgers

They stomp us with their
desires.

These rioters
Cities on Fire

Fiends and criminals
Non-white idlers
Begging nations
insatiable cravings

They want
just want
and want and
want
and want

They want to rule
They want to be
They want love

                (Smirks.)

Like cries in the mist
these wanters want to be
all this

             (Gestures all.*)*

            MASO
But tonight the stand will be made

            SADO
No further steps these wanters will take

            MASO AND SADO
We are the final takers!

HAM
(Applauding.)
Yes—The News! What speaks as future?

MASO AÑD SADO
(Laughing maniacally, trying to saw as THEY *roll.)*
Future?

MASO
How presumptuous of you.

SADO
How presumptuous indeed.

MASO AND SADO
We are in charge of the past.

SADO
And the Future.

MASO
And as punishment for this wild wanting, this aggression all around.

SADO
We have decided not to let them *have* a future!

MASO
No future, after all . . .

HAM
(As if HE*'s hearing something grand and mysterious.)*
No . . . Future . . .

MASO AND SADO
No future at all!

HAM
And That is . . . the News.

MASO
The News.

SADO
The last News anybody will get!

(Lights up on the TWO MUSICIANS.*)*

WOMAN
You don't recognize me—because you don't even recognize yourself.

THE MUSIC

MAN
(Musing.)

Lightning in the sky
The building shaking
The ground like water

    (Musical background: the violins, flute, etc. Piano and sax.)

WOMAN

What do you remember?

MAN

A wave of lost souls. The Blinding
Light. A world full of screams.
Oceans of Fire.

    (It becomes like a reenactment. Lights—slides.)

WOMAN

Explosions Explosions. You were running.
The sky behind you was white with Horror.
A figure alone. You were running
Toward me. I was fixed in the
heat storm, the thrashing on all sides.
I had screamed myself into a silence
of jagged edges.

MAN

A ring of the murdered flashing across
the sky. The murderers' voices whining
over radios televisions newspapers
blown by with their lies screaming

WOMAN

I saw you race past me.

MAN

I escaped alone, the dirt on fire.

WOMAN

You carried the horn in two pieces
Like I found it. The survivors had
scattered. I hid in the shadows.
You paused to look round. I
could barely see your face.

MAN

The world seemed midnight permanently
Hell uncovered to Burn
hideous like that in an eternal night.

WOMAN

You stood there staring
into red darkness
as if fixed yet
already flying

MAN

It had been an evening
of music, amusing
conversation
The Money Gods were

    whining we
    tried to change
    the station

    They said there'd be
    no future
    That the world
    had been
    canceled

(Tableau of MONEY GODS *as* THEY *approach their last press conference.*

  Violins and Flute come in as death imminence sound. The MONEY
    GODS' *voices:* BUY SELL *are a rhythm form for the song.)*

WOMAN

Remember that ending
Blind death mounts light
Blackness and fire the
Blown-up world weeping
as it flies out into
emptiness

MAN

The panic The death—Yes
I ran ran.
        (Covers eyes, then looks.)
  And where
were you then? When
they blew up the world?

THE MUSIC

WOMAN

I was there as you came
flying out the fire.
I was there in the shadows
weeping for the world.
Too tired to run farther
I lay there watching as you decided
I felt your mind searching
But I heard a music in you then
that lifted me
and moved me toward
you.

MAN

And what did I do? Just run
half mad, afraid . . .

WOMAN

And I ran
in your direction
I followed you
I led you
I advised you
like nature

MAN

And I never
saw you

WOMAN

You always
saw me

MAN

Always?
Then what
did
I do?

WOMAN

What you're doing
now, what
we're doing
now
Reconstruct
till fresh winds

blow your brain
clear again

At that moment
you go back
to the Fire
The mad night
they blew up
the world

Then you stare
like a mad thing
and cover your mouth
with silence

Then you wander out
into
the dark
trying to
find the old world
like a Zombie

MAN

Dreams
Hideous Dreams
The horn
in pieces
The world
on fire
my hands
burning
the ground
screaming

WOMAN

Where I lived
we were close
to each other
My family and
me.

We worked
and fought
them
worked
and made

151

THE MUSIC

love
and picketed
worked
and sang
Made beautiful songs
out of poems
we danced
we painted
we spoke the words
of genius
we also
worked
struggled with
the Money Gods
with their stooges
and hatchet persons
Yes, the Money Gods!

I knew you then
I'd heard that sound
that beautiful horn
Carrying memories and humanity's
future
I'd heard you
You'd seen me
You'd looked in my eyes
I thought
or were you staring
past me into
this

Like a black
crazy bird
scrambling out of
Smoke

They'd blown up
My home
my city
my family
my life . . .
all our lives

All our futures
I'd come East

152

toward the
water
Then you flashed
out the black fire
night

A broken horn
in your
hands

Trying to sing,

(SHE comes closer.)

You were standing there
peering into the hot
dark, trying to find
a song.

MAN
(Sings.)

Another life
like this, caught
a life looking for
your kiss

There must be
another life
somewhere

Someone take me
there

WOMAN

Yes, like that
A romantic thing
Why, I wandered
In this craziness . . .

You saw me then and fled
You thought I was a nightmare
An illusion. You had not
tasted me
then

MAN

The shadows
were
warm

153

Like humans
lived
there

Now a soft face
the brown skin
lovely under
some sudden
moon

The lips there
I touched
them

WOMAN

We were running
together. A wind
caressed us. I
hadn't felt a
breeze like that
so gentle
full of Music

All loveliness
seemed alien
in that
world

MAN

This world

WOMAN

Except

MAN

(HE *reaches for her, takes her to him.*)
Except even without that memory you are
all that loveliness
means!

WOMAN

Except, remember!

MAN

I do

WOMAN

What's my name?

MAN

Naima

WOMAN
(Begins to play that tune on the piano.)
You remember nothing.

(Lights up on the STATESMEN.*)*

HAM
(Slowly accelerating rhythmic speech.)
No future . . . What a coup!

MASO AND SADO
Of course—This'll teach them

HAM

It will It will

MASO

And you, Ham, will go down in
history

SADO

Ha Ha. If there was any more
history! We've canceled it,
remember

MASO

Oh, Yes, Ha Ha! Canceled
History. I always wanted to do
that.

HAM

I'll announce it!

SADO

Be Firm

MASO

But Loving

HAM
Tell Them The Buck Stops Here
(Points at the MONEY GODS.*)*
Right here!

MASO
You see this little pink button I wear around my neck?

THE MUSIC

SADO

I, of course, have one too. Simultaneous
Inspirational Destruct Switches.
For Him and Him.

HAM

Oh, how thrilling. But, sirs, ahem,
In my ignorance I thought such
buttons were red!

MASO

Fiction writers' conceit. We hate
anything *red*!

SADO

Better Dead! Ha Ha

MASO

You might say it's our message
to the world. Ha Ha

SADO

But let us be serious   (THEY *pose*.)

MASO

As befits world creators

SADO

And world destroyers

(Flashing flicks identify them seriously.)

HAM

This will be a special bulletin?

SADO

Of course. Stop all transmissions
and fire away

HAM

When?

MASO

Now—It's now the whole thing goes
                    (Imitates studio.)

HAM

Special Bulletin! We interrupt this program—all programs—all activity
of any kind—with this special bulletin

156

(A rap.)

The Money Gods have
decided because there's too much Wanting,
and Needing too I might add, that
society itself has become a pest!
The MG's are sick of it. Life
with you boobs. You people You
nations You countries. So
because you continue to make your silly demands
for life, liberty, sovereignty,
independence, liberation,
heaven forbid, revolution,
and various rights of all
sorts. Because you complain
and make noise. And Strike. And Vote
and Fight. And will not go peacefully.
Or die
The MG's have decided to
  Cancel the World—
  Until Further Notice!

(A roar of anguish—from the people—heard over a TV monitor.)

MASO

(At monitor.)

Look at them out there, scrambling
Crazy with Fear!

SADO

Turn it forward slowly
so we can see the Approach
of death to them all!
Let us watch the end—how
Thrilling

HAM

Awe-inspiring

MASO

Slow Forward—Look
Suicides, mobs searching
for us. Flags. Committees.
Nasty people cursing.
Look as it gets later
they're trying to rush the

Gray House looking for you,
Ham. Ha Ha.

How vulgar. They're
Shooting cops. Drowning
politicians. They think
they'll take over—but
the world is done.

We've decided

SADO

Fast forward. Let's look at
the very very end. The madness
and explosions.

>   *(A big monitor shows explosions, agony, blood, dying.)*

MASO

Now! Now! Now!

SADO

Even the Gray House went up!

HAM

Wonderful! Wonderful!
They thought I was still in it!

>   (MASO *and* SADO, *looking at each other meaningfully, laughing harder*
>   *still.)*

Is the whole world blowing up?

MASO

Of course.

HAM

Where do we hide—um retreat
till the old world's blown up and
a new one is created?

SADO

A new one?

HAM

Yes, isn't that the plan, to create
a new world?

>   (SADO *and* MASO, *laughing like at a child.)*

SADO

Why would we want that? A New World
Full of what? New complaints?

MASO

New wants and New Wanters?
No, enough is enough.

HAM

Enough—yes—of course
is enough. And . . .

SADO

And . . . you mean yourself and
property

HAM

Uhuh

SADO

Are you asking what about, Bux
and I?

HAM

Uhuh

MASO

As for you—you have ultra
super bomb shelters five hundred feet
under the soil. You'll survive
of course.

HAM
(Dutifully smiling.)

Yes—but

SADO

If we told you you'd find it hard to
believe. We're serious. We're through
The World's too old too full of
rotten wanting

MASO

We've found a way to change into the
very stuff of the universe, the very stuff
of the world!

THE MUSIC

SADO
(A bloodcurdling scream.)
The Insect Is Supreme!

MASO
(Secret admission.)
Ants Are the Hippest!

SADO AND MASO
(With violins screeching . . .)
The Energy

(. . . up mad screech sound!
THEY *begin to babble, like a vactic scat abstracting the facts the reality,
to a tale of their own making. Instruments used to accent their
deteriorating sense of reality. A voice and violin with flute piece—The
voice screamed, moaned, growled, screeched, sung, etc.)*

MASO
The ultimate energy—Computer mind
insects.

SADO
The Holy Scarab!

MASO
(Clack Clack.)
Buy!

HAM
Ultimate . . . Energy.

SADO
Time is energy—power—wealth
   control
Nobody would ask an ant for anything.
Ha Ha Nobody could want anything from
an ant.

MASO
Eternal Master Glorious Warrior
Gloriously beautiful

*(SADO, like HE's been turned on by the OTHER's rhetoric—a love song
to insects.)*

(Waving photos.)
The complex eye
ultimate historian

SADO

Most of all, survivor!

(A sudden blow.)

MASO
(As if praying.)

Master of Creation.
. . . I Shall Not Want . . .

HAM

Freedom—The Transparent Responder.
(Crawls, bumps into monitor.)
Ohh! But what's this—fast forward the world's blown up
the fire cross the sky. Dead people
toe up everywhere. Skeletons and
desolation—What fire didn't
kill, radiation and disease—
But still I see—shadows—
Shadows—No, what is this?
Money Gods, What is this we see?

MASO

Prayer to the Insect Master

SADO

You see only insects the holy ant
building beyond the
rationalization of broken human desire

HAM

I see the ants—
But the future—these shadows—
like living—humans

MASO

What?

HAM

Look here

MASO
(Moving to the monitor.)

There is somebody

(The MUSICIANS.)

MAN

I do remember . . . life. You are life to me

                              WOMAN
From no knowledge to life itself

                               MAN
No, the nightmare defined it
          What was
                alive.
          (Closer to her, SHE *is running* randomly *up and down the piano.)*

   Lost in the dark I thought
        I cd not grow
   Now I live
        among the
            stars

                              WOMAN
   What memory A kind of
        being there when you
            enter yr self
                conscious
                yr very senses
                    demanding
            all of what Life is
                every minute

                               MAN
   We're lucky to be alive
        Is that a Song?
                    (HE *bends to kiss her.*
            SHE *plays a brief very melodic ballad.)*

   But we cd be a Song
        two poems
     in search of a
            home

                         (Piano.)

                               MAN
   You smell like life!
                         (Musing.)
            That light beyond—
                    (Remembering.)
                was you
            That flow of lovely
                words
            The tremble the air is

162

```
        as it sings
           to us
        as quiet
          beauty
        was you
I remember we lay there whispering
        under the music
  I said I loved you
you smiled and let me
  caress you slowly—
        it was like
        a song
```

WOMAN

What name did you call me then?

MAN

Naima

WOMAN

Then you remember

MAN

I always remembered

WOMAN

```
That word I tossed at you
  Yr eyes upon me heating
       the air
    through which
  I returned yr stare
```

MAN
*(Playing lightly, the same ballad,
humming the end of some phrases.)*

```
It seemed we were below
      the surface
      of the earth
A black sky with holes
 Music seeping everywhere
   It was Sun Ra
```

WOMAN

```
If there were scientists of this
      life as lived
      measuring that space
```

                    we came to each other
                            in
                    They'd measure the
                            heat
                        & music
                    Their dials wd say
                        MAGIC!

                                            MAN

            All of that you said
                to me
            It was Africa
            I said to you
            Naima

                                        WOMAN

            Yes

                                        MAN

            I said, "Naima
            can you
            love me?"

                                        WOMAN

        I said, "Yes," I remember
        I sd, "Yes,"
            and you breathed
            the air into harmonies

                                        MAN

            My blood the
            rhythm

        I remember . . .

        I was warm and
            dark

                                        WOMAN

            We were already in each other's
                    language
                    Passion Eyes
                You said, "Come
                    with me"

                                        MAN

            You smelt like
                music

WOMAN

It was
 like a
  Song

(Duet out, lights dim to suggest lovemaking.)

(In the Chamber, the MONEY GODS *watch ever more frantically. But* THEY *are already Mad. Though the Madness has been already made to seem the "norm.")*

MASO

(Exchanging masks as rhythmic device—a bizarre game.)
Hey, it's only niggers! No people. Ha, you scared me for a second.
The Ants survive. *Forrrrrrrrr—everrrrrrrrr*—Insect Deities.

HAM

Niggers? Will They not . . . reproduce?

SADO

I see your point!

MASO

You mean, these blobs of distorted protoplasm would have the nerve
. . . to survive.

*(*MUSICIANS *repeat Song and Playing.)*

SADO

We cannot permit it.

HAM

It seems contradictory—
(Musing.)
Five Hundred feet below the earth!

SADO

Send heavier waves of death—

MASO

But even better, kill them before they arrive.

HAM

Death Music Future!

SADO

Of Course

*(*THEY *begin to get various instruments* axes *out to wail against the living future.)*

165

THE MUSIC

MASO

So we prepare The Final Assault.
As Death is launched. The bombs.
The Fire

SADO

Even beyond that!

*(Song like shrieking—like a mad person humming mood music out of
tune!*

*The eerie trio gets together, the expressionist masks of faces contorting,
a happening of craziness attacking!*

We see now a music war begin. The MONEY GODS *and* HAM, *like
invading Monsters. Blow a piece called "War of the Worlds" which
sounds like laser death beams from alien maniacs!)*

(The MAN *and* WOMAN MUSICIANS *suddenly feel the presence of the*
MONEY GODS *and* HAM. THEY *are attempting to destroy them. At first,
the* TWO *stagger under the attack. It is danced by the weird* TRIO *like
ballet and burlesque; showing their ass, then leaping crude pas de trois/
tour jetés, etc.)*

MAN

What's happening. Of a sudden, this air is clawing at me.

WOMAN
(Touching her throat and eyes.)

Juke Box Death Ray!

MAN
(Closing eyes.)

In Boats. A horse.
The Whip. He's . . . galloping
Crown Prince . . .

WOMAN

Like Bela Lugosi's theme song

MAN
(Shouts!)

FRANKENSTEIN!

(They are making ready to play.
The WOMAN—*An explosive piano run, like machine-gunning
colonialists from the high ground, on a very clear day!*

166

The MAN—*a solo, like the horn is talking! It's trying to identify the* MONEY GODS *and attack them murderously.)*

(The MONEY GODS *jump around, attacking, retreating. Sneak attacks, deadly rockets launched.*

We see a tableau of struggle. The music: an extended piece.

The struggle seems a balance, back and forth—like a surreal cutting session—with death as the penalty for losing!

The three dance around to get better leverage, advantage. THEY *try to spread out and then gang up. But it is clearly a war, all out, with exchanged solos and wincing on both sides like they're* hit.

But then from the dark, a thumping, a deep and thunderous rumbling— the drum[s].

The MONEY GODS *notice, the* BROTHER *and* SISTER *are animated,* get down *harder, at the sound.*

The drum sets the music *from Africa, to Latino, to low-down Blues, to traditional New Orleans, to Big Band to Bop to Hard Bop to a throbbing dynamic solo, with the* bombs *rocking the* MONEY GODS!

Now a straight-ahead, impossible tempo piece, which is the beginning of

A Suite: 1. Tension 2. Explosion 3. Terror 4. Death 5. Silence 6. Time

SILENCE—*weeps of violin—horn snorts—like temporary quiet on the battlefield—and suddenly a pounding on the* MUSICIANS' *door.)*

MAN
(Instinctively.)

The Drummer

WOMAN

Who's that?

(The MAN *swings open the door. Violin screeching wind poison wafts in. Black jump-suited goggles, carrying all kinds of percussion instruments, and, of course a brace of congas under wraps.)*

DRUMMER *(Heart)*

I saw lights, I heard . . . music . . . two musics fighting back and forth.

MAN

A drummer?

WOMAN

Who are you?

167

THE MUSIC

DRUMMER
(HE thumps an answer, the talking drum which accompanies the verse/
song.)

They try to blow up
the world
Turn night
to poison
day to fire
But I am Man

MAN

If the world survive
  A drummer
    must be in
      it!

WOMAN

Man

MAN

Yes, they try
to turn the world
back to animal
rule
Gorilla time
Ape era
Monkeys' business

WOMAN

Even past that
before that
Crazier than that
they in the past
killing our future

(The MONEY GODS' *laughter spits in eerily. Their faces for a second are*
creeping across a wall.

Drum accompanying—Drum popping.)

MAN

And they here around us
now. Blowing Mickey Mouse
as vampire insect

168

WOMAN

Yes, like they worship
some hideous . . .
insects

DRUMMER

Yes, I've heard
recently the cries
of Killer insects

WOMAN

We've heard them
praying in their
craziness—to insects
to be insects
and to kill off
human life

DRUMMER

No one can kill
life. It live
Its heartbeat
It live!

WOMAN

Yes, you survive
the lonely darkness

DRUMMER

I'm not alone
My name is Heart
I search for lovers
. . . like you

What's a drum
without a horn and
box

(They laugh.)

I search for more life
to go with that
I've found

MAN

Life, out there, still?
More life?

THE MUSIC

WOMAN

Life?

DRUMMER

Every day, more life
We're hiding out there
Waiting for the air
to clear

A giant *orchestra* building
all of us, rainbow people
blowing more life in
the world

WOMAN
(Musing.)

Like there could be a world
after all.

MAN

But that mad shit
we heard
that screeching
like Mickey Mouse
hatchet murder

WOMAN

Madness of the past
trying to kill
our future

DRUMMER

Yes, we know them
death figures
We heard you
Fighting them
Knew you was life
I come
You heard me
Coming

(DRUMMER *plays licks* HE *played.*)

MAN

Life go on go on
          (Plays note of direction, then goes to the corner.)
and look my man
Black Heart

170

(HE *uncovers yet another instrument, the bare frame of trap drums.*)
I found these—
Knew I'd need
some Heart music

                              DRUMMER
Heart Music!
                         (Rushes to set up.)
Heart here.
I need to call
some of the others
be with us
when the final
go down
get down

                              WOMAN
When the war
gon start
you need
your heart

                              MAN
                         (Touching her.)
        Lovers' music
        the soul
        of the
             world . . .
                  Naima, my name is . . .
                       (About to embrace.)

                              WOMAN
I know your name, Mtu, I know your name.
                       (THEY *embrace.*

The screeching of the MONEY GODS *begins again. We see them.* THEY
look like THEY*'ve been attacked, faces raw, wounded, background in
                              shambles.)*

                              MAN
Get ready

                              DRUMMER
                         (Calls.)
        Music Lovers
        Soul People
        Heart Companions
        Ready To Get Down

                                                            171

THE MUSIC

WOMAN

This the final go
Life or death

(Kissing her PARTNER, sitting at piano.

But as MONEY GODS begin their screech, Death Attack of the Money
Gods, THEY look changed. Their faces are altering, changing to insects,
large hideous insects, buzzing [violins], chirping, etc. HAM jerks around
like some weird gorilla.)

DRUMMER

The Past versus
The Future!

WOMAN

Yes

DRUMMER

Yet I am the past
that lives to be
future

MAN

But not
the dead past
the past of horror
terror
madness
stupidity
the past will
die and stay
dead

WOMAN

You are no past
man, you are
only
tradition

(MONEY GODS, now raising their axes in combat. The Final Conflict.)

DRUMMER
(Calling to his COMPANIONS.)

Music Lovers
Heart Companions
Soul People!
All Who Love Life better than death!

(BLACK WOMAN, HEART's WIFE, *a* WHITE *and* LATINO, *push warily through the door. They have instruments in their hands, the* Life Orchestra *formed meets this final challenge. The Music War, a long final suite beginning with:*

1. *Tension*
2. *Explosion*
3. *Terror*
4. *Death*
5. *Silence*
6. *Time*

But then, as a kind of ReBirth, like a history of music, the whole suite, but particularly the Life Orchestra *plays:*

1. *ReBirth*
2. *New Life*
3. *Lovers*
4. *Sweet World*
5. *"Great Peace"* [Reds and Blues]

The last music confrontation shows the insects turning in circles, made mad by the music, their monitors and machines smoking and exploding.

MUSICIANS *finally are playing, embracing, and dancing, life victory movement. Final chorus is all together and get audience to sing/chant gigantic:)*

ALL

YES TO LIFE!
NO TO DEATH!
YES TO LIFE!
NO TO DEATH!

(And at each chant, MONEY GODS *and* HAM, *dead feet straight up in air, shrink and die deader. And finally ending in unison joy laughing shouts.)*

ALL *(Continued)*

YES!
YES!
YES!
YES!

Essays

by *AMIRI BARAKA*

Where's the Music Going and Why?

A general answer to that question, if we're talking about African-American music, would be, "Wherever the masses of the African-American people are going or have gone." And I would hold that as an accurate and verifiable insight. But at the same time there is such a constant flow of new or altered trends or recurring patterns that sometimes it might seem that there are simply too many things happening to analyze.

Under the broad rubric of black music in the United States, in recent years we have seen the continued significance and endless stylistic variations of the Funk (on one level simply the restating or re-expression of the basic African-American blues impulse, in most cases the intensification, the speeding up, the re-instrumentation of the rhythm that be with the modern instrumental urban blues). This aspect of the music was sucked up immediately in its formula corporate form *Disco,* a commercial mostly mindless flattening of black urban rhythms into dollar-producing hypnosis. The popular Afro-American music of any period is the blues, and the most significant styles of the music are rooted in and connected to the blues. But when the heavy corporate hand is laid on the music, any aspect of it, blues included, can turn it into dead formulas which have much more significance in the corporation's financial records than in the real aesthetic and emotional life of the people.

The Funk explosion in the early seventies was also accompanied by a period of death and transformation of important trends in the sixties' avant-garde music. The deaths of innovators like Trane, Ayler, Dolphy created a vacuum that sometimes saw their disciples carrying those trends into dead ends of mysticism or commerce or both at the same time.

A trend arose that in much the same way as the fifties' cool development expressed emotionally and historically a change in the society (the letdown of a post-revolutionary age) in which now the funk bottom or rhythm was harnessed gently to the cooled-off top or melodic and harmonic lines, and the result was Fusion. A corporate composite in its worst incarnation, though like everything else there were all kinds of Fusion from the highly commercial to the highly experimental. But mostly it was dollar-sign music.

We could credit Miles Davis for the mainstream creation of Fusion as a jazzlike trend. His Bitches Brew bands and Post-Bitches Brew bands read like a who's who of Fusion (Corea, Hancock, Weather Report, Tony Williams, etc.). But like Cool, not only was the rhythm, blues, and improvisational fire cooled out in most Fusion, for the sake of formulas and commercial charts, but a whole royalty of performers, mostly non-African-American, was raised so that it was possible on the defunct WRVR to listen nonstop to a so-called Jazz Music, hour after hour, that made little reference to the greatest names and musical tradition of the African-American experience, except the obvious golden straw stuck into the ear and jabbed deep in the brain of that same tradition like an electric cord stuck in a wall socket.

But so trendy and faddish was the Fusion mini-epoch that it was possible to trace its ebb very clearly, and the morning that WRVR turned hillybilly right before our ears was simply evidence that the trend had risen and fallen on greenbacks. It is interesting in the face of this that Columbia would then urge Miles out of retirement, and his *Man with the Horn* is in one reading simply a further restatement of the Fusion trend.

There was by the downturn of the Fusion trend a reawakening, it would seem, of a neo-BeBop voice. In much the same way that Hard Bop, pushed by players like Horace Silver, Art Blakey and the Messengers, Sonny Rollins, Max Roach, reappeared to do battle with the Cool school in the early sixties, trying to restore the heart and soul to the music. So in the late seventies, BeBop had made a distinct comeback (not that it ever left among a lot of folks), and reissues of records and some new clubs indicated the artistic reinfusion as well as some commercial interest. To me this was a healthy sign, concrete evidence that Fusion, for all its great sweeping trendiness which saw a few of our greatest musicians turn out a couple of new-style mood-music albums and bands, could not erase the deeper mainstream traditions of the music.

But there was also, at the same time, a restatement, a new coming together or just an initial breakthrough of musicians who had heard the new music revolution of the sixties and early seventies, younger musicians in most cases, who had been turned around by the Coltranes and Ornette Colemans and Cecil Taylors and Albert Aylers and Sun Ras and Eric Dolphys and Pharoah Sanders and now were ready to make their own further statements. Their clarifications and refinings, their new expressions rooted in the profundity of the African-American musical tradition, which has always borrowed from whatever and wherever it wanted and at the same time remained itself.

The Art Ensemble of Chicago, Air, World Saxophone Quartet, Olu Dara's Okra Orchestra, David Murray's big bands and Octet and

Henry Threadgill's sextets, the consummate artistry of Arthur Blythe are some of the obvious examples and pluses of this period which extends until today. This is like a second wave of Avant-gardists, coming out of Chicago and St. Louis and California and other places to be sure, but a generation of players that not only sounds the most contemporary note of the music but brings a great deal of respect and knowledge about some of the oldest of black American musical traditions.

The present situation sees the newest black music developing within a social framework that is, as is also traditional, oppressive and exploitive. But at the same time there is an even broader range of influences and cross-currents in the music than ever. Advancing technology, especially in communications, makes it possible now to sample a whole crush of world cultures, and the movement and relationship of people in the United States and internationally add to this. There is a broadening of the palette created by a welter of different trends and influences (e.g., reggae, new wave, etc.) and also the corporate drummers whose general approach to art (and especially progressive art) is always, first ignore it, second coopt it, then water it down and formularize the weakest version. For the African-American artist and his art there is also the added opposition and ignore/coopt cycle set up by racism. So that in rhythm and blues it is Bill Haley, Elvis Presley, or for that matter the Beatles, Rolling Stones, or the various instant superstar white teenagers, rather than black blues players of any generation.

A neophyte listener to alleged jazz station WRVR a couple years ago would think Chuck Mangione, Weather Report, and Phoebe Snow were the High Art creators of the music. Somehow it always seems strange or untrue to some people, especially in corporate and media posts, that the major innovators in African-American music would be African-Americans.

No one would question that the major innovators in European concert music are European and that if the various non-Europeans who have played that music were somehow not talked about it, would not change the essential history of that music. (World influences would be more to the point, including African.) So too for African-American music; if the non-African-American who played the music had not played it, it would not change the essential history of African-American music.

The problem for the Creators of Black Music, the African-American people is that because they lack Self-Determination, i.e., political power and economic self-sufficiency, various peoples' borrowings and cooptation of the music can be disguised and the beneficiaries of such acts pretend they are creating out of the air.

179

The absence of African-American-owned concert spaces, theaters, clubs, recording companies, publishing companies, and periodicals means that black music, like black people generally, is then left to the tender mercies of white racist monopoly capitalism.

The creation of such institutions by any nationalities independent of monopoly capitalism is obviously important to most of us!

African-American music like the other profound expressions of that culture can only be strengthened by the whole people focusing in on the struggle for Self-Determination for the African-American Nation!—whether black artists or black businessmen, black workers or progressive people of any nationality. The only way for the music to achieve self-determination is for the people to.

Greenwich Village and African-American Music

(A paper delivered at the Greenwich Village Jazz Festival)

My first investigation of the Village was in the middle fifties while still in college. Wandering around stunned and awed and turned on by the variety of strange images to my still teenaged mind.

I was then being drawn into the world of artists and writers, intellectuals and bohemians, the struggling and the poseurs.

My introduction to bebop was at the very beginning of the fifties when my cousin made the mistake of lending me his Manors, Guilds, and Savoys. I met Bird, Miles, Max, Diz, Getz, and I was on my way, barely a teenager, into the ever-opening world of The Music. A few months later I had a skatebox with a picture of Diz I painted on it complete with bebop glasses and beret—we called them tams—and a caption painted under it, "To Be or Not To Bop." I still remember my father asking me the loaded question, "Why Do You Want to Be a Bopper?" For me, it was like saying, "Why Do You Want to Be Conscious?"

I finished college in 1954 and went into the Air Force and during that period, in New York State, Rantoul, Illinois, and finally Aquadilla, Puerto Rico, I was listening to the music. But I'd started to come down to the Village, as I said, even in college, because a friend of mine I'd idolized in high school had come down and was making the bohemian scene, so I'd heard. I wanted to know what that was about.

During the Air Force, whenever I'd have leave I'd come downtown and wander and gawk and stare. Try to interpret what was happening, and also try to learn. That was my credo I'd developed isolated in the middle of heathen Illinois, Learn Or Die!

It was during one of these leaves that I first peeped The Open Door, which Bird played at, a club opened by Bob Reisner who wrote the book *Bird Lives*. And my friends in the Village gladly gave me all the current Birdlore. One night on leave I hung out in front of the Door most of the night, peeping in trying to see Bird, or whoever, and watching people coming out. One poet friend of mine told me how

Bird was known by all the painters and writers in his circle. How he was giving alto lessons to painter Harvey Cropper in exchange for painting lessons. They also used to talk about the loft on West Twenty-seventh Street where Buhainia, Art Blakey, lived for a while, along with Bird, and poet Carl McBeth.

By the time I actually got out of the service and moved to the East Village, 1957, Bird was dead. Murdered by America!

In the trends that I perceived, I had followed the music as it moved from Bop to Cool. In fact *Venus de Milo, Move, Budo, Darn That Dream* was the main music I dug just before leaving high school. Throughout college the cools, Brubeck, Chet Baker, Shorty Rogers, were in vogue. When I moved to the Village, hard bop had come out to try to restore the primacy of improvisation, the fundamental thrust of blues, and the heavy rhythmic flesh and blood of classical African-American music to jazz. Art Blakey and The Messengers, Horace Silver introducing the gospel, Max Roach and Clifford Brown (in my opinion the high point of the hard-bop rectification and reform), and Sonny Rollins had already emerged to stop the drift of the music into elevator obscurity.

One of the earliest clubs I started going to, mostly standing outside of, was where what was to be the classic band of the late fifties played, Club Bohemia on Barrow Street where the great Miles Davis Quintet and Sextet played. The Bohemia was one of those uptown nightclubs downtown, at least it seemed to me in my impecunious position. But Miles's great classic group was so heavy because it contained all the elements of the period, both what had gone before the cool and bebop and the hardbop revival in something like perfect balance. Cool, hard-bop plus echoes of what was to come, New Music and Fusion. Cannonball seemed like he carried Miles's thrust into pop blues with cool top. Miles was one of the most important popularizers of both cool and later fusion. It's no coincidence that Cannonball and Zawinul in Cannonball's later bands made *Mercy Mercy* and *Jive Samba* which take the hardbop revival full of its churchisms and softens it, popularizes it—this is early fusion and you should note that Zawinul, Tony Williams, Herbie Hancock, John McLaughlin, Wayne Shorter, Chick Corea are all Miles's alumni and fusion leaders.

The other side of that was, of course, John Coltrane, from whom can be traced the heaviest of the avant-garde thrusts of the following period. Trane was the fierce muse of thousands of young musicians, certainly tenor players, but all kinds of other players who heard that band or him in person or on records. So that the avant-garde of the sixties leaps out of Miles's classic sextet as well, that's why it was classic.

We'll talk about the sixties in a minute, but we should set up a historical framework as well. First of all we should ask, Why the Village? What is the Village? Probably many of you do not know that this Village community was first settled by eleven black men who had arrived as indentured servants in what was then the small settlement of New Amsterdam in 1626. Eighteen years later these servants demanded manumission (all the men had taken wives by that time and so they were families), and in 1644 the Dutch settlers granted these blacks' request but made them move to the outskirts of the settlement in "a tangled swamp" known later as Greenwich Village.

The Village was the earliest black community in New York City. As a matter of fact, the African Company at their Grove Theater called the African Grove was located at the corner of Bleecker and Mercer Streets and performed Shakespeare regularly there led by the great Ira Aldridge, one of the world's most famous Shakespearian actors. This was in the 1820s! There were also black theaters with orchestras at Houston Street and Spruce Street. And later a whole string of clubs called Black Bohemia which stretched up into the twenties. The Village was the center of New York's black community until just before the Civil War when Irish immigrants and other poor whites, egged on by northern merchants who were in sympathy with the South because the South owed them money, set fire to the black community, including the black orphan asylum. This was in July 1863; over one thousand people were killed and wounded. This was the end of the black community in the Village. They subsequently moved uptown into the West Forties and Fifties in the area later known as San Juan Hill [and Black Bohemia], where Theolonius Monk was raised. (See *New World A-Coming* by Roi Ottley and *Black Manhattan* by James Weldon, Johnson/Arno Press.) Harlem was not the center of New York's black community until early in the twentieth century!

So that the Village has had a legacy of black music, both the show biz and gambling club variety, as well as the more blues-oriented music that was created when the great waves of black immigrants came north after the Civil War in the latter part of the nineteenth century.

Bebop sprang out of the Harlem after-hours experimentation with small groups to escape the by-then monotony of strict scores and charts of the big swing bands at places like Monroe's Uptown and Minton's (right across the street from where I'm currently in jail). Bebop saw the first movement out of Harlem or a black community by the musicians and the music en masse. The Street, West Fifty-second Street, was one famous strip for late swing and bebop giants. Fifty-second Street, at one time, was the heart of the black community removed from the Village, and if you walked west on that strip far enough you'd find yourself in the black community.

But the post-World War II years saw bop spread widely for the first time (since the war had stopped recordings). These years were marked by upward motion of blacks in society caused by the relative prosperity of the war years. It also saw some of the strict ghettoization of both the people and the music broken down. In the twenties non-blacks journeyed up to Harlem to check the music. (They're getting ready to make a movie *The Cotton Club* with Richard Gere—will they play Duke Ellington and Florence Mills?) But by the late forties some of the music could be seen on the strip midtown Fifty-second Street and also, as Morgenstern points out, in the Village.

Bebop had many elements of nonconformity, musically as well as socially, in it. It was, in some senses, a music of rebellion. Part of that rebellion had to do with reversing the stereotypes or escaping them. Black people began breaking out of the ghetto, and the music did too.

The Village had been identified as early as the twenties with this nonconformity and openness that black music always suggests in relationship to the formal culture of America or its official highbrow and lowbrow music. (Actually, as early as the seventeenth century if we look at its founding.) Though the music of white workers and farmers, country and western, has always been closer to the blues than the official expression, the so-called "classical" music which is not even American but European.

The Village was looked at as a place where there were fewer restrictions of the absolutely square (locked in and blunted) ideology of Uncle Sam, which is monopoly capitalism and racism. Just as the corporations could turn swing from a verb to a noun and put out twenty different orchestras bearing the same leader's name to rake up profits from an increasingly straitjacketed music, the boppers were the artists (they began to think of themselves not just as entertainers but as artists), so in the flight out of the various ghettos, mostly black, but some Jewish or Italian or Irish or even white ASP middle class, the music was always identified as being outside the mainstream. When the American apartheid was broken down enough for blacks to move more freely in society, places like the Village became the theoretically freer liberated zones where new art and new society hopefully would flourish.

As I said, Miles's bands were the classics to open up the late fifties and the sixties and even the seventies and eighties for the music. The soft software that became Fusion was Miles's creation, but the fire and brimstone of the avant-garde came from one of his sidemen as well. Miles's militancy as a person in the fifties (Miles boxed—he wdnt take no shit) became overtly political in the sixties, and there is the further social continuum.

The late fifties and early sixties was a transitional period. On one hand, after the open rebellious forties in which bop was born, you had the fifties, best characterized by Dwight Eisenhower, the Cold War, and the madness of McCarthyism! On the other hand, you had the civil rights movement beginning in the mid-fifties signaled by the 1954 *Brown* v. *Topeka Board of Education* decision which smashed the so-called separate-but-equal doctrine of American apartheid, at least theoretically.

The rebels and innocents and naifs of the Beat Generation, located primarily in the Village and San Francisco, were a local signal of a general progressive outburst in the late fifties that would give rise to even heavier fire in the sixties. The music was also identified with this rebelliousness and social upheaval. The way-out society of Kerouac's *On the Road* and *Subterraneans* is connected heavily to the jazz expression, which it sees as nonconformist and as outside the mainstream, as the beat movement itself aspired to be. Jazz and poetry became a common attraction. Langston Hughes and Charlie Mingus were among the most intriguing practitioners.

The music itself could only reflect in its various expressions the being and spirit of the period. So that where hardbop had come on the scene to restore some reconnection of jazz with classic Afro-American music, it, in turn, became a norm, a statement against which new departures had to be played. Because there were new reactions, new expressions, new ideas, further refinements of old ideas, neonate and ancient philosophies introduced.

Trane's "sheets of sound" and then his endless explorations of harmonics investigating chords by playing off each note of the chord singly, each variation one way then backward then upside down, all meant that there was something more to be said than the framework of hardbop or even Miles's classic sextet allowed. Rollins's work of the period, his *Freedom Suite,* the innovation of extended improvisation, opened up new musical horizons, but the very title suggested social stands and an opposition that had to be overcome. The music comes from the people and their lives, it cannot be separated. Max Roach's *Freedom Now,* his and Abby Lincoln's explorations in form and content, added not only new musical extrapolations but a clear social stance that could not be misunderstood. Charlie Mingus's *Pithecanthropus Erectus* gave us the contemporary redefinition of Ellington, and his *Fables of Faubus* showed that his social focus saw the need for rebellions just as his musical choices were rebellious.

New forces came on the scene and most times they came downtown, the Village, where all was supposed to be open and possible. The Eisenhowers and Faubuses were supposedly without meaning except to be jeered at. Cecil Taylor, armed with Duke, Mingus, Tatum, and contemporary European concert music, smashed open the definition of what jazz piano is. At Arthur's, right up the street, and later at the Five Spot, then on the Bowery where the abstract expressionist painters had reclaimed an old Bowery bar, got the owners, the Termini brothers, to put up their art-show posters, and got the Terminis to bring in music.

The Village itself had to be redefined as the new forces, unable many times to find places to play, burst into the East Side, the so-called East Village. The older clubs like the Vanguard handled some of the bigger names—Rollins and Trane—but the new people had to find other places to play. Archie Shepp arrived to play in Jack Gelber's *The Connection* at the Living Theater and later hooked up with Cecil. Cecil's group, Dennis Charles and Buell Neidlinger, and later big Sonny Murray, another innovator on drums, and Cecil rehearsed every day in one loft or another, even though work was hard to find. Ornette Coleman arrived with Don Cherry, Charlie Haden, Billy Higgins, later Eddie Blackwell, and made his earth-shattering debut at the Five Spot. Monk's historic eighteen-week stay at the Five Spot when he brought Trane on board (with Wilbur Ware on bass) and gave JC his doctorate, marked the music's rising to still another level as one watched in awe as Monk helped transform Trane from a fantastic player into an innovator of the new music.

There were other new forces in the music arriving, all carrying to various degrees the elemental changes that were occurring in the society itself. Just as the civil rights movement was transformed (and we can identify Malcolm X as its catalyst) into the Black Liberation Movement, so the music went from hardbop to the avant-garde. And along with Ornette, Sun Ra, Eric Dolphy, Pharaoh Sanders, Oliver Nelson, Ted Curson, Freddie Hubbard, Bill Dixon, Henry Grimes, Wayne Shorter, Bernard McKinney, Jimmy Lyons, Scott La Faro, and many others moved onto the scene. And later innovators like Albert Ayler, Don Pullen, Milford Graves.

The music was trying to get away from the restrictions of tradition without reason. To break out of unnecessary fetters of chord changes and the banality of the so-called popular song. The new music wanted to do what bebop had done and then some. It wanted the music back to its basic African rhythms, blues orientation, the primacy of improvisation, introduce the extended form of Ellington and Mingus and Rollins. The search for the new expression of Coltrane.

During this period the older clubs could not hold this music in transition. The Vanguard, to some extent the Gate, handled Trane and Rollins too. The Five Spot became the new mecca and moved to a larger site at St. Mark's Place. Later, the Terminis even opened another barnlike affair further east on St. Mark's called the Jazz Gallery, but they made the mistake of thinking that their downtown audience wanted to hear the same names that the uptown and older clubs specialized in, and they went under.

This was the period when the lofts and coffee shops came into prominence as places where the music could be heard simply because there were not enough club owners open to the new music. There was also a bunch of nonjazz clubs that would feature the new music for one or two sessions. But the lofts and coffee shops had to take up the slack. This was the sixties loft period as different from the late seventies loft period. Places like the White Whale on East Tenth Street, Take Three, Avital, Metro, the Ninth Circle, Harouts, the Cinderella Club, the Speakeasy were some of the coffee shops and nonjazz clubs that took up the slack. (See "Loft and Coffee Shop Jazz" in *Black Music* by LeRoi Jones, 1963, William Morrow.) Later a club in the far east called Slugs became the new center of the very new music. And clubs like the Half Note on Hudson Street got in it. But for the most part nameless lofts on Great Jones Street, Marzette Watt's loft on Cooper Square, and Clinton Street housed the Cecils and Ornettes and Dolphys and Cursons and Cherries. Lofts where liquor and coffee and food might be sold and where occasionally the air turned to the smell of burning leaves.

But there was much good music to be heard, much that was daring and actually new; and the real tradition of the music, that it be a thrust of the Afro-American masses, no matter who played it, somehow outside the mainstream of American society, was continued, but now in out-of-the-way downtown lofts and in obscure coffee shops and one-shot nightclubs.

At a certain point the social motion of America itself went off into a turbulence of confrontation and conflict. The sixties are synonymous with this basic class and national struggle of United States life where the majority is in constant struggle to seize its means of existence from a tiny minority of bloodsuckers. At one point many people left the Village, going in all directions trying to get closer to the real struggle to transform this society. One remembers that period when innovation and conflict locked into each other and screamed at the top of its voice all over this country. Just before I took my leave from the Village (although I had left a month or so before) I produced a concert at the Village Gate to raise money for the Black Arts Repertory Theater School, which a group of us, mostly ex-Villagers, had opened in Harlem. The concert, called "The New Wave in Jazz" and was recorded live on Impulse by Bob Thiele, featured Trane's classic group Jimmy Garrison, Elvin Jones, and McCoy Tyner; Albert Ayler with Joel Freedman, cello, Lewis Worrell, bass, Donald Ayler, tpt, and Sonny Murray, drums. Grachan Moncur's group with Bill Harris,

THE MUSIC

drums, Cecil McBee and Bobby Hutcherson. Archie Shepp with Reggie Johnson, bass, Virgil Jones, trombone, Marion Brown, alto, Roger
Blank, drums, Fred Pirtle, baritone, and Ashley Fennel, trumpet. And
Chas Tolliver's group with Cecil McBee, James Spaulding, Billy Higgins, and Bobby Hutcherson. The new wave it was called. It was announcing something, the opening of something, but at the same time it
announced a departure, the closing of another era. The newly born
and newly gone!

What was new in the art and music produced by the sixties most
times was also pointed and direct as far as its social reference. But it
also prepared forms that were coopted or legitimately extended by
other later artists. Some of those innovators who were identified with
the new and the Village died or were killed or disappeared. Trane,
Dolphy, Mingus, Monk, Ayler, Ware, LaFaro are all gone. How many
of them were even in their forties? Some of those sixties' Village forces
have turned into money-making machines and the question of art is
moot and long past. Some hide in colleges, improvising toward tenure.
But some continue and still struggle, still try to innovate and put out
the new and pay homage to excellence and art itself. Many hooked
themselves up with the people and still try to bring the basic change we
need, using their art as weapons of transformation and revelation.

By the middle seventies a new new wave had come on the scene
downtown, many who had been inspired by the sixties forces; and
since the sharpest vectors of struggle and change had been cooled out
by the middle seventies and the torpor of commerce triumphant had
raised again its lazy ugliness, a newer new had to be. Cooled out, yes.
How? By the progressive forces' own immaturity and lack of information. By assaults by the state (between 1963 and 1969, six years, John
Kennedy, Malcolm X, Robert Kennedy, and Marthin Luther King
were all assassinated! Any mumble of change was to be squashed by
the powers of far-right capital). By the absence of a progressive organization capable of, at the same time, running a jazz club, publishing
books, electing people to public office, or assaulting the precincts of
capital itself.

A new wave of lofts opened in the middle seventies, again to pick
up on the music in transition—places like Sam Rivers' RivBea, and
Joe Lee Wilson's Ladies Fort, the Brook and Environ, and so many
others. A newer force was emerging, and for a time the clubs couldn't
quite hold it. But by the late seventies clubs like the Tin Palace and
Sweet Basil, and later most of the clubs involved in this Greenwich
Village Jazz Festival, began to find some way to include the new. The
Vanguard and the venerable Max Gordon were still on the scene and
still doing some very hip things. Max has always approached the music
from a more rational and sincere direction than many club owners,

188

hence the longevity of the Village Vanguard. But now there are a host of new clubs, though never enough, to deal with the newest new. Air, the World Saxophone Quartet, Old and New Dreams, Arthur Blythe, Art Ensemble of Chicago, Sun Ra the great master—who still expands, still holds out his various arkestras as examples of what the new is really about. The Archies and Cecils and Ornettes and Pharaohs are still around and the Don Pullens, but look at the list and schedule for this festival and you can see some of the newest of the news whom the clubs must now find room for.

At the same time, as a legacy of that forties breakout from the ghetto, there has now developed a more substantial black middle class, one that can even live and grow up outside the black ghettos. This is even more so for all the other ghetto dwellers of other nationalities. So that now within the music, a struggle is going on that often centers in the Village between the legitimate tradition made new of Afro-American music, called jazz, and middle-class elements who think the music needs to be defunked and deblacked and creep around as an exotic tail of European concert music, or as elevator music fused with corporate prostitution. So sometimes we hear "avant-garde," we hear Webern more than Duke or Schönberg (or maybe Spoke Jones) over Monk. Alas and alack, but not to worry, the music will last as long as the people do, and it will always emerge in the openest of places, as the Village is supposed to be, and definitely where the masses of the Afro-American people are.

Milestones 1

by Jack Chambers, University of Toronto Press

Mr. Chambers' book, alas, is a product of this time in its most unattractive aspect, i.e., the return to primacy of white chauvinism, a backward ideological outgrowth of the sharp movement toward the right by the so-called "Free World," led by the United States. It is a general period of reaction and conservative counterattack.

I said in an essay of mine given during the Kool Jazz Festival in New York City in 1983 that jazz writing, like everything else in the society, has shifted toward the right. White chauvinism in jazz writing has in large part replaced the tentative thrust toward "ethnomusical" and socially aware analysis that were evident in the sixties and the seventies with publications like *The Jazz Review*, that period's *Metronome, Cricket, The Grackle, Kulchur*, and to some extent even in *down beat*. Nat Hentoff, Martin Williams, Frank Kofsky, Larry Neal, A. B. Spellman, Jim Stewart, Larry Gushee, Ron Welburn and others have been replaced by right-wing journalists, e.g. Len Lyons who recently wrote a book called *Great Jazz Pianists*, which includes derivative and largely aesthetically indifferent players like Chick Corea, Joe Zawinul, Jimmy Rowles, Keith Jarrett, Paul Bley, Ran Blake, Dave Brubeck, Marian McPartland, Steve Kuhn, Toshiko Akiyoshi. But at the same time, Lyons leaves out Duke Ellington, Thelonius Monk, Bud Powell, Art Tatum, and Fats Waller (not to mention James P. Johnson, Willie "the Lion" Smith, Meade Lux Lewis, Count Basie, etc., etc.)!

The strange inclusions in the volume are, of course, white pianists whose name commerce can make quasi-significant (Corea is Latino; Akiyoshi, Japanese). The excluded and to me obvious candidates for such a book are black pianists. They are also acknowledged historically as "great pianists" (even by the pianists in the book!). What would make a person supposedly knowledgeable about the music, come up with a list of such assembled mediocrities touted as "great" except white chauvinism? The same chauvinism that could make old-time critic Whitney Bailiett say in *The New Yorker* that the most influential female jazz singer of the recent period is Anita O'Day (who he claims influenced even Betty Carter). Bailiett does not even mention Sarah Vaughan.

The *Illustrated Encyclopedia of Jazz* says that "Benny Goodman is . . . the most technically accomplished clarinetist to play jazz." The same Lyons in another abominable tome called *101 Best Jazz Albums* includes two Chick Corea albums and no Bud Powell albums (even though Bud Powell is one of the creators of bebop and a true jazz innovator)!

Endless examples of this tendency can be cited. The essence of this chauvinism proposes that the greatest creators in the music were white, even though jazz is one of the richest developments of African-American culture (albeit of American culture as well—one is not possible without the other—i.e., African-American culture is not possible without the American experience, but then American culture does not exist without African-American culture).

Earlier, the chauvinist tendency in American life dismissed jazz, and African-American music in general, as inferior. The childish and primitive diversions of a subhuman species. Europe's consistent opposition to this view, based on its distance and a more developed social democracy, made this U.S. white chauvinism part of the hickish stereotype of Americans, still remnant as the leavings of eighteenth-century European colonialism (vis-à-vis the "thirteen colonies," etc.).

In the sixties, as part of a general upsurge of democratic struggle in this country, jazz criticism reached some impressive heights of intellectual and analytical importance and social relevance. The backward motion of U.S. society in the eighties provides the social context of current attempts by racists to rewrite the history of African-American Music so that it is in reality created by whites. Since the music cannot be "inferiorized" out of existence, the next best move is to *claim* it!

Ordinarily, no one would get upset that the principal creators of European concert music were and are Europeans (regardless of Leontyne Price, André Watts, or Ulysses Kay). But because African-Americans are still an oppressed people and the ideological justification for their oppression, white chauvinism, cannot allow the true stature of African-American culture to surface, the authentic "greats" of the music must be hidden. "Covered" is the word used in the record industry.

If U.S. citizens were educated to the real identity of Duke Ellington, for instance, it would weaken somewhat the psychological addiction to white chauvinism many Americans are affected by. The critical role of black culture in helping shape the whole of U.S. culture, if properly understood by the majority of people in this society, would reorient the population and throw the U.S. social order into psychological shock. But racism is necessary (as psychological mindset and as social organization) to ensure superprofits gouged out of the "inferior" because they are not completely citizens! That is, since they *require less* of the collective social wealth.

Mr. Chambers is a very boring, colorless (literally) journalist. His "analysis," such as it is, besides being gnawed through by white chauvinism, barely exists. Except the fundamental theme of *Milestones 1*, as far as I can see, is that Miles Davis was really great through his association with white musicians!

As far as any concerted analysis on the whys and wherefores of the music itself, any illumination of the *history of ideas* associated with the music, there is very little. There is no real understanding of the complex and many-headed aesthetic of the music, no clarity on its social significance. There is not even any real comprehension of the variety of styles characterizing the music.

What Mr. Chambers does do is posit that Miles's initial influences were Bix Beiderbecke and Bobby Hackett! Also, that despite Miles's history of playing with the great bebop innovators, Charlie Parker, Bud Powell, Thelonius Monk, Max Roach, etc., Miles didn't really make the great music until he linked up with Gil Evans, Gerry Mulligan, Lee Konitz for the famous *Birth of the Cool* sides.

Mr. Chambers also thinks that the next great phase of Miles's playing was when he linked up with Gil Evans, e.g., on *Miles Ahead, Porgy and Bess,* etc. In fact, Chambers thinks Evans is as great an arranger as Duke Ellington. He quotes André Hodeir, "No other jazzman can compare with him as a harmonizer and orchestrator." Since Evans has composed relatively few tunes, Chambers stops short of making the claim for Evans as composer but does say that Evans's work "perhaps" places him alongside Ellington"! (Evans is an important arranger, but only a chauvinist would say that he was Ellington's equal!)

Mr. Chambers's musical commentary is limited in the main to putting discographicals information together in chronological order, but he is so "academic" he does not list the various dates under the commercial album titles generally associated with them. This makes the discographical information somewhat confusing.

The author generally deprecates the efforts of black musicians, and cites incident after incident showing how childish, irresponsible, depraved, overpraised, and primitive they are. Aside from the dull and confusing discographical information, much of Chambers's book is a stringing together of rumor, gossip, and rehashed slightly incorrect innuendo and plain out b.s.!

Can we really learn about the most important aspects of Beethoven's or Mozart's music by reading stale drolleries disparaging their character? Then why should this be true for Charlie Parker or John Coltrane?

Alongside the listing of negative habits by the musicians, Chambers also lets us know you can't trust a jazz musician because he or she is childish, irresponsible, etc. (see above).

Mr. Chambers is a resolute enemy of bebop, having the ingenuousness to say things like . . . "bop suffered by comparison to the cool chamber jazz of the nonet, and bop already had more enemies than it needed." Or what about, "In Gil Evans and the other members of the salon, he [Davis] found the individuals gifted in theory and harmony who could continue his own education beyond what he had learned from Gillespie, Monk, Webster. . . . He also discovered a musical setting that suited him better than the hard-core bebop he played nightly with the Parker quintet. . . ."

Chambers thinks that Duke, Count, Lady are an "ersatz royalty." He chides Mingus for "passing himself off," on a record, as *Baron Mingus*. He thinks that scat singing is composed of "nonsense syllables." That Earl Coleman was second-rate. That Kenny Dorham was a Dizzy Gillespie imitator and that Red Rodney was more suited to replace Miles with Bird. He thinks that even though Miles first wanted Sonny Stitt for the Nonet albums, he was "fortunate" that Stitt couldn't make it so that Miles had to use Lee Konitz. He tells us that Mike Zwerin thought the Nonet date was Gil Evans's gig! He tells us about Billy Eckstine's "mannerisms" and that Pancho Hagood was not much. He tells us that Tadd Dameron was a kind of "Carmen Lombardo" steeped in "Tin Pan Alley clichés."

He also quotes John Hammond on bop that "it didn't swing . . . including Monk and Trane." Also that Dizzy Gillespie acts "clownish because of the compromises of show business." That Billy Taylor was Horace Silver's principal influence. That the American song form was created "by Jerome Kern and Irving Berlin." That "pimping" is the occupation of many jazz players. That R&B has "bawling mannerisms." That Sarah Vaughan has a "flashy vocal style."

He also lets us know that Al Cohn and Zoot Sims were "solid musicians" in the context of the irresponsible boppers. That Cohn's charts were "bright, friendly, extroverted . . . a bit of an oddity for Davis." That Joe Carroll was a "hip vaudevillian" unskilled at "low comedy."

He skips through the style hard bop, the Black antidote for the white-dominated "Cool Style," as if it hardly existed. But he lets us know about the white-dominated 3rd Stream style; as well as that he thinks Lester Young, the president of tenor saxophonists, was a "taciturn alcoholic of unpredictable musical prowess" . . . "a great talent

193

smothered by his apparent indifference not only to music but to life."
He quotes J. Lincoln Collier that Bill Evans was the piano player who
has had the most influence on contemporary stylists. All these bursts
of inaccuracy and chauvinism stitched together with dull reprise, sordid
hearsay, and mundane technical reportage. This is a bad trip, but one
right in tune with the neo-chauvinism of much of the current crop of
jazz literature.

It is an indication of just how far to the right everything in this
society has moved and how much struggle must be waged to turn it
around.

Woody Shaw/*Woody Three!*

Woody Shaw's reputation has gianted itself in the last year. He is beginning to get some widespread critical and popular recognition, and there's even a *chance* (remember that, *chance,* 'cause this is a lottery for most of us) he might eventually make a little money.

A lottery for most of us. I mean we don't even know if we gonna *make it,* in the totality of everything that means. Like the survivors of a catastrophe.

Woody hails from Catastrophe City, Newark, New Jersey, where the wicked witch of the west has located her largish urban commode. In one sense he's even "lucky" to have "got outta there alive." (Though the living dead call themselves Mayors and Councilmen and Superintendents of Schools—Presidents of the Board of Education— loyalists to terror and decay: Capitalism's Cute Coons!)

Ironically, some of Woody's "luck" consists of his having gone through the Newark "school system" at a time when music was still part of the Elementary School curriculum.* Because it was in public school that Woody turned and was turned to music as a principal means of expression, rather than hot flight from the long hairy arm of the law behind ghetto "j.d.-ism," the horn of frustration.

In many ways Woody is a typical product of the urban ghetto called Newark, but since he is *the* Woody Shaw, obviously there's some things about him not altogether typical. This much *is* typical of a large part of Newark's overall community, but particularly its Afro-American community—Woody is the son of a factory worker. His parents are from the South, where 80 percent of all blacks in the United States were born, where 52 percent still live today. Woody himself was born in Laurinburg, North Carolina, in 1944. Laurinburg itself seems like it has a special connection with places like Newark because of the Institute there that serves as a secondary boarding school for quite a few

---

* At this writing Newark's black Mayor, Superintendent of Schools, and President ot the Board of Education have removed the regular programs of art, music, and physical education, industrial arts from the elementary schools—reduced library service so that one librarian serves four schools, three being closed when one is being served. Also, after-school recreation program has been dropped, closing playgrounds in the name of back to basics.

youth out of places like Newark. Grachun Moncur, another Newark-reared musician, went to school in Laurinburg.

But the urban gray of Newark rests behind the eyes of any of its natives—probably no matter where else they might get to. So pulverizing and depressing is this "worst city in America" (according to *Harper's* magazine) that too many times it is able to injure those condemned to live in it, principally because of the incredibly mean limits of its official social organization. Black immigrants from the Afro-American nation in the black-belt South; jobless refugees from America's colonial prison, Puerto Rico; working-class Italians at the lower rung of "well, it was supposed to be better than this for white people" -ism; the second largest concentration of Portuguese in the country; and a buncha other folks, mostly working class, mostly doughless, are all here under the yoke of sham democracy pipsqueaked by the well-paid bureaucrats who run it!

When Woody Shaw came along, there were a few more middle-class folks in the town, a few more whites, less urban blight and suburban flight. Still, even then, the joint was already over the hill toward the crazyhouse. But Woody could go to a Cleveland Junior High and get one of the best trumpet teachers on the scene, Jerry Ziering, who could recognize the seriousness and promise Woody had then, and transform him from a one-valve bugler with the Masons and junior Elks to a hard-blowing session-making musician with classical underpinning.

(Ironically, at a meeting a couple of weeks ago, of parents and students and concerned persons to oppose the almost complete emasculation of the Newark school system, one sister spoke for days on the fact that Cleveland Junior High is about to fall on the children's heads. And now there are no more trumpet teachers, great or otherwise!)

The pressure to be broken by incredible odds by the poverty, ignorance, violence, indifference—that is, one's day-to-day environment in the town—is immense. It's like a gray haunting presence one feels pushing against the outside and inside at the same time. But even so, a few fortunate people like Woody Shaw who are not stronger or brighter than the struggling masses of the city, but simply more consistently focused in a direction that can provide a shield and exit from the ghetto horror, do manage to make it out. And many times the stories they carry, told through whatever medium or form, are staggering in their brutality and shattering in their beauty!

Woody Herman Shaw, oldest son of Woody Shaw, came up out of Laurinburg a couple months after he was born, when "good" work in the urban North catapulted many of the black immigrants out of the Black Belt. Work, because the United States was at war, and as in

World War I, jobs opened for blacks. *Woody Three* speaks of Three Woodys, however, and the third and most recent Woody (born 1944) is Woody Louis Armstrong Shaw. The eldest Woody, like many working people, especially black ones, still managed, according to Woody 2, to have "a very creative mind" which he exercised for many years as a member of the famed Diamond Jubilee Singers, early spellbinders for Woody 2. Woody 2's brothers are both athletes, football players. One with a college scholarship at the University of Iowa (Cedric), the other (Pete), already in the pros, with the San Diego Chargers. (Now there's not even gym classes for elementary school kids in the town!) Woody's sister Toni works for the International Royalties Department at RCA. So Woody 1 and Rosalie got all their kids up and out. Woody 2 says about the original Woody, that he is still "dap and handsome," a very cool dude. And a very happy one too to see all his children escape the crawling death, sometimes while still alive, of narrow ghetto existence.

One thing is clear, that within these stagnant graveyards the rich lock us in to make their maximum profit, the will and fire of life burns and throbs anyway. Woody 2 is proof of that. And only one proof among a bunch. Today, as the young trumpet player (thirty-four) with the best jazz album of 1978, *Rosewood (down beat),* as well as being named the best jazz trumpet of the year *(down beat)* ahead of legendary figures like Dizzy Gillespie, Miles Davis, as well as Freddie Hubbard, Maynard Ferguson, and even ahead of WRVR and commercialism's main man, Chuck Mangione, Woody has the world ahead of him. He even got a couple of Grammy nominations out of *Rosewood* for best jazz instrumentalist and best group.

Woody's been playing since he was nine or thereabouts and took up the bugle at Cleveland Junior High and W. Kinney and later at Arts High. Woody says, "Jerry Ziering prepared me . . . he wanted me to play with the New York Philharmonic, but I heard Clifford and said, 'Fuck this shit.'" But that preparation still can be heard and the seriousness of those good teachers' concern. But for many young people, the driving rhythm messages of American improvised music are stronger than the call of the European classics. Especially for the young Afro-Americans whose whole lives are surrounded and interwoven with the Afro-American popular music, blues, and one of its more international offspring, jazz.

Woody at fourteen was already hanging out at famed local cutting joints like Len and Len's and Club 83, because he had already developed good chops. In just five years, based on a combination of passionate regard for the music, good formal training and encouragement, and coming in contact with some fine musicians and musical guides, Woody was moving into full-fledged apprenticeship. Earlier he had got propelled into the music almost accidentally (except for the heavy black music background of the United States and English working class). Involved in a typical frustrated ghetto youth trip, busting out lights in Newark's Hayes Homes Projects (an area outlined as having the highest population density in the United States—nearly 20,000 people in a square mile!), Woody, "legally blind," and admittedly slow afoot, got caught. But instead of the bust, and maybe, like nowadays, being "tried as an adult"—which will surely end all our problems except the real ones, the cause of all this shit—one security guard had enough relationship to positive human reality to send Woody, once he had asked him what he *really* wanted to do, over to old Lavozier Lamar at the Jones Street Y. *Mr.* Lamar, as we all most certainly called him, rehearsed a big band made up of ghetto youth with professional big-band arrangements. And he didn't stand no faking or shucking. Mr. Lamar also had pointed people like Wayne Shorter and Walter Davis in the right direction.

The profusion of hip musicians to spring out of Newark, and out of bands like Mr. Lamar's or Nat Phipps's and Jackie Bland's teenage bands, or out of the public schools, is enormous. Let's just begin with Tyrone Washington, Grachun Moncur, Wayne and Allen Shorter, Sarah Vaughan, Melba Moore, Betty Carter, Scott LaFaro, Larry Young, Eddie Gladden, Gloria Gaynor, Dionne Warwick, Hank Mobley, Walter Davis. Woody picked up the trumpet the same month Clifford Brown was killed (1956). This is ironic because Woody's music is definitely Brownie-shaped. Before that, Woody had played the bugle with the Junior Elks and the Junior Masons, where you could find dudes who could play one-valve bugle like Freddie Hubbard played trumpet. By the time Woody started playing in school he wanted to play trombone, and people were trying to mash the violin or clarinet on him. But a chance hearing of Perez Prado's "Cherry Pink and Apple Blossom White," Woody was convinced he needed to play trumpet, so he got "an old silver martin" went home, and, by his own account, "learned to play in a week!" He was then in the sixth grade!

The flashy stratospheric trumpets of Harry James, Ray Anthony, and the implied good chops fascinated the young boy. He was drawn by the charisma of Louis Armstrong (hence Woody 3's name). "I loved jazz and the first time I heard Bird it was the most fascinating thing I'd heard in my life. I heard Diz and thought, 'It's impossible'!"

About the time Woody was beginning to sit in around the town, he also began to get gigs at fourteen and fifteen with prestige Newark bands like Brady Hodge, Nat Phipps, and through another Newark native, Eddie Gladden (now with Dexter Gordon), with Allen Jackson. He also began now to meet other young musicians and some with already established reputations. Saxophonist Jimmy Anderson, still known as one of Newark's finest players, pulled Woody's coat to classical music. "It's good for the brain," Jimmy told him. Woody was listening to records and imitating them, learning the hot licks. He was also picking up the "legit" training on pieces like *Bolero* in Cleveland. At fifteen and sixteen Woody was already able to get as much as thirty dollars a night some weekends through another Newark legend, bassist Art Williams, who later on opened the *Cellar,* an outgrowth of the Newark Jazz Arts Society, where many of the new musicians played in the sixties. Woody met Art through Jimmy Anderson, as well as good musicians like pianist Bill Harris, tenor man Bernie James (who some think was one of the finest tenor players to work around this city). "There is a distinct Newark tenor sound," says Woody. "An urban cry." He was talking about people like Anderson, James, Herbie Morgan—who's still playing beautiful horn—Wayne Shorter, pre-Weather Report, Tyrone Washington.

Woody claims his major influences are tenor players, and of course he mentions Trane, along with the Newark players. But he also talks warmly about Newark trumpeter, Johnny Coles's influence, calling him a "mentor." It was Coles who told Woody to play long tones so he could develop a pretty sound, and to learn to read so he could get all kinds of gigs. Coles would also bring news of Freddie Hubbard and Lee Morgan, who came to be a couple of Woody's idols.

By the ninth grade, even though previously he had got good grades, Woody started messing up in school and finally quit, to the horror and surprise of all his music teachers and family. Woody was having a bad case of "the adults," which carried him into his first confrontation with the ladies as well as having him declare that he only dug jazz. "I didn't dig anything but jazz, and after this woman put me down, I considered suicide but went deeper into jazz." This was around '57–'58–'59. The music was Lee Morgan's "Moanin," the album *Dig* of Miles's, especially "Paper Moon." Diz on "Night in Tunisia"; Rollins at the Village Vanguard; Jackie McLean on "Beau Jack."

"I started working pretty regular with Brady Hodges. I even sat in with Hank Mobley and Kenny Dorham, with Larry Young on organ. Geronimo [a near-legendary slickster-musician-promoter from Newark] introduced us and was playing drums. This was at Len and Len's."

By seventeen, Woody tried to form a band, which included Larry Young (who died last year of pneumonia, which has supposedly been conquered in most modern industrial countries—but Newark is in the Third World) and Tyrone Washington, whose name in those early days was "T-Ball." This was also at Len and Len's, whose Tuesday-night sessions were well-known carving nights for some pretty heavy musicians. During this period Woody would meet Benny Golson, Yusef Lateef, Betty Carter. Woody describes this as "a healthy period," because he was getting to the music, and hearing some of its most distinguished practitioners. But, of course, his parents were seting him on fire for leaving school and issued the ultimatum, go back to school, or go to work. Woody went back to night school. Although whenever he could now he would slide over to the Apple and sit in where he could.

At eighteen, he got a gig with Willie Bobo. He was checking the Messengers, Phillie Joe and Maynard Ferguson heavy, and started hanging out at Birdland. Junior Cook, Blue Mitchell, and Freddie Hubbard let him sit in at the Blue Coronet in Brooklyn. He also ran into Booker Little, who "scared me to death, but I could always relate to Lee and that sassy, urban style." In the Willie Bobo band at the time were Chick Corea, Larry Gale, Joe Farrell, and Garnett Brown, who also scared the young dude to death, but he recovered in time to get down. And then one night Eric Dolphy came in and inquired who was the young dude on trumpet. And just about that time Woody started checking out the music called New Thing or Avant-Garde, in which Eric Dolphy was a giant. Dolphy's *Our Man in Jazz* turned both Woody and Tyrone around, and edged them further to the "left" of many of the straight-ahead trumpet types coming out of the Clifford Brown, Lee Morgan, Freddie Hubbard syndrome. The Dolphy influence on Woody was profound. Eric had him over to his house and they talked music, and he showed Woody some of his music. "I played it . . . but slow . . . it was hard . . . hard." This one tune called "Miss Anne" was so hard even Booker Little had trouble with it. Hard because it contained new elements, and steps past the already given experience of bop and hardbop. Yet the hardbop development was the necessary antidote to the "cool" and "third-stream" diversions that crept up as a reaction to the new fire of bebop. The hardbop was the restatement of the basics the Horaces and Buhainas and Rollinses, the Max and Cliffords, had to make to redirect the music on up a little higher, beyond crass commercialism on one hand, and sterility, catatonia, and meek pootbootyism on the other.

The media had announced the coming of the Beat Generation, and Woody was sitting in at places in the Village like the Cafe Wha. Folks like Zita Carno, the pianist and critic Clifford Jarvis, Al Cotton, Hubert Laws, Morris Edwards, steered into these joints many times by Melba Moore's brother Wilson Moorman, a drummer. There were very few musicians as serious as Eric who could be heard some days in a huge loft he stayed in down on Water Street practicing from dawn till the sun went down. The band Eric got together during that period was Woody; Bobby Hutcherson, vibes; Eddie Khan, bass; J. C. Moses, drums. This band gigged very little but did do a gig at Crawford's Grill No. 2 in Pittsburgh, which was a regular stop. But work was scarce for Eric, and they didn't work much. But they did put together the album *Iron Man,* which is a great example of Eric's fantastic creativity and virtuosity. The date included the band that went to Pittsburgh plus Prince Lasha on flute; Sonny Simmons, alto; Clifford Jordon, alto; Garvin Bushell, bassoon.

Eric left the country with Mingus because he couldn't get enough work with his own band. That was June '63, after he'd already made the classic Coltrane sides. After a while Eric sent for Woody—he wanted to get the old band back together. He wrote a letter to Woody that Woody describes as "beautiful," but before anything went down, Eric was dead! Cause, even now, unknown. Woody had been "rigorously studying" Eric's music, from books and records, and expanding, even though Buhainia turned him down as Freddie Hubbard's replacement with the Messengers for Lee Morgan. But now, with Eric's death, Joyce Mordecai, Eric's fiancée, summoned Woody to Paris anyway to make the gig, and he stayed, stretched out psychologically and musically, until May '64, and then returned.

When he got back, this time it was Horace Silver who picked him up and they returned to the same Crawford's Grill No. 3. By now Woody's music was developing, as he said, to "relate to the whole spectrum, the whole kaleidoscopic version of jazz. I could play bebop and avant-garde." And he talks about "Tyrone, Eddie Gladden, Les Walker, and Larry Young" when they would have sessions "to play free . . . turn lights out and go mad . . . Couple bottles of beer and some wine and look out!"

Horace's band was another one of those important learning experiences for Woody. Joe Henderson got him the gig, and with them were Teddy Smith, Roger Humphries; but soon Joe Henderson quit, and Woody called on his man "T-Ball," now at Howard University, to fill the gap. "The Horace gig got me a firm basis in musicianship. . . . Learned about chords, voicing, and style from Horace. And I tried to write like him." Traces of this are still evident in Woody's writing, even on this album, as are the influences of Eric Dolphy. In fact it is Woody's adeptness and smoothness at combining diverse, sometimes contradictory-seeming influences in an imaginative "mainstream" framework, that makes his work as interesting as it is, e.g., *Woody One. The New Ark* seems straight-ahead swing, *almost,* yet there is an originality to the approach, an echo of advanced harmonies (harmelodic sez Ornette) that makes the music, at its best, zesty and open, hipper than just hardbop.

Woody and Tyrone Washington had a radical effect on Horace's music. (Tyrone is one of the most interesting of the post-Trane players; his name is now Bilal Muhammad Abdullah, and one wishes he would be more available musically because he is now so deeply involved in religion!) But it was an effect, caused by the two young musicians following behind influences like Sam Rivers and Pharaoh Sanders, that Horace did not altogether appreciate. "Horace's thing is tight and formal, to be so funky." Anyway, Horace let both of them go. For a taste of the Shaw-Washington collaboration that is sometimes free, sometimes like Horace, listen to *Natural Essence*. It's Tyrone's date, but Blue Note's Alfred Lion wouldn't give Woody a tumble.

No matter, Woody slid on, dipping into the Slug's scene, in the East Village, now in his early twenties and unfortunately, around the same time he drifted off into Scagville. The real promise America holds for the creative, like the promise it holds for the working class and oppressed nationalities in general, either takes you out of life, or takes the life out of you. The rulers want us to submit to their madness, their slums, in the midst of incredible riches . . . their unemployment in the midst of work crying to be done . . . their maximum profit in exchange for our bones and blood. So that dope addiction is a form of submission to them . . . and, dig, they encourage it!

Woody lay for a while around the Slug's scene, became almost like the house trumpet player. One important influence on him then was Jackie McLean whose "unique personality" Woody greatly admired. He played at East Village Inn, Pee Wee's, Rafiki's, and began to take on a more personally identifiable style, coming in contact with musicians like Herbie Hancock, Clark Terry, Andrew Hill (who was also music coordinator for the Black Arts Repertory School in Harlem), McCoy Tyner. And again, Woody credits Hill and McCoy Tyner as having important parts in shaping his musical conception, as well as Jackie McLean. Archie Shepp and Pharaoh Sanders had come on the scene a few years before and were starting to smoke, and Woody sat in with them as well. But by the late sixties he temporarily succumbed to Uncle Scag's Habit routine. With Max Roach in '68–'69, Woody remembers sadly how Max had to let him go because of his weakness before "the heavyweight champ," as a dude I know used to call the shit.

He worked for a while with Joe Henderson's band, and for a while got caught in the whole dope mystique, but still contributed to Henderson's *Lighthouse Live* album as well as "Either You're Part of the Problem or Part of the Solution." Finally Contemporary signed Woody, and he played with Herbie Hancock at Fillmore East as well as opposite Rock Groups in San Francisco's maniacal paradise. Woody also gigged with musicians like Gary Bartz, Bennie Mauphin, along with Henderson, until finally he and Joe reached a parting of the ways. And so he was brought low in sunny California, strung out and broke, but finally caught on with Art Blakey and went off on a brief European tour, then back to the United States, more recording with Contemporary. He and Bobby Hutcherson briefly collaborated but, says Woody, "Our egos got in the way," plus they were both, at the time, "fuckin with that mud." So they split, but Woody stayed out in the Bay area for almost two and a half years, picking up odd gigs where he could, sitting in with any and everybody, but mostly paying dues. And even in the middle of Scagout, Woody practiced and sat in, tried to pay attention; even through the mist of dope dopiness, he tried to pay attention to the music. He got weary and restless on the West Coast; even as he started to come out of the dope-frustration trauma, there seemed to be no place to play. He could go and sit in with dudes like Rahsaan. (One night Rahsaan, who was blind, said to Woody, who is "legally blind," that they should, while they were playing, "walk around the club." Woody refused, and Rahsaan embarrassed him by strolling and tooting all over the joint. But then, Ornette Coleman told me that one day he knocked on Rahsaan's door and this dude came to the door, opened the peephole and "peeped out" at him!) So finally Woody split for the East and signed very soon with Muse, "the Bluenote and Prestige of the sixties."

Woody began to draw a steady group of musicians around him. Players like Azar Lawrence; Steve Turre, the dynamite young trombonist; Onaje Gumbs, he of the silken touch; journeyman bassist, Buster Williams, and hard-driving drummer Victor Lewis. He did *Moontrane* on Muse which got four and a half stars from the lottery called *down beat*, but it helped. Some other gigs started to fall in place, like the now disappeared Boomers on Bleecker Street. He also began sitting in all over New York. He and Louis Hayes put together a band which featured Junior Cook, Stafford James, and Ronnie Matthews, and did five or six albums with Muse, some four of which have already been issued. His first album on the charts was *Love Dance* with Cecil McBee, Vic Lewis, Billy Harper, Rene McLean, Steve Turre . . . "but nobody pushed it." The record got five stars. The Hayes-Shaw band was a tight swinging number; also it was a cooperative band with everybody getting the same salaries. But Woody was not satisfied. He knew his own head was bulging with things he wanted to get off, new expressions, and to his credit he did not just want to replay and play again the standard hardbop licks (even à la Max and Clifford). Out on the West Coast Rene McLean replaced Junior Cook.

The band was working steady, but one night, in Woody's words, "Elvin was sitting in the audience. We were playing in the Concerts By the Sea, and I asked him did he want to play. He came up and that blew it. I took off after that because I heard some stuff playing behind Elvin that I knew I wanted to do. A freer approach to the music, and I had to split. I didn't want to quit . . . but I felt also that the band was making it off my name. About the same time I'd met Maxine [Gregg, who is also his very capable manager] and altogether the band broke up."

Woody's music is something different from just hardbop à la Max and Clifford, though for everything's sake, we know that Max and Clifford's music is lasting and still dynamite. But it has already been done . . . art is to learn from not imitate. Woody's approach is more modal; he is also given to utilizing Afro-Latino effects and percussion in a manner that he says brings him closer to the roots of the music. "My music is a continuation of what other cats did, but on *Woody 3* I feel finally uncompromised, like I am finally making the statement I want to make. *Rosewood* got me over—critical acclaim, but this is my statement" . . . as of now.

And this statement is a pretty clear evaluation of where Woody Shaw is at. Any conversation with him about the music is apt to bring out some pretty controversial statements about what's happening with it, his direction and others'. He has made already fairly well-publicized putdowns of some of his ex-idols like Herbie Hancock, Freddie Hubbard, for conning with fusion. He is equally acid about excellent players like Gary Bartz and Mtume, who seem to have drifted away from hard-blowing improvised music for sounds to inflate bankbooks by. The music on this album can stand up clearly as an example of where Woody Shaw is coming from musically. *Rosewood,* in his own words, was *hip* but slightly predictable, and therefore hugely successful. *Woody Three* is more daring, more personal, more innovative, and as always when one deals with Brother Shaw, it swings its ass off. Especially dig the side with the Three Woody's, this is Shaw's best and most interesting appearance on records to date. *Woody One* reminds one of *Rosewood,* but there is more of a modal and minor feeling, and while it is funky and bright there is a sly Latino feeling. Check the way Onaje comes in like a classic Red Garland funk setup, and dig too Carter Jefferson, who registers his appreciation of the master, John Coltrane, even while moving us into his own time-space swing world. And that last chord, resolution (yet what is resolved, it is all beginnings; as Brecht says, the serious artist notes the "moment of *becoming* and *passing,*" i.e., the change(s)).

Woody 2 reminds us of Eric Dolphy, the voicing and space between the horns. Parallels, minors, echoed dissonance. Buster Williams's full articulate solo is a real highlight on this cut. But Woody is strong and open on this, as he was fleet and rocking on *Woody One.* James Spaulding (it's good to hear him again) and the muscular off-funk of Steve Turre (who is really a find) all contribute to some very good music.

"Woody 3" completes this first side, and it is, I think, a total, almost a suite, connected, yet each piece stands by itself. "Woody Three" is a poignant ballad, a presage, like the "real" Woody 3, of things to come. Above all, it is *serious,* aware of itself as an awareness of all that has gone before, indulging in its fantasies (a bright "Parisian thoroughfare" section that pops in intermittently), yet by its own existence affirming the promise and progress of the future. The three Woodys are a real accomplishment, a reflection of the accomplishment of the three Woodys from Black Belt South to Plantation North to freedom future.

To Kill a Brick and *Organ Grinder* are more or less typical of the kind of all-out blowing sessions Woody is already well known for. *Brick,* however, is very Milesian, and reminds us that Miles Davis (to whom *Rosewood* was dedicated and who is a great partisan of Woody's) is also one of Shaw's influences, even though the debt to people like Brownie, Lee Morgan, and Freddie Hubbard most times seems more direct. But Miles was in it too, Miles, in fact, spoke up at Columbia to help Woody connect with the biggy, and the instant success of *Rosewood,* and the musical strength of this current album speak of Miles's correctness in pulling Columbia's coat.

The group that Woody has pulled together seems an up-to-date expression of him Shaw 'nuff. Both the smaller group that he is apt to use in the clubs (as witness the hot swing of *Escape Velocity,* lifted live from the Village Vanguard). The larger, concert ensemble is more Woody, but on an expanded scale. Adding horns and percussion allows him even more complete expression, more musical depth. He combines young heads, some well-traveled ones, and the mixture is hip. It is a sure music that woody Shaw makes, a classic Afro-American improvised style that is straight up, straight ahead, and in its sassy wide-open funkiness apologizes to no one. It is refreshing in this terrible disco fusion land, when WRVR (what passes for the local jazz station) plays Mangione more than Miles, Phoebe Snow more than Betty Carter and Sarah Vaughan combined, to hear someone who still wants, as he says, "integrity in the music." Woody, quoting McCoy Tyner, says, "We can't mock the music," and he adds his own caveat, "We've got to preserve the music. Yes, it's about playing our music with integrity. I wanted to show it could be done."

The cockiness of Woody Shaw is a combination of Newark swagger (necessary to survive in a wilderness of desolation and frustration) and plain out self-confidence. The last quality the result of accomplishment gained through fierce struggle. "Hey, man . . . I can play my ass off!" He can!

Masters in Collaboration

Everyone here to consciously get in on history. Years later the references to this event will let you know how heavy twas that you and we could get together like this, to hear this. Because, I'm sure, for most of us here, we have come to witness the collaboration of two masters. One, a master of source, the other, a master of elaboration. One who goes back further to the great crossing and extension of our collective historical lives (as America and as African-America), that crossing where the corporations had conspired to come up with the formula to turn our verbishness into quiet nouns of commerce—so that suddenly one day we would look up and swing would no longer mean the soul's uttering itself into music, the most sensitive among us transforming the seeming quiet air into what is always, *rhythm*—no, the fiends had conspired to turn fire notes of our human striving (and anguish) into bank notes of flattened sensibility and (un)sophisticated intention—suddenly there was ten Casa Lomas or twelve Kay Kaisers (as the market dictated); you see, they meant to inundate us in the death formula, which they, so confident in their infamy, dared call Swing.

It means as soon as the little money bums come up with the right stuff they canned it and shat it out everywhere at once to kill off the real, as the theory says that gold can be diminished in its life by cheaper metal pushed for that purpose. Corporation NonMusic to make profit from the black prophets and sound scientists who could not fully explore their own consciousnesses because of the national oppression of the African-Americans, so they had to settle for *genius*, while others had their works taught at universities or made millions imitating these exploited musical workers.

We understood that it was White Man (Paul, to be exact) who had created jazz, despite what Jelly Roll Morton might say or Duke Ellington might play! We was hipped that it was Good Man (full of Benny) who had founded that desperate brightness called Swing. But we still wondered (excuse us, yo' infamy) who we ourselves, excuse the expression, was!?

So involved did we become in this quest that we sent certain scientists and aesthetes of the real, some cultural workers, off to the side, after hours, so to speak, to check out if we were still we (even though we knew we had not got free). You see we had in mind those kinds of advanced artists who carried our whole history in their consciousness, who could conduct some sound experiments, so to speak, to obstruct and finally foil the demonic plan of suffocation the corporations had laid out to turn us all into furniture, as the only correct audience for the nonmusic they invented from watering down our own.

Thus, at certain laboratories and city *do*-tanks these artists gathered to explore the outside of the inside and recreate us for ourselves. Minton's, Monroe's Uptown were some of the in/sites. It was there that these heavy musical explorations took place. It was there that certain Birds, Monks, Kooks, and Dizzys gathered to reinvigorate the African, who alone among us did not come to these shores voluntarily, but trapped in slavery transported in the holds of bloody slave ships, had for all that, by the nineteenth century, involved his/her sensibility in America by means of English, Spanish, and French whips and chains, at the same time picking their brains, and then sometimes in flight, hanging out all night with certain Native Americans, so that by the time of the appearance of the Slave Narratives and the black conventions, there was a people a culture that could be called *African-American* (which later, them/itselves became a Nation in the black-belt South). So that the African-American, its source and basic content African, wired up with English, French, Spanish, Native American language, culture, logic, and history comes to exist to be heard as grunts against the wind, for the picking of cotton. We made the work song. For the worship of the God (from the old African one in the storefront to the Jeeeee-zuz of AfroXtian design) we created the spiritual; and then to celebrate our real lives blues was willed into being, and to show we could hook our matrix upon these new instruments we encountered on our tour of the southern U.S. (loitering around New Orleans we spied these aesthetic weapons of European design, we encountered also certain marching bands such as those Dessaline had wasted in Haiti, we heard also certain harmonies that were, after all, interesting. Yes. And so we thought we would introduce all these to our own heartbeat, there in Congo Square, Master Drum was allowed to infect us, and anybody calling themselves American once more.

And inside the ho houses—ho ho ho—whilst involved in jassing, did certain immortal journalists respond to the elegant wailing that accompanied the sliding up and down of their pants, to certify their profound understanding of these events and that time and place by saying, hey now, that noise is good for jassing. What do you call it, sir? (It was Jelly Roll so addressed, and he went off to the Library of Congress and responded to the question in twelve long-playing records, now out of print!)

We know that the music came up the river, the Mississippi, when the people did. How else would it get there? We know of the funeral stomps and the small group classics. How black blues got in them gold horns and set fire to foolishness. We know about King Oliver and Louis. And ragtime and boogie woogie. How the urban spaces where we showed up with our buckets in our hands trying to get some guts still had the shadow of the plantation chained to the streets. How blues came up, and that old blues and old jazz were carried up there wrapped carefully by certain Fletchers and even royal personages like Dukes and counts unfolded the gift and extended it in suites and riffs and tone poems of our historical, social, and artistic consciousness.

And each time, the same corporations that had got over exploiting the African's tragic willingness to sell off pieces of weself to anybody who had the necessary trinketry, these same villains would reappear to scoop out the insides of our hearts and sell them for super profits and then convince us that the scooped-out portions of ourselves existed as such because we had never been whole, never, we had only and always at any time in anybody's history been simply *Niggers*.

But to get back to this evening arumm let me see. . . . Yes, we had alerted these scientists to experiment, and they had, and their experiments were successful. And the results of these sound workings could be picked up by the sensitive. The drum master here, Brother Max, as a very young man was turned on by the fertile whispering rhythms set loose in the environment by these revolutionary cultural workers. The period the forties, the Second World War, brought a prosperity to Bloods, new jobs, a new higher consciousness in the cities, rebellions in Harlem and Detroit, the Black consciousness movement, "Don't buy where you can't work," the Negro National Congress, Margaret Walker and Theodore Ward and young Max Roach picket it all up in the throbbing of the rhythm.

Max Roach in a long line of masters of the art, in the African-American tradition. As an incredibly young man/boy working with Bird in 1946–8. I came up the street and my cousin mashed some Savoys and Dials on me. I heard also Max Roach's BeBop Boys. Later I understood what it all was, what they called *BeBop*. To restore us to ourselves, to restore the polyrhythms of Africa, the primacy of improvisation and the blues, and the fundamental AFRICAN-American reidentification of ourself back to ourselves as Industrialized Africans of the West.

And Max has never turned his back from the initial fire and attack of the original bop revolution. That was a fundamental rejection of the corporate values—values that included our own slavery. So the boppers were weird, America. They had dug that it was America that was fucked up, not we ourselves. Like most black people if you could dig it. Play advanced African-American music on the airwaves all day everyday and watch what this country will turn into!! I became a BeBop-per (I didn't even think of it until my father asked me why I wanted to be one). It was like somebody asking you why you wanted to be conscious.

But that act of saving the music and removing it to yet higher planes of thought and action was revolutionary. That music sounds as fresh today as then. And Max was among the primary creators of that music even in his youth. He is the master of polyrhythmic construction. To speak of classic modern drumming is, of course, to speak of Max Roach.

Interesting also, and again to further make the point, when the music was attacked again (as it is always being) that is, when the corporations again gathered the antarctic renegades of dollarocracy to attack screaming as they came at us COOL COOL COOL (meaning, "we mean to get rid of this *hotness* you niggers are stirring up"—we answered that hot shit with the cold war on one level, with McCarthyism on another level—hell we even indicted DuBois as agent of a foreign government, humiliated Langston at the HUAC hearings, sent Richard Wright into exile, and placed Paul Robeson under house arrest). So now we going to stomp those hot rhythms flat, we gonna banish the blues, we gonna create ubiquitous charts that sound like mechanical organ grinders—aha yes, to grind out the bux—we'll injure you niggers and our code word of attack is COOL COOL you want emotion we'll give you non-motion, you want fire we'll give you ice—you want life we'll give you death. "COOL COOL COOL," pretending all the while to be admirers of Lester Young, not understanding that we had already heard *Taxi War Dance*!! And dug, that underneath Pres's distance he was very very hot.

But then among those of the next generation who saved the music once more was Max. When cool seemed like it would rule, here came Horace bringing the church in it. I guess he figured if they wanted to fight, we can go get some really spooky hot shit for ye to deal wid mister. Horace, Art Blakey from Messenger University, what they called hardbop, to bring back the real and oppose the steal. And amongst those groups called hardbop was perhaps the high mark of that, Max Roach-Clifford Brown-Sonny Rollins. On the high level, showing the direct vector from the sound scientists of the forties to raise it to another level for battle in the fifties. It was bad! bad! Another classic.

Throughout the years Max has always communicated high consciousness. Not just directly inside the music but in himself as African-American artist and man. Whether it was revolutionary music or revolutionary thought, it was joined together as a whole, as the whole the man is. When the cool fifties turned hotter and the African independence struggles came full up and the civil rights movement raised more open cries for democracy Max said WE INSIST—FREEDOM NOW. He told us about the "Driva Man" and made us cry "Tears for Johannesburg" even while we were loading our guns. He tells us "Deeds Not Words." "It's Time." "Speak Brother Speak." Or looking deep in our eyes he might know we need to be told to "Stay Up" so he'll say "Members Don't Get Weary." Or tell us about the "Long March." Or very recently he made us weep with him about our children's murders in "Atlanta-Chattahoochee Red!"

The percussion group MBeam is innovation on still a high level. Uniting some of the most impressive percussionists of the period to show us the extent to which percussion can be totally expressive. The totality of Max Roach's consciousness is what we hear when we listen to him. Everything that needs to be said is coming out, pointing at everything, always in motion, creative and transforming, aesthetically powerful, and politically revolutionary.

I came upon Archie Shepp in New York City in the early sixties. He was playing at the Living Theater in the play *The Connection* and I was startled by the newness trying to get through and organize itself. Archie was linked up to the same forces of tradition. Tradition in Transition. Was it Sonny Rollins who'd shaped him or Ben Webster or John Coltrane or was it the whole of that tradition trying to carry him with it through that horn?

Archie too comes from the revolutionary aspect of the tradition, like Max. Archie emerged as a professional in the hot sixties. The music had already been restored by Max and Clifford and Sonny; its base had been reidentified and held aloft like a red flag. Archie came out when Trane had finished Miles Davis's prep and was about to enter Thelonius Monk University, then held at the Five Spot. When Ornette Coleman came to town with a plastic horn and Eisenhower jacket trying to send BeBop into outer space and cut it loose from the popular commercial song. When Pharoah Sanders was a youngster from Arkansas everybody called Little Rock and we used to get on both of them about who had the worst feet, him or Archie.

I think I first heard him with Cecil Taylor, who invented the Five Spot. Cecil was a revolutionary player as well. He had dashed through the conservatory screaming BUD POWELL IS WHAT'S HAPPENING, LAMES! So Cecil's intense pianistics, which made European concert form stand up and be counted as possibly hip if it could only be extended to include the fire and funk of the man who hipped Stravinsky and Gershwin to the blues, in combination with Archie's new raw snarling grumbling ultrablue wail made a sound of those times that seemed to be able to say what actually was happening in the streets and in people's heads and hearts.

It is critical that we understand that there is in Archie and Max the open link of art to life. That these are both revolutionary artists, who will not bite their tongues aesthetically or politically. And that is what makes their art so hot. So that their own collaborations like "The Long March on Hat Hut" celebrating the triumph of revolutionary China and which includes Max's *South Africa Goddam* is simply among the near recent homages to the progressive spirit of world transformation. The piece "Sweet Mao" made together after Mao's death is more essential contemporary world comment at a high level of aesthetic accomplishment. Yet, get to this, both the albums with this music have had to be produced in Europe, as the corporate villains of America continue to fight revolution all over the world, usually with our money!

Archie came out in a revolutionary period, a hot time, and so he was shaped in his deepest heart by that process, the liberating force of struggle, the ecstatic revelation of victory, and always as contradiction to the powerful forces of reaction that constantly threaten any of us with elimination. In his playing one can hear black tradition recalled and absorbed and set in motion at the next level. All those midnight urban horn men and dudes stomping on the bartops like Trane did can be heard in Archie's sound. All those solitary blues players creating a world by waving their fingers across strings. All that history and pain and beauty and meaning, it's the blues, quiet and loud as the world.

Archie and I were comrades in struggle during those early years. We were in organizations together whose focus was to destroy the system that had tried to destroy our people and most people. We were openly antiimperialist, and even discovered that hid off not too well, right up in the middle of the so-called art world, were some of the worst racists and running dogs of monopoly capitalism that we had ever checked, disguised as artists and what not.

We knew that our art had to be a weapon in the struggle for black liberation, if it was going to be worthy of our people's memory. We found out also that there were people like us struggling all over the planet against exploitation and oppression and we tried to organize people as well as make our art.

Throughout Archie's career, in the titles of his pieces and the public stance he has taken, one can see this commitment to struggle, this willingness to take chances. It's in the music clearly. The Malcolm pieces, the focus on older more traditional lynchings, crying out about contemporary mass lynchings like Attica. He has incorporated African liberation struggles, African-American contemporary battles for democracy, the cry of the old and the scream of the new. He is traditional and at the same time avant-garde. And for that reason the mainstream of the African-American aesthetic tradition. Archie was part of the Black Arts Movement, wherein we tried to make an art that was African-American rather than Euro-American, an art that was public and open that was intended to move and be moved by the people. It was an openly agitational art, meant to get people hot and make them do something about the ugliness of what is. It was meant to be a revolutionary art, a people's art, fuel for social transformation. As Mao said, Artistically Powerful and Politically Revolutionary. So Archie was among the artists who played at the Black Arts programs in the streets that hot summer of 1965, where thousands heard the new music and thought it as funky as the old music. The music for *Slave Ship,* my play about our original transportation problems, Archie did, and made that production perhaps the most memorable for me. So moving for us all that many stood in tears shaking hands to the strains of Archie's music for "When We Gonna Rise/UP When We Gonna Rise." Which is still a good question. At one point in the sixties Archie and I even made appearances in forums at local nightclubs showing that not only was our art connected with struggle but we ourselves were also. We wanted Malcolm poems and Malcolm music.

All this to say that you are in the presence of two great artists, two masters. I hope you can dig it!

Cecil McBee/*Flying Out*

There's a group of musicians who everybody seems to use. They seem to work pretty regularly, because word of their professionalism and ability to adapt to different musical settings has become widespread. Among bassists, Art Davis, Percy Heath, Walter Booker, Charlie Haden, and Fred Hopkins come to mind immediately and, of course, Cecil McBee. (Quiet as it's kept, Billy Jabali Hart is in that group as well, among drummers.)

But Cecil seems to work or to have worked with mostly everybody who's saying anything. His recent work with Chico Freeman is outstanding. Cecil has worked with Jackie McLean, Roy Haynes, Grachun Moncur, Wayne Shorter, Charles Lloyd, Yusef Lateef, Freddie Hubbard, Miles Davis, Sam Rivers, Bobby Hutcherson, Pharaoh Sanders, Alice Coltrane, Lonnie Liston Smith, Charles Tolliver, Sonny Rollins, Michael White, and believe me, this is only a partial list.

Musicians swear by Cecil, citing his ability to jump right on a chart plus that solid tone and swinging facility. Just recently Cecil and Billy were part of the rhythm section for the Jazz opera *Money,* which George Gruntz and I put together. Watching Cecil and Billy at work going over some brand-new charts, and quickly bringing the music up to a very high level, was an eye-opening experience. I could see right away why they are both in such demand, whether from the "outest" or the "innest" of band leaders.

Cecil, as band leader, has also made the same wise choice that so many others have made, viz., Cecil McBee, bass, and Billy Hart, drums. Cecil's last album for India Navigation *Alternate Spaces* showed the kind of broad spectrum of musical emotion out of which Cecil functions. It was a very impressive album. Now *Flying Out* shows Cecil in a rather new context. The instrumentation, not only bass but cello and violin (plus drums and trumpet), represents a departure for Cecil. In one sense, this is string music, obviously because Cecil would be most sensitive to the stringed instruments. In fact, according to India Navigation producer Bob Cummings, because Cecil had never worked with this sound before, as the session started, "there was some tension/apprehension . . . but as soon as things got under way" . . . smiles and pleasure soon took over as everyone (particularly Cecil) realized it was working. Billy Hart was eating during the trio piece "Into a Fantasy" and put that down and listened and then said, "I've played with him for twenty years and never knew he could do anything like that."

Another departure is Cecil's piano playing on the stark, searching "Truth-a Path to Peace," first against the unison front line and then dark chords under John Blake's pensive yet finally romantic violin.

But departure or not, what is evident in all the music on the album is Cecil McBee's firm, mellow tone and the easy graceful flow of his fingers over the strings. "First Impression," the most swinging of the pieces, begins with a hushed announcement by the strings, but soon goes right up over Cecil's ever-smoking line and Billy Hart's relentless swing, which become the launching dynamic for trumpeter Olu Dara. And in brother Olu, Cecil has tapped one of the new stars of that instrument for this date. There's no doubt in my mind, and I think there are already a great many observers who would cosign this, that wherever the trumpet is going, Olu Dara will be among those who bring it there. His recent work with Henry Threadgill at Avery Fisher Hall during the Kool Jazz Festival was moving, stunning, and absolutely gorgeous!

"Into a Fantasy," as stated before, is a string trio work. In this sense, it is more nearly "contemporary American music" than it is a jazz piece. Violinist John Blake and cellist David Eyges collaborate with Cecil to create this quiet lyrical music, yet there is a brooding "darkness" to this chamber work that speaks of perception beyond the often illusionary concept of "American."

"Flying Out," the title piece, is more string music, but this time transformed by Billy Hart's hot drums and Cecil's agitating insinuating bass. From the ostinato bass line with cello and violin over, and then the swelling of Hart's cymbal accompaniment, there is a rushing, rumbling evocative quality to this piece that gives it a "flying" feeling. The solo violin over running bass line with Hart under and then the emotional almost percussive attack of the cello with its spreading overtones, still underpinned by bass and drums make this one of the album's high points.

"Blues on the Bottom" is just what the title suggests. The head is reminiscent of a slightly quirky Messenger-type blues, maybe one of Wayne Shorter's or spiced with a little Dolphy. So that violinist Blake has to come on a little like Eddie South or Ray Nance, over Cecil's ever-supporting and always warm bass line. Olu Dara is on this too, which is exactly where Olu is always coming from, directly or indirectly, Bluesville.

Flying Out is not only a showcase of master bassist Cecil McBee's instrumental skills, it is also a vehicle for his composing, arranging, and orchestrating talents. It also shows him off to good advantage as a band leader. It is becoming clear that not only is Cecil McBee a much-in-demand and accomplished "featured player" (having left the ranks of "sideman" years ago), but that he is already a leader-musician of rich and varied accomplishment.

Craig Harris/*Aboriginal Affairs*

The word is out—the new sound on trombone is Craig Harris! If you're given to frequenting the places where the very contemporary African-American music is made and played, that word, that name, Craig Harris, is in the possession of the hip and the would-be's. And what's more impressive is that these accolades are both deserved and accurate. At thirty, Craig Harris is more than a new voice on the scene; it is already clear that he will make some indelible impression on the music of his time.

This first album is just a bare introduction to what Craig can do and only a hint of what he will do, and this will be obvious after you hear this music recorded here. First, Craig is already formidable on his instrument, the trombone. And he has chosen to come by way of an older tradition on that instrument. For a long time, most trombonists were simply J. J. Johnson clones, even some very imaginative ones—but clones they remained. Craig said, in an interview, one of the negative things about the sixties he thought was that except for Grachun Moncur and Roswell Rudd, there were no trombonists. "Why weren't there any trombonists on Trane's *Ascension*?" he asked.

But Craig hears the old big heavy sound on trombone. Not just the quick slippery sinuous noting of J. J. and company, as hip as that can be. Craig wants the trombone sound to be big and funky, a daring, raucous thing. When asked who his influences were, he said, "Everybody," and proceeded to name a half dozen great bonemen. "I got a personal thing for Benny Green, his sound and spirit . . . but J.J., Jimmy Cleveland, Duke's folks [meaning "Tricky" Sam Nanton, Lawrence Brown, and Juan Tizol—Tricky Sam's influence, and Bubber Miley's and Cootie Williams's too will be obvious on "Down (As in Under)"], Jimmy Harrison, Curtis Fuller, Grachun, and Roswell." All heavyweights, and from such a nonsectarian list it should also be obvious that Craig Harris has picked up whatever from whomever, in the pursuit of his own sound and vision.

Another thing about Craig that is not only distinctive but very welcome for this listener is that Craig Harris comes to *swing*—he plays very very *hot*! Too often, nowadays, in this era of an expanded black middle class—some of whom are so victimized by cultural aggression that they think they have to make African-American music an appendage of European concert art—it is extraordinarily refreshing to hear a young aggressively "avant-garde" musician so clearly expressive of the hot tradition of black music. And far from apologetic for it, Craig says, "I'm proud of my R&B background. I want to touch people with my music. There are musicians who always talk about not wanting to have their music retarded by having to play down to the people. You have to be strong enough to raise the people *up,* not play down!" The music on *Aboriginal Affairs* is a case in point.

The title is part of the heavy influence that a trip to Australia made on Craig a couple years ago, when he toured Africa, Australia, and Europe with Abdullah Ibrahim (Dollar Brand). Drummer André Strobert, and guitarist and electric bassist Alonzo Gardner were also on that tour. Alonzo and Craig have known each other since kindergarten. André and Craig have known each other ten years. Also there is a Westbury connection, since both Craig and Alonzo were students together at SUNY at Old Westbury, and André Strobert and Ken McIntyre still teach there.

One engaging aspect of the music is its easy accessibility at the same time it is complex and challenging. Ken McIntyre's contribution to this engaging musical whole is important, and the minute you hear McIntyre it brings back the screaming sixties when he was one of the new avant's most promising and erudite innovators. It is good to have him back!

All the music on this album was influenced by the trip to Australia with Ibrahim. The titles testify to this quickly, but the content of the music does as well. There are two "Dreamtimes." "Dreamtime (Dawn)" is the quiet, meditative piece, where we hear Craig's full, strong, yet stunningly mellow quality on his instrument. The sound is so deliberately evocative, it is possible to glimpse some of the meaning that the Aboriginal people of the land called Australia symbolize by the term, "Dreamtime," which is the time, the period, the mood of creation and creativity. Their belief has it that the world is but a dream of some things. Donald Smith's deep, rich piano sound is perfectly complementary. He is still relatively new to many people, but folks had better stop sleeping on Donald; as you hear on this album, he can play—and sing (he plays the flute too but not on this album).

Dingo is the desert dog or wolf of the aboriginal land. Some communities believe that when they die they return as the Dingo, so they are very seldom killed. The music begins with a swift announcement of swiftness to come—straight ahead—Donald Smith's sinuous line and André Strobert's driving drums. Craig demonstrates why he is known as a swinger, a hot man. Strong tone, driving, yet fluid and smooth. Alonzo Gardener adds a blues feeling to the whole, languid at times, at other times a contemporary "no wave" R&B touch. Ken McIntyre in this too brief but "Dolphyesque" pronouncement makes it clear again why he was so highly thought of in the sixties. The ensemble of block improvisation is as heavy and as swinging as you can get to these days.

"Down (As in Under)," with its insistent bass call, is a piece Craig says was influenced by Ibrahim, but it is obviously also deeply influenced by the black church. Listen to Craig's gorgeous work with the plunger (Duke's influence), and Donald Smith's trilling soulfulness. This is some of the most beautiful music I've heard in a long time.

"Dreamtime (Dusk)" is a "rhythmic exercise" to quote Craig Harris, but it is something much more. Strobert's in 3/4, the guitar and bass in 7/4, then the horns come in 4/4 and the piano and bass to 4/4. It is an example of cross rhythms, with the solo form 7/4 against 4/4. Craig says it is the "essence of African music," inspired by a trip to Africa for the FESTAC, where he was turned on by the African polyrhythms.

"Awakening Ancestors" features Craig Harris on dijiridoo, the traditional Aboriginal instrument, which is a long wooden tube that has to be leaned on the floor to be played, with its deep wind-instrument sound. It is sometimes played with clapsticks and accompanied by singing. Harris went into the Queensland area of "Australia," where the Aboriginal people are kept like the native Americans in the United States, on reservations. These are even worse than the so-called homelands of apartheid South Africa!

The whole tune is built on the dijiridoo which is an E, and all tones pass that E, and at the bottom of all the other sound remains the dijiridoo with all the other instruments "suspended above," McIntyre's flute is moving and lovely on this, a "sky" statement that still broods in its relationship to the dijiridoo's "earthy" consistency.

"Dijiridbludu" is still another impressive Craig Harris chart. (All the music is Craig's!) But this time featuring the hip blue vocal by multitalented Donald Smith. Donald, who is the brother of the well-known Lonnie Liston Smith, shows that he could make it as a singer alone, but when you add his piano to it, you see what a huge talent is about to emerge! The words are Craig Harris's as well; they tell of the Aboriginal people's black and blue life under colonialism. "Cry your song blue/Scream the sighs/Shout the whys/We die." A lament against third-world oppression.

Craig Harris has, since he moved to New York City in 1978, moved very quickly into the public's eye. After a two-year "postgraduate" course with Sun Ra, inspired by reed man Pat Patrick's teaching at Westbury, Craig came to New York where he has been practicing "getting your stuff together." He is getting it together very rapidly. He worked with many of the AACM musicians in the late seventies and early eighties, worked a year with the Lena Horne show on Broadway; gigged with Beaver Harris–Don Pullen's 360 Degree Musical Experience, Don Moye–Josephy Jarman, Muhal Abrams; and most recently he has been stirring things up with David Murray's great Octet, after George Lewis moved on, and the Henry Threadgill Sextet.

Aboriginal Affairs will be your introduction to a young musician with a fantastic future and a pretty fantastic present. Check it out!

Jay Hoggard/Solo Album/*India Navigation*

For a little while now people listening to the *new music* have been mentioning Jay Hoggard's name when it comes to vibes—at the top of the list of folks to check. (Another name people conjure with these days on vibes is Khan Jamal.) And once checking, people tell you about Jay's technique and speed with the mallets—they also talk about his overall musical approach, melodic and tuneful, yet equally characterized by sustained rhythmic and percussive effects. (Check "Samba pa Negra.") Jay also has a beautiful sound, making us think of the last two innovators on the instrument: Earl Griffith, who made his brief impressive career public, most memorably, with Cecil Taylor; and the incredible Bobby Hutcherson. Jay makes us think of them—his musicality, innovation, e.g., the sureness and beauty of his handling of dissonance and minors and modal approaches, while still managing to *swing.* But he also, even now, very early in his career, lets us hear something *new,* a personal and unique approach to the instrument, which is warming and inspirational.

Actually, Jay is part of the newest wave of innovators to emerge on the jazz scene. The consolidators of the New Thing avant-garde of the sixties led by Ornette Coleman, Cecil Taylor and co-experimenters on each and every instrument, such as Eric Dolphy, the perennial avantist; Sun Ra; Sonny Murray; Milford Graves; the great Albert Ayler; Norman Howard; Archie Shepp; Don Cherry; Pharaoh Sanders plus countless others who caught that spirit and fire and brought us "the music" on a higher level. Made it New! And all these were guided by the most searching and creative spirit of the older generation, John Coltrane, who was both link and spearhead for a new direction.

Hoggard and many of the musicians he is most often found with are the newest generation. Picking up where Trane, Cecil, Ornette, Albert, and the others brought it (with C.T. and O.C. still bringing it) and trying to take it even further. Another very important quality Jay has (so important I mention it again—and will probably mention it another 'gin) is his *swing*—Hoggard can swing! Yes, as the Duke of Ellington musicked to us in his succinct aesthetic credo, "It don't mean a thing . . ." etc. It needs to be said a few times, because there is one sector of Jay's generation (as there was to every generation up under national oppression and its resulting cultural aggression) who think that in order to be "intellignk" they have to strip the Afro-American guts out of the music and let us know they have EUREKA heard but also been stunted by Cage, Webern, Berg, etc. and recent European concert music! Not so with Hoggard, who is new and avant but understands what Duke meant. Or as Stanley the Crouch said recently in conversation, "Some dudes don't know Duke solved the problem of what to do with European concert music forty years ago." And the truth of that can be witnessed easily, if you can check *Diminuendo & Crescendo in C, Transbluesency, KoKo,* etc.

But not only does Jay Hoggard know that, second-generation players like David Murray, Hamiett Bluett dig it consistently and *most times* the most interesting players out of the Chicago, St. Louis, and L.A. West Coast funk brigades know this as well (talking about players like Oliver Lake, Julius Hemphill, Olu Dara, James Newton, Steve McCall, Art Ensemble of Chicago, Lester Bowie, Chico Freeman, and many others).

Jay Hoggard was born in Washington, D.C., September 28, 1954, and moved up to New York (Mount Vernon) at age six. He is the son of an AME Zionist bishop father and schoolteacher mother, which places him jam up in that miniature socioeconomic stratum, the Afro-American middle class. Obviously, Jay is not the first significant petty-bourgeois jazz musician; we can name a bunch who have admirably conveyed the advanced improvisational music of the people consistently. Nevertheless, the heavy odor of brain damage still lingers among us from various "upward mobility" types who have gone off into the lotus land of "3rd stream" or "progressive jazz" (or what's the latest term, Jo Jo?) or other such projects to make the music square (and boring).

The powers that be will give out grants, and concerts and slick tours, and residencies and great reviews for such capitulation faster than it takes to say, "Our music has nothing to do with bebop or other Afro-American musics that preceded it."

But Jay Hoggard is bringing all of the tradition with him and raising it to a higher level. From Hamp to Bags to Earl Griffith to Bobby Hutcherson—and now Jay's got the chance to run with it. And that is not only a heavy responsibility but a *challenge,* a commitment, a rest of your lifetime gig! (If you up to it!)

Hoggard studied at Wesleyan University in Connecticut, ethnomusicology. Sam Rivers, Clifford Thornton, Jimmy Garrison, Bill Barron were teaching there, a course called World Music (1976). Clifford Thornton gave Jay his first big-time gig. And right after he got out of school Hoggard taught in a New Haven high school.

Since that time he has played widely among the newest of the new musicians, like multi-talented reed man Chico Freeman (on the beautiful *Kings of Mali* album); with trumpeter Ahmed Abdullah, the Art Ensemble, Anthony Davis, Sam Rivers. Recently Jay's been rehearsing with Cecil Taylor for a record and a tour in a group that includes Jimmy Lyons, alto, Ramsey Ameen, violin, and Kenny Tyler, drums.

Jay, who is still very very young, only reached the Apple in June of 1977, and this soló album marks his debut as other than a member of the ensemble. (Although he is planning a "more commercial thing" with Don Moye, on Arista in the near future. Jay mentioned that folks like "Chick Corea and Keith Jarrett were making money" off the music. Though one gets the feeling that the young musician wants to make a *popular* album, in the sense that it will be more accessible to the audience, rather than the purely commercially oriented right-wing fusion pushed by superhustlers like New York's WRVR. But plainly, a musician *ought to* be able to make a living playing music—but one soon learns, if one is awake at all, that in a society where only a few colossal Porkers have all de bux tied up, all most of us get is a hard way to go—artists included!)

One very positive side of Jay Hoggard is that he realizes that his music must be addressed to an audience. His concern for the makeup of that audience shows a high degree of social sensitivity. And so he wonders out loud how can the new music reach more people. Specifically he is concerned about it reaching a much larger segment of the black community. Hoggard lamented the fact that most of the places the new music played there are "few black people in the audience." Talking about places like Tin Palace, the loft scene, Ali's Alley, Joe Papp's Public Theater, or recently the La Mama Theater. This is true, though the TP and Ali's audience is made up of a fairly good percentage of blacks (counting all the musicians downtown looking for work). But the owners of the bars in the Harlems, Bed Stuys, Newarks want these bars *only* for Maximum or even Super profit and the idea of Art-Music never would enter into that. The Village and SoHo and Lower East Side have reps that the landlords and criminals feel they can exploit and so the offerings are somewhat broader since they feel the downtown audience can support such weird stuff and they still make money. But in the main *most* audiences are played down to, and suppressed by commercialism, even in the artsy Village. The almighty aesthetic dominating the United States is, of course, the buck. And everything is sacrificed to it, even (no, especially) people's lives!

Jay wants to reach a wider and blacker audience, "like church music or R&B," and to do that he feels he has to construct "a bridge" so that even "more exploratory stuff" is accessible. This present album features both the more exploratory and the accessible, but finally even

Jay's most adventurous thrusts are excitingly accessible, despite the solo form which can be very restrictive. Recently, the solo perform-ance, both live and on record, has come to popularity among the new musicians (and producers too, I would imagine—dealing with the bud-get side). On one hand, it is really fantastic when musicians are such strong and inspired players that they can sustain an audience through a whole set (or album) by themselves. (David Murray's *Sur-real Sax-ophone* is a dynamite for-instance.) On the other hand, however, the solo format in the hands of the less skilled becomes quickly mundane and merely an excuse for criminal self-indulgence. Part of the cult of the individual falsely "celebrated" at the expense of the majority.

Jay Hoggard's selection of tunes for the recording (made live at the Public Theater) demonstrates from the very beginning his sensitivity to his audience, trying to reach them and teach them! The pulsatingly rhythmic Afro-Latino (Brazilian) "Samba pa Negra." Hoggard is both the spinning melodic line as well as the get-down rhythm section, driv-ing throughout.

"Comfort in the Storm" is reflective, quiet and introspective with some hard beating and a hint of dissonance reminding us of the menac-ing storm—yet at the center all is calm and balanced. Hoggard paints with his mallets and the sweeps of sound easily draw us into his straightforward yet subtle progressions.

An important element of Jay Hoggard as performer, composer, art-ist is his consciousness. Because, in any artist, that is finally what you hear, or see, or read and respond to—their total consciousness—how they have perceived reality and what they have chosen to tell us—and whether we have *learned* from them.

Hoggard's song "May Those Who Love Apartheid Burn in Hell" was inspired by a piece of Ntozake Shange's *Soweto Suite,* for Steve Biko, when they worked together earlier in the year. Hoggard's piece was accompaniment for the suite, which he then developed even fur-ther. It is the most striking work on the record. Wild, furious, surpris-ing, yet a well-structured whole building to a series of screamed dissonant confrontations that puts spears of goosepimple sound right on your body. There remains, however, a *lyricism* to it, an abiding rhythm and song melody that keeps it in our memory like a work of heroic preaching art.

But the stance that would see that, Yes. Apartheid could be as-saulted with music too; that art must be in the world like an exploited worker fighting back. And raise that perception to a rational stance and then play it. The music *means* this, like when Trane called a piece of his "Alabama" during the Selma marches. "Focus on this, and hear me putting my soul's energy to the task, so that even in the music world the people's enemies are opposed and attacked." Yes, it is hip! And necessary. Swings too!

Ditto, the last selection, "If You Believe," from Motown's much maligned (by reactionary critics and their camp followers) *The Wiz*. Actually, *The Wiz* is hip! Sidney Lumet put it in the black ghetto and restored its *original* political overtones. (Frank Baum, the author, was an old populist and intended *The Wizard of Oz* to convey a very specific political symbolism, which Hollywood in *Wiz 1* tried to erase.) Hoggard has seized on Lena Horne's flick-stealing number which she sings after Dorothy helps black workers out from under the clutches of the Wicked Witch of the West, the owner of a subterranean sweatshop! And while Lena sings, Lumet directs the cameras to focus on black children, telling them to believe in themselves—no matter what b.s. the WW of the W tries to put on y'all.

Jay sees himself being influenced by a wide variety of folks and things. He mentions Sam Rivers and Cecil Taylor prominently, and adds quickly, Trane, Hamp, Bags, Cal Tjader, Lem Winchester, Gary Burton, Jimi Hendrix. In 1975, the young vibist got to Tanzania, East Africa, and studied xylophone music (the African xylophone played all over Africa). He opened his solo performance in Newark with a demonstration and lecture about African rhythms. Part of the reason he wanted to do a solo album is because he feels the vibes, and its African antecedents are instruments people don't know about. He calls what he plays Creative Music, or New Creative Music, which is apt, and also is the functional and moving, opening our selves (together) and helping those selves grow (together). Jay said he has trouble with "Art for Art's Sake," which is how it should be. Art is for the People, and quiet as it's kept, created by them. Watch Jay Hoggard, he is at the beginning of an important career.

Jay Hoggard/*Mystic Winds*

Jay Hoggard says of this album that it is his first album concentrating on composition. Meaning that the compositions on this album were the basis of everything else that we have. That they occupied a central place in the construction of the total musical product.

Not just as a set of musical relationships, but also the thematic emphasis and continuity. All the tunes on the album are Hoggard's except "Listen in Silence," which is Anthony Davis's.

In essence, all the Hoggard pieces on the album comprise the parts of a single whole. Like the separate pieces of a suite. The thematic focus is Africa and most particularly the trade in human beings emanating from there from the sixteenth century on. The music is Jay Hoggard's personal insight, his personal musical way into so huge and far-reaching an event as the slave trade, slavery, and many related questions.

Jay says that the catalyst for the pieces, or piece, was the television series *Roots*, as well as his reading of the book. Particularly, it was the rendition of the African experience, both pre-slavery and during the earliest grim days of the slave trade, that captured Hoggard's imagination. *Mystic Winds* and *Ashanti Gold* tell of an Africa before slavery. He is speaking, he says, of "a cosmology and ritual" that pre-date the slave trade. The music means to invoke a "normal" African world, before the coming of traders in human flesh, and before whole nations and empires perished because of the fatal diminishing of productive forces caused by various African rulers selling their own black flesh into slavery.

"Winds" has a buoyancy and swing that have pre-slave trade Africa popping its fingers, with Hoggard wailing on marimbas. The band that Jay hooked up for this date also tunes in with the infectiously swinging line. Anthony Davis has gained the reputation as one of the most interesting and multifaceted of the second wave of avants, and he continues to put out a very high level of performance with all kinds of different groups, as well as his own. Cecil McBee must be one of the most sought-after bassists among the most modern of the moderns and among the mainstream as well. Cecil's clear throbbing lines collect the music in its forward motion.

Billy Hart is very similar to Cecil McBee in the sense that everybody wants him to gig with them. And this is a tribute to Billy Hart's skillful swinging. He is driving, yet tasty and open.

Percussionist Don Moye is keeper of the drum with the Art Ensemble, which means that he is a musician functioning at one of the highest levels in the music. And he is perfect for this album, because his well-known attention and focus on Africa translates into swinging music. He is a very moving player.

Wilson Moorman adds tympani to give yet another dimension to Hoggard's ensemble. Not yet a household word himself, Moorman comes from a musical Newark family that has already given the world Melba Moore, and he is beginning to appear with more frequency on albums and in clubs.

Dwight Andrews is a multiple accomplished musician and reed man. And not only does he bring a deep keening polished artifaction to the music, he is a musician of great intelligence and learning, teaching at Yale University and associated with players like trumpeter Leo Smith.

Hoggard, from Wesleyan as well as teaching school in New Haven; Davis who comes out of New Haven, as well as Andrews, all come out of that richly intellectual tradition associated with New Haven, Yale, etc. And they have made music together there before.

Ashanti Gold has the overall feeling of a "freer" African percussion, but the piano and reed line repeated in consonance with the drum makes for a new music dynamic with deep African roots. There is a brightness to the swing, yet there is a kind of brooding, a shadow, perhaps of the opposite, the contradiction, which Dwight Andrews insinuates and Hoggard echoes with his undercurrent of dark marimba staccato.

Hoggard says of these two tunes that they "explain themselves." Which is true for the best "programmatic music," i.e., music that tries to reflect a particular theme. But all music is, to a certain extent, program music in that it cannot exist except it reflect the composer's perception of reality and social life. People who call for "pure" music call for an impossible abstraction of an abstraction.

The piece "Other Side of the Ocean," is "program music" in the best and most aesthetically rewarding sense.

Jay says he wanted to give that experience, in music, of pre-slave Africa, and then the horror, the madness, of being captured by a slave ship. What would be the human emotions in such a context, after the initial hatred and agony and fear, in trying to wonder what one's fate would be? And so he begins with the gongs, cymbals, tympani, and bass speaking of the eerie, the unknown, something weird in the air. This is called "Clouds of Terror." Bass resolves to piano after the horrific cry of the reeds and then bass clarinet. These announce the second part, "Struggle," a frenzied stomping of piano, percussion, and vibes, in reflection of the life-and-death battles played over and over again until half a race of people had been chained into slave ships or sacrificed to the hunger of rising Euro-American capitalism.

It is then that the bass clarinet lays down the hideously calm death/life of "on the slave ship." It is like a horror movie with the vibes digging into psyche to reveal the still-existent image of this African holocaust while Moye gives us everything from the bells of the death ships to the rumble of chains and water under our feverish stomachs chained in the dark. But even here there is a rising, a rumble, a held-in fury, perhaps of dark realization and what else? What would it be like to lie at the bottom of the fetid vessel knowing you are bound for hell?

The immensely effective compositions remind me not a little of the Hoggard piece "May Those Who Love Apartheid Burn in Hell," on his solo album. The brilliant young vibist shows us how indeed music can and does express ideas.

Ironically (but perhaps not so much) Anthony Davis's "Listen in Silence" seems relaxed, almost "laid back" in comparison with the Hoggard charts. But it is a necessary relaxation, a reflective peacefulness that permits one to analyze events and situations, to hook up the expressive with the reflective and the intellectual. We are listening in silence, maybe, to all that makes sound. And it is in this state that we contemplate, that we dream, that we plan.

Jay Hoggard, yet a very young man, continues to make extremely rich music. Music that makes us feel and think. Music that not only demonstrates his increasing maturity but all of us who are conscious, here in the last part of the twentieth century.

To Be or Not to Bop: A Biography of Dizzy Gillespie

by Al Frazier

Around 1948, when I was about fifteen years old, my older cousin gave me (actually "lent" me, but he blew—'cause he never got them back) a bunch of BeBop records. This was my first up-close exposure to the new music. Before that I dug the Ravens, the Orioles, Little Esther, Dinah Washington, Larry Darnell, Louie Jordan and his Tympany Five, basically the popular music of the Afro-American people, contemporary blues. But now my cousin laid the real heavies on me, Max Roach and His BeBop Boys, Charlie Parker's ReBoppers, a mess of Guilds, Savoys, Dials, Musicrafts, the riches of the new world! Whether that was my first consciousness of Dizzy Gillespie is difficult now to ascertain because I think Diz was getting some publicity (as he points out in his book) around the nuttier aspects of what the media could draw out about the music, in *Time* and *Esquire*, etc. But I know once I got hold of the sides my conversion was complete. I know I must have seen pictures of Diz earlier, but at one point during that period or earlier I painted a picture on one side of my skating case (though I never could skate) the picture of a Diz-like figure with lop-sided beret, and horn-rimmed glasses. And underneath the picture I painted *To Be or Not to Bop.*

What was so thrilling about that music was that it took me places I had never been, made things go through my head that I wasn't before hip to. And then those windowpane BeBop glasses and goatee and beret, now you knew that was hip! But the music, itself became for me the passport and vehicle for a head trip which I still make every chance I can. BeBop was a different music for me because it not only reached me rhythmically (And with what rhythms!) but it seemed to me *deeper, heavier;* it not only moved my body but got hold of my mind!

To Be or Not to Bop is a must acquisition for anybody interested in the music from more than a surface, strictly entertainment point of view. The book is part of the music's history—an important document adding to our understanding of the development of modern Afro-

American improvised music, from the point of view of one of its major innovators.

When I first approached the book I had more than a little trepidation because peeping the format, mostly interviews with Diz and Al's running commentary as the overall collecting form, I thought that like a few other jazz books I'd read that this form would tend to disperse the insights and dribble too frequently off into trivia. But the spookwriter (which is different from a ghostwriter) Al Frazier does a good job laying the various interviews and comments by the host of commentators on Diz's life and music in places throughout the book that do actually serve to move the narrative forward, and give real insight into Dizzy's statements. Frazier places Diz's comments and corroborations and even opposition to the interviews so that they're interesting and funny.

There *is* more than just a taste of trivia and exaggerated detail, e.g., about Diz's early and home life, his relationships with various people, his many knuckle-drills with all kinds of dudes, etc. *In fact,* Diz got enough stuff in this like that to make a good novel; he and Frazier need to get together on that. But in spite of this and Diz's occasional ego trips, the book comes across as an important work because it tells us so much about the real life history and development of the music. For instance, there is enough purely musical discussion vis à vis the technical innovation that BeBop made to satisfy all but the straight-out technique freaks who are so into form they blow the content and feeling. We also come to understand much more about the life of the black jazz musician in the United States, how the national oppression and racism that all blacks suffer in this capitalist paradise specifically obstructs and exploits and many times even kills black musical artists, especially would-be innovators.

And Diz is a very conscious artist-historian; there are things he wants to make sure get said. One of these is the whole evolutionary-revolutionary historical process of black music's growth and development. Where the music is coming from, where it's been, and why it sounds, at any time, like it does. He cites the Buddy Bolden, King Oliver, Louis Armstrong, Roy Eldridge, Dizzy Gillespie trumpet succession many times to make his point, how each contributed and brought the music, with a revolutionary turn, to a higher level, which then set the evolutionary process at work with new materials, new directions, with new stories to tell. He also lets us know that Fats Navarro, Clifford Brown, Miles Davis, Lee Morgan, and Freddie Hubbard, who he sees as his successors, are really carrying a message that he, Diz, got from others and gave, like the relay racer's baton, on over to them. When people dig them, he says, they're really digging me, and all those others before me as well—which is real, and heavy.

The book moves from Diz's early days in Cheraw, his family, his first exposure to the trumpet and the music (checking Teddy Hill's bad orchestra on a neighbor's radio—and thereby coming in contact with Roy Eldridge—his early model—Chu Berry, Dickie Wells). Along with this life motion we also grow to understand who Diz is a little better, how John Birks Gillespie got to be known as *Dizzy* and why he wanta be like that. The move up north to Philly; his learning of the piano which he cites again and again as a major tool in his harmonic innovations on trumpet ("'cause you can see all the chords and the notes in them"). We go on fantastic trips with the many bands Diz played in, and follow his personal and musical ups and downs with interest, not only getting educated along the way, but cracking up repeatedly over the essentially comic verve of Dizzy's*ness*.

Lucky Millinder, Cab Calloway (and the famous spitball/Cab-Diz rumble incident), the Savoy Ballroom and earlier Newark hipsters like Al Kooper's Savoy Sultans, Diz talks about all of it. The emergence of the new music, BeBop and its "flatted fifths," and chord substitutions, and new virtuosity, along with Diz's collaboration with the other giants who appeared during that period, Bird, Monk, Bud, Oscar Pettiford, and what a portion of their life was like hooked up to the music is material that historians and the regulation "down" listener will go back to often, because it is laid out by one of these great artists themselves. As Bruce Franklin said in his need to be read book published last year, *The Victim as Artist and Criminal* (Oxford), Afro-American culture is central to American culture, not peripheral, the fact of African slavery is perhaps the key to understanding what the United States is in reality if not in White House theory. So as Diz runs down the development of the music, and the lives that changed and developed with that, as he talks to us about the great Earl Hines's band which should have played in the major concert halls of America, or the fantastic Billy Eckstine band, in which Diz was the musical director, and which featured, among others, Bennie Green, trombone, Fats Navarro, trumpet, Gene Ammons and Dexter Gordon, tenor saxophones, Sarah Vaughan and Billy Eckstine, vocals, and a weird dude named Charlie Parker on alto . . . another band which should have played in those same million-dollar concert halls but was washed out by the corporate aesthetic that bathes most of America in commercial mediocrity—today they're conning us with fusion and disco—these things make us contemplate and yearn for an America that would really utilize its human product for the growth of that human product rather than maximum profit for a minority, and the frustration can bite us in the butt, even while we follow Diz's exploits and discoveries and the sinister implications of the artist's life and the people's lives momentarily trapped in a sham democracy where Bird and Trane or for that matter Malcolm and Martin King can be dead in their thirties while toothless titty-milk-drinking dudes like old man Rockefeller can live into their eighties!!

But the book is a good experience; it makes you feel good and tells you something at the same time, that's a lot. Dizzy's big bands were also of major importance, and we should *still* be hearing them with the likes of John Coltrane, Paul Gonsalves, Jimmy Heath, J. J. Johnson, Al Mckibbon playing with them, and the Gil Fuller, George Russell arrangements—or with BeBop Joe Carroll singing "In the Land of Obladee" or "Schooldays" or "Swing Low Sweet Cadillac." We get to know Diz the innovator with Bird playing together "like a thing with two heads," the startling revolution that shot the music to where it still is today. Diz pioneered use of Afro-Latino polyrhythms, using great musicians like Chano Pozo and Candido or bringing in new things like Samba and its child, Bossa Nova. (Not to mention all the many musicians that Diz helped and taught or sent off to commercial success like Quincy Jones, or Lalo Schifrin!) This is a very rich book; it will be a standard reference book, of various kinds, musically, historically, socially. It tells us something about America North, about some of everybody in it. It has obvious flaws and shortcomings, and some of its political summaries are shaky as Jell-O—like Diz talking about what a great person Ladybird Johnson was—yaknow?—but you can walk with that, and, what's more, Diz probably don't even believe that stuff, privately! At least, we hope not.

Dear Roger Riggins

Wow, Roger, I didn't realize you were such a stiff type. But just a couple responses, having heard your letter by phone. First, I was not putting down Anita O'Day, Benny Goodman, etc. in my piece. I was merely reporting what white chauvinism was rampant among jazz writers. Apparently, because I sought to point out that Anita O'Day should not be cited as *the* major influence on modern jazz singers and certainly not to the *exclusion* of Sarah Vaughan, you think I am attacking her. Or because I do not think that Benny Goodman was "the most technically accomplished player the music has produced" or that Phil Woods is "Chief alto of the Jazz Tribe," you think I am attacking them. In other words, if such chauvinist distortion is not upheld I am attacking these musicians? What seems more likely the case, Roger, is you don't see such chauvinist characterizations as incorrect!

Secondly, to say that you uphold "the artistic party line" as distinct from the "political party line" is, by your own written example, the sheerest nonsense. But a kind of nonsense that is famous among petty bourgeois intellectuals. There is no such thing as an "artistic party line" independent of the particular aesthetic, i.e., social and political shaping of what is beautiful or good, etc., that sees it as such. Your aesthetic is created by your deepest politics, whether you are *consciously* making political choices as such or not. In other words, what you think of as "hip" is essentially a political choice!

Next thing you know you'll be telling us that *Birth of a Nation* is aesthetically hip but its politics are irrelevant!

As for saying you're not certain or you question whether there is an erosion of democratic values in the U.S. during this period of Reagan Rightism shows again that you are some kind of naive *centrist;* that is, you think you are neither left nor right, but objectively (as with such a statement) you support the right. If you don't think Reagan's attack on blacks, other oppressed nationalities, women, the arts, social programs, public education and his determination to start World War III constitute an "erosion of democratic values," what are you waiting for—the U.S. version of Dachau to open?

As for your contention that a "populist line is not adequate." I am not a populist (which is simply giving the appearance of appealing to the majority while still maintaining bourgeois views) but a Marxist-Leninist. But from the tone and content of your remarks you're not even a populist.

Dennis Moorman/*Circles of Destiny*

Dennis Moorman is yet another member of the Newark, New Jersey, Moormans, though Dennis now lives in Brooklyn. (Two others, his sister Melba, who shortened her name to Moore, and Wilson, an increasingly better-known percussionist, who is a cousin.) This is relevant, not simply as still another indication of how much artistic talent has been developing in the city across the river, much of which has near instantly got away, but to the depth and broadness of Dennis Moorman's musical background.

In Dennis's foreground is a growingly impressive list of credits, including recent work with new star tenor saxophonist Chico Freeman and with premier bassist Cecil McBee. He has also performed at jazz festivals all over the world, e.g., Montreux (Switzerland), North Sea (Holland) among many others.

Dennis, who has both a B.M. and M.M. from Manhattan School of Music, has not only a family background in music, but an academically sound one as well. He is certainly no stranger to European concert music, and his work with the Harlem Opera Society and with the Society of Black Composers speaks to his contribution to an Afro-American presence in the world of western "classical" music. He performed the premiere of Carmen Moore's *Gospel Fuse* with Cissy Houston, Sam Rivers, and the San Francisco Symphony. He has also written and performed *A Jazz Mass*.

Dennis is a versatile artist, as pianist, composer, arranger. And his academic background is only one aspect of his musical equipment and personality. He has already criss-crossed a substantial part of the jazz club circuit—NYC's Sweet Basil, Palsson's, Tin Palace, Boomer's; Maiden Voyage in L.A.; and even Caesar's Palace in Las Vegas, with names like Carter Jefferson, Billy Hart, Reggie Workman, Dave Liebman, Freddie Waits, etc.

He has been a pianist/conductor for vocalists like Sammy Davis, Jr., Melba Moore, Brock Peters, Thelma Carpenter, and Novella Nelson. Moorman's Broadway credits are equally impressive: *Sophisticated Ladies, Comin' Uptown, Evita, Timbuktu, The Wiz, Stop the World, Louis.*

Circles of Destiny is Dennis' first album as leader. This is a solo album of his own compositions, and perhaps it is the nature of such albums that they tend to be introspective. *Circles of Destiny* is a very personal, even intimate statement, but at the same time there is a "concert tone" to the music, a performance-conceived improvisational style that can be eagerly listened to.

Moorman's mastery of the instrument is obvious from the opening phrases of the fiercely staccato "Three to Go," with its repeated motif which reminds one not a little of some earlier "Moormen" who used to hang out in Spain.

Throughout the album, Moorman's sweeping arpeggios and big blocks of dazzling chords and his aggressive pianistics talk to us of his extensive technical preparation. But one is made quickly aware of the musicality and artistic relevance of what he plays. He is not just "playing his music lessons," his considerable technique is the given and the catalyst by means of which his musical aesthetic is expressed.

"Suite" is a gentle ballad—searching, even quizzical—that gradually builds an ever more heavily mood-provoking statement, a subtle chordal voice, that just as gradually fades to quietness.

"Fourth Composition" is somewhat jaunty and reserved at the same time. It has echoes of Broadway tastefully blended with jazz. But Moorman's specialty—repeated motifs often restated in any number of ways and contexts—give this a bittersweet depth that seems to characterize much of his compositional work.

"Ballad" is in some ways similar to "Suite" in that both carry heavy layers of quietness and introspection. But "Ballad" seems a kind of earnest love song asking all those questions that only the future can handle. The piece has a concertlike expansiveness, filled with tenderness and wonder.

In "Third Composition", the "classical techniques" and "compositionally improvisational" style seem to come full out. The repeated motifs with their variations, theme and variations, create a work that is tight and formal, yet open and spontaneous. And the variations carry evidence of the statement (Is it faintly "Latino" stretched way out?) as music and emotion, not just an arrangement (of notes).

"Me'N" is the funk entry of the album. It is "pop" plus bouncy and bluesy, indicating still another facet of Dennis Moorman's musical capacity. Moorman has said that he is trying to develop an entirely new kind of improvisational style, linked to a broad musical tradition and expressing his own personal ear and understanding of the music. *Circles of Destiny* shows that he is well on his way.

Gil Scott Heron

In 1970, when many of us were using up our energy and time working to get rid of Hugh Addonizio, who was then mayor of Newark, a couple of young poets came into the city to help that effort. They were part of a great many college students who got bussed in, drove and flew in, walked in, got here somehow, to help with that great struggle.

The two I'm talking about were Ron Welburn, who now works for Rutgers Institute of Jazz Studies, the other was named Gil Scott Heron. They were both from Lincoln University, the black college in Pennsylvania where Kwame Nkrumah, liberator of Ghana, and Langston Hughes, the great black poet, went.

But these two brothers came in, not only to help us but to show us their poetry, a poetry they had been working on in school, trying to hook up with the magic. And it showed promise even then, even more than promise.

I guess in those days we were all full of promise and idealism. We had a vision then, not only in this city but throughout the country. Malcolm and Dr. King had already been murdered by the same butchers who brought us here in slavery chains from Africa. But the talk was still about Black Power! Self-Determination! Freedom Now!

The 1967 rebellions in Newark came at the same time as the second Black Power Conference. I came right out of jail and went immediately over to the House of Prayer church to speak as part of that black-power conference.

And the vision and dynamism of Martin Luther King flowed through many of us. The heroic strength, commitment, and will to be free of Malcolm X flowed through many of us. You could see that in the people's faces, you could hear it in what they said. You could tell by what they said they were gonna do, that we had focused in on that centuries-old tradition of African American struggle and resistance.

You could see that in Gil Scott Heron's poetry even then, even as a college student, that he was part of that movement of the masses of black people to liberate ourselves to destroy the legacy of slavery and humiliation which has always been our lot in white racist monopoly capitalist America.

And thanks to the will and struggle of black people and the Latino people in this town (coming out of our history black and Puerto Rican convention) and even the white people of goodwill, we, the majority, took this town. Thanks also to the support and hard work and intelligence of the many students like Gil Scott Heron, we took this town, reclaimed it, kicked out the corrupt racist politicians and elected our own. Or so we thought!

But all the people who promised that they were working for People's Power, that they were struggling for Black Power, did not tell us the truth. We took the city, we did. We did take it. But because we elected corrupt negro civil servants and not Black Leaders, the town was given back to the same forces we had snatched it away from.

Hopefully we can correct that soon! If you get my meaning!

But Gil Scott Heron did not turn his back on his promise. The early commitment and vision are still everywhere visible in his work. From the pieces like "The Bottle" or later like "Angel Dust" trying to keep us from being programmed by our slave masters willingly self-destruct. If you kill yourself ain't no need for them to do it!

Or his exposés of this corrupt unworkable system like "H_2O Gate" pulling the covers off evil capitalist America. We need to get him to do an exposé of this town called *NeegroGate*!

Or what about "Winter in America," which tells us about the historic exploitation of the people, all the people from the Native Americans to the African slaves to the wage slaves of today and how it's all called for in the con-stitution.

Or what about Gil's exposure of the instant unreal revolutionaries with pieces like "The Revolution Will Not Be Televised."

What makes Gil Scott Heron such a consummate artist is that he is in the great tradition of black artists, the African-American tradition of resistance and struggle. We have never submitted to this madness. Our artists, the greatest of them, have never submitted to this white supremacy oppression.

It is with great risk to his own career and even his own life that Gil Scott continues to say the things he says, continuously, without biting his tongue. He is part of that great tradition, who know like Frederick Douglass said, that without struggle there is no progress! And he tells it to us, poets it to us, sings it to us, plays it for us, so we will never forget. So that when we walk down the street instead of singing, i aint got nothing, i aint nothing, all i want is dope and to be dopey and to be drunk. i hate myself. and my woman too. Instead of that standard American rock lyric that is common on our blood-aimed stations (even tho we dont own most of them) Gil has us humming and singing about Third World Revolution or how those racists are going to be driven in the sea when they have to get out of *Johannesburg* (the pan-African struggle from South Carolina to South Africa)!

238

Or he will tell us that for strength we must go to our tradition like Lady Day and John Coltrane, who will help sustain us in the face of the infamy of monopoly capitalist and white supremacy.

His latest album, *Reflections,* is a masterpiece. And just in time. Right in the face of the strong rightward movement, the movement toward a neofascism led by Bonzo's buddy . . . check out "B-movie"—the creativity and political insight. Or his version of Marvin Gaye's "Inner City Blues." Or the reggae funk of "Storm Music." Gil Scott has not abandoned that promise of twelve years ago; he has matured into a fine artist, one who as Mao says is both *artistically powerful* and *politically progressive.* In the stifling rightism of the Reagan era, this is a matrix of consciousness and commitment we need more of from American artists. Gil Scott is right on it.

Bob Neloms/*Pretty Music*

Bob Neloms's "new" name belies the fact that this impressive pianist has been around, laboring with the music, for quite a while. Bob was born in Detroit, but raised in Eureka, California. Believe it or not, one of his earliest gigs and influences was country and western, but by 1959, at the age of eighteen, he had won a *down beat* scholarship to study at the Berkelee School of Music in New York City, so he came east at that time. After that, he stopped back in Detroit, where between the years 1961–3 he was the house pianist for Motown. So you can see the varied influences at work. Listening to Bob you can also hear traces of the hip swing pianists and even the older stride style, probably as reflected through the swing giants like Earl Hines.

Bob went back to the coast during the middle sixties and got married. (He and his wife Marie have two children and they live currently in downtown New York.) But before they got back, Bob had come back to Berkelee to study another year, then gone up to Boston where he got a succession of gigs that lasted him well into the seventies. He led the house band at Wally's and worked at places like The Jazz Workshop, Inner Workshop, Paul's Mall, and with various leaders and groups that came through the Beantown area. He also worked with Elma Lewis at her arts center in Roxbury, teaching music, and worked at community programs at the Boston Conservatory.

In 1973 Bob came back to New York to live and began to work with some of the most serious and even best-known names in the music. In the last few years he has worked in many and varied hip settings, working with Roy Haynes, Freddie Waits, Pharaoh Sanders. He's also worked what he and his wife called a great many "instead of" jobs, where if one pianist was not available, a whole lot of people would send out word to get hold of Neloms. Bob could be booked at as a kind of "Mr. Sideman," having also worked with people like Pepper Adams, Jr., Cook-Bill Hardman, Buddy Tate. He was just about the house pianist at the Jazz Forum and Jazzmania, two of the most interesting of the loft spaces.

But many people will remember Bob for his fine work with the last Charlie Mingus's band from 1976 to 1979, with Jack Walrath, Ricky Ford, and Danny Richmond. And more recently, at the Tin Palace before it closed, he had one of the hippest bands I've heard on the scene, with Ricky Ford, Jame Newton, Ronnie Boykins, and Michael Carvin—a real smoker!

It was with this last band that I began to get a real sense of Nelom's abilities. He is of that newly matured set of pianists (and other instrumentalists) who can go "outside," but who also have a strong sense of where the main road is "inside." A pianist like John Hicks comes to mind immediately, or Donald Smith, or Hilton Ruiz, able to get hotter than hot, funky, but at any moment capable of relating to the kind of rhythmic avant pianistics that Cecil Taylor first exposed us to and that Don Pullen has developed to blue perfection.

This album shows us both aspects of the Neloms's aesthetic, his piano-room lyricism on pieces like "This Is How I Feel About You" or "I Thought About You" or the deeply introspective and delicate touch of "Mother Love," as well as the two-fisted new-dance new-music flights that we hear in "Non Sense" or "Black Light."

Neloms has been playing both sides of the music for quite a while and he moves from one pole to the other effortlessly. Working in piano-room settings like the Charcuterie on Fifty-second Street or Kaspar's or Nobody's he has developed an intimate, delicate touch that sometimes almost makes the piano sound like bells or vibes. Wailing away as he has done with Gary Bartz (whom he toured Europe with), or on a forthcoming album with maximum avant baritonist Hammiett Bluiett, equips Neloms to deal with the incredibly swift pianistics the new pianists have developed.

It is this feeling of completeness that animates this entire album. One gets the feeling that you are listening to a *complete* pianist, and since all the tunes on the album are Bob's except the old beauty "Who Can I Turn To?," you are also listening to an inventive composer whose charts are deeply rooted in piano music and an overview of jazz tradition that make it impossible for him to be characterized as a one-sided musician.

This is another aspect of Neloms's piano that I thoroughly enjoy, and a feature of many of the more serious younger musicians. They are interested in the whole scope and history of the music. So that you hear, for instance, on "A Flat Blues" not only a good slow introspective blues, but echoes of boogie and stride that make the blues as hip as it really is. This was one strong characteristic of Charlie Mingus's music, that he could play and go through the whole history of the music at any given moment. Groups like Air, Art Ensemble of Chicago, World Saxophone Quartet, Arthur Blythe have made this wide-ranging knowledge and ability to play the whole history of the music their hallmark. Bob Neloms, in both his compositions and his playing, can do this too. And very well.

Pretty Music is a fine introduction to Neloms, his compositions and his instrumental technique. "Non Sense," with its Monkish off-beat head (waltzlike, but something else again, a kind of tipsy syncopation) which sets up the long and fantastic runs, is a good example of this. Full of quotes and jokes, suddenly crashing chords and deceptive simplicity. The soft rolling ballad that "The Mystic" is Bob stretches easily into his pianistic dynamics. Neloms has a feeling for the "American Song Form," the ballad, as John Lewis called it. He knows how to make a ballad swing gently or pointedly. "The Illusion Waltz" keeps throwing out a waltz rhythm that at the same time is filled with dashing jazz nuance, while "Bobby's Bossa Nova" is half Bossa half bouncy, like a light straightforward children's romp. The mounting dynamic and huge block-building chords on "Black Light" which give way suddenly to skipping, almost delicately voiced funky phrases, which then go back to the powerful deeply sounded "concert" pianists, show you just the kind of thing Bob is already doing, and where he is moving too. The dazzling thousand-fingered piano heaped on top of bass not underpinning and that running dynamics announce a pianist of tradition and originality, an independent spirit that knows all the hip runs as well. This is Bob Neloms's first album of his own. It is, obviously, the first of many. In a short time Bob Neloms will be one of the most sought-after "box cookers" on the scene. He has taste, musicality, daring, and a strong sense of tradition. He makes *Pretty Music* and much more than that.

New Music/New Poetry

Amiri Baraka, poetry
David Murray, tenor saxophone, bass clarinet
Steve McCall, percussion
at Soundscape, December 1981

Poetry, first of all, was and still must be a musical form. It is speech *musicked*. It, to be most powerful, must reach to where speech begins, as sound, and bring the sound into full focus as highly rhythmic communication. High Speech.

The poetry of the dying epoch (racism and monopoly capitalism, imperialism) exists mostly on paper. It is print bred and bound, and actually intended for a particular elite. It, like the structure of the economy itself, is not meant to reach or benefit large numbers of people. English poetry died when the empire died; it was spent by the beginning of the twentieth century. Some Americans went over to rev it up (Pound, Eliot, etc.) but the baton had passed to the Americans because at that time they did not have to cover up as much madness and lies as did the Empire. And the various cultures inside the *American* experience—African, Latino, Native American, Asian, European immigrant—pumped it daily full of reality and its complex living rhythms. Combined with the Anglo-American worker and farmer rhythms, American poetry, writing, the culture as a whole became truly formidable as a force in the world. (Though obviously spread by the search of the American rulers for profits all over the world. Like when you turn on the Voice of America or Armed Forces Radio overseas somewhere you do not hear Brahms, but stevie w or bobby d or various clones therefrom.)

Black poetry, in the main, from its premise (unless the maker be considerably "bourgeoisified") means to show its musical origins and resolve as a given. Just as Blues is, on one level, a verse form, so Black poetry begins as music running into words.

Black poet laureates like Langston Hughes are compelling examples of black music running into high speech. He said he wanted "to grasp and hold some of the meanings and rhythms of jazz." And in more recent generations poets like Larry Neal, Yusuf Rahman, the

243

Last Poets, Askia Toure, Jane Cortez write a poetry that brings the words into music and the music into words, reflecting the most contemporary of both expressions, made one.

"Poetry and Jazz" I first saw being done in the Village when I got out of the error farce in 1957 or so. But Langston Hughes was the first poet of any reputation I saw using this form, at the Five Spot in the late fifties. But he had been doing it, by that time, for years.

It never occurred to me that there would be any reason not to read poetry with music. And the clearer I got on my own legitimate historical and cultural sources, the more obvious it became that not only was the poetry supposed to be as musical as it could be, but that reading with music would only enhance and extend its meanings and give new strength to its form.

The poetry I want to write is oral by tradition, mass aimed as its fundamental functional motive. Black poetry, in its mainstream, is oracular, sermonic; it incorporates the screams and shouts and moans and wails of the people inside and outside of the churches; the whispers and thunder vibrato and staccato of the inside and the outside of the people themselves, and it wants to be as real as anything else and as accessible as a song—a song about a real world, full of good and evil.

The music is also Afro-American, as are the players and the poet. But the music has borrowed from whatever in the world interested it, but it is still itself. David Murray and Steve McCall are fine artists of Afro-American contemporary music. It is a music whose African origins are expanded by its American experience, like the people. It has come from work song and spiritual, and blues is its common personal speech.

Murray and McCall are part of a current generation that has taken these basic historical and cultural bases and given the startling innovations of folks like Mr. Armstrong, Mr. Ellington, Mr. Young, Mr. Parker, and Mr. Coltrane have continued to tell us the second, minute, hour, day, month, year and epoch of our reality.

David Murray, still young, is already acknowledged by serious listeners as a significant new voice on the way to becoming an innovator. His work on albums like *Flowers for David, Let the Music Take You, Live at the Lower Manhattan Ocean Club* Vols. 1 and 2, as well as his writing and playing with the World Saxophone Quartet (a quartet of major saxophone innovators) make it clear that he is an important player.

Steve McCall is one of the Chicago second-wave avantists who have been giving the sixties' black music revolution new meaning and strength in the seventies and eighties. He is a drummer of consummate precision and complex artistry, one of the most sensitive percussionists in the music, alive to the most subtle nuance, yet able to carry the big rumbling funk fire of nigger-in-the-street-rebellion. (Yeh, that's in it!) Steve's work with Air, one of the most impressive of the new groups, also Chicago sprung, like Murray's work with the WSQ, shows that he has got to be included in any list of who's really doing it ca 1980.

Together, they are the tremendous wings for the poetry/music flight heard here. We wanted the music and words to extend each other, be parts of the same expression, different pieces of a whole. And the work to produce this product seemed effortless—it was a pleasure, a beautiful experience. Sometimes working with other, less skilled musicians, trying to put poetry with music is hard draggy work. The musicians might not want to deal with the poetry, might not be able to understand that for the music to be right it must begin with the spirit of the poem and put it into hot sound. But that's something else. On this record we tried to express some of the joy we had in making the *poetrymusic*. We also wanted to say some things.

Chico Freeman/*The Outside Within*

Freeman, tenor sax, John Hicks, piano
Cecil McBee, bass, Jack DeJohnette, drums

Side One—"Undercurrent"

Side Two—"The Search/Luna/Untitled"

Chico Freeman is part of the second wave of modernists who are pick-ing up the banner of the sixties' new music revolution and taking it straight ahead. Still a very young man (thirty-one) he has already re-leased some records of such accomplishment that one wonders what he will do next. In fact, there are many musicians who will never make the kind of music Chico has made already in a career that's really just getting under way. And if you want to know what Chico will do next, check this album out. It'll tell you both where he's been, like they say, where he's coming from, but also where he's going!

But if Chico (real name Earl) is very advanced, this is not to be mistaken as the result of some mystical process. He's the great sax-ophonist Von Freeman's son. And if you needed more of a leg up than that, it'd be hard to come by. At six he was playing piano, at seven, composing. He's already got a master's degree in composition and per-formance. But on top of all that he can really play. And not just play, but go past performance and instrumental excellence into the realm of deep expression. Moving expression. And this is the important thing.

The album *Kings of Mali* was voted record of the year by some folks, given five stars by funnytime *down beat,* and generally raved about. It should have been because it was an album of uncommon beauty. What was so heavy about *Kings of Mali* is that it seemed like it was fully conceived, as if it was the work of some mature master. Yet that record appeared in 1978, when Chico was in his twenties! And if he never did another thing, never blew another note of music, that album will certainly endure, which is, yeh, I know, very heavy praise.

What is so interesting about Chico's music, and it is very evident on this album, in fact he has given a title to the album that could sum up the attraction of his music, is that Chico has found a way to be clearly melodic and musically swinging, yet searching, daring, and experi-mental. In some cases people think that to swing and be melodic one has to bathe in clichés. On the other hand there is folks who think to be modern or serious one has to be dull. There are even a small group of assimilados who believe that for the music to be really way out it has to be a dead appendage of European concert music.

Chico shows that all those extremes are simply backwardness of one persuasion or another. He is a musician who openly declares his tradition and its roots (*Mali,* his obvious affinity and extension of Trane) yet he can give us straight-out ballads so convincingly moving that we are moved by the musical daring of such simplicity. Again, it is like Trane's *Ballads* (Spirit Sensitive), yet it is of this specific time, the updated link and presence. But also like great players Chico is never afraid to take his music wherever it needs to go to tell us something new about the world.

"The Outside Within" seems a whole piece. Though "Undercurrent" is Cecil McBee's tune, all of the music seems to come together as a whole emotional and musical experience. It is time to stop talking about Chico as "post-Trane" and deal with him as now-Chico. "Undercurrent" shows this. Moving from a quiet Afro-blue feeling, a steady rhythmic buildup, from the lyrical and elegant to the full-out shouting. And in that shouting it is already clear that Chico is not merely repeating Trane but has cleared out a space for himself, and when it is fully cleared it will be awesome.

Chico's choice of sidemen adds solid accompaniment and support for his sound. DeJohnette's work as bandleader and instrumentalist have received a great deal of critical acclaim in recent times. Freeman has worked before with John Hicks and Cecil McBee. McBee's reputation is steady and he is always in great demand by a host of different kinds of bands. In John Hicks, Chico has picked himself not only one of the most popular young piano players among musicians, but a shonuff cook guaranteed to add some real heat to any proceeding.

Especially in "Undercurrent" is the strength of this all-star rhythm section heard and felt, as the music steadily rises and stretches out. Each rhythm player backing Chico individually, and then later soloing. "Undercurrent," with its haunting Afro-Latino presence and terrible terrible Freeman solo, with brilliant backup and extended statement by the rhythm is alone worth the price of the album.

But the other music is intriguing as well. The haunting eastern mysterioso of "The Search" opens with McBee on bow and Chico's bass clarinet. This all gives rise to a simply stated quiet ballad feeling tenor solo. But with John Hicks's insistence this ballad comes full-out transforming itself into a kind of blues march of tragic power.

"Luna," another Chico Freeman composition, has the same kind of "eastern" scalar quality to it. And with John Hicks setting the emotional foundation backed by McBee, the music is introspective but

247

pulsing as if at any moment it might leap into an up-tempo screaming. The simple statement made complex and dramatic because it is openly attached to real feelings, and the music of these feelings, so well articulated, is consistently moving.

The untitled piece is similar in this last respect. It is a simple repeated scale, becoming an ostinato that lifts itself and the players to a furious yet controlled agitation. The improvisation is controlled by the form, and so it seems that all kinds of passions are swooping and challenging within the repeated phrase because of the repetition and the sharp interplay between the musicians, especially Chico and John Hicks. The music is free, yet it is never loose or chaotic or so rhythmically deficient that it is abstract. It is funky, melodic, and swinging at the same time.

Finally, that is the mark of Chico's musicianship, his playing as well as his composing and arranging. And judging from his choice of fine musicians, it is also the mark of his bandleading. That he can unleash all the fire and mystery and *otherness* of the outside, but within the unifying and compelling vision of the carefully made. And this is what we look for, what we listen for, in any genre or style, the care and attention of the skilled craftsman along with the fire and passion of the exquisitely sensitive. They are both indispensable in high art, form, and feeling. Chico Freeman unites them impressively.

Ricky Ford/*Future's Gold*

Ricky Ford is a young man, but already he's been on the jazz scene long enough, and playing hard enough, to have made a significant impact. In any list of young musicians, particularly saxophonists, if you were hanging with a generally knowledgeable crowd, you'd have to hear his name.

Yet Ricky is only twenty-nine years old, now in New York for his seventh year. He was born in Boston, lived most of his young years in the Roxbury section. Like so many other musicians who go on to careers of more than passing significance, Ford is the product of a musical family, his early environment providing, as he says, "a subliminal" entrance into the music, even when he wasn't quite conscious of it.

Ricky's grandmother, Ucil Joseph, he is quick to mention as a seminal influence. She played rhythm guitar around the Boston area, but also was a member of the famous Sweethearts of Rhythm and even "slinked," i.e., danced and played, at Harlem's Apollo Theater.

His grandfather also played guitar, and when they had those warmly remembered sessions they got Ricky to play drums for them. Ricky remembers his father had records and worked the subliminal perception on him. His father also worked at Storyville when he was in law school and took Ricky one evening to see the great Dinah Washington.

Ricky eventually attended the New England Conservatory and actually just graduated in 1983, "with distinction," doubling up on courses, because he had been well aware that it was time for him to go out into the world of gigs and dues.

But aside from formal study, Ricky has also been a sideman with some of the great names in the music. He has already worked with Walter Bishop, Lionel Hampton, Betty Carter, Nat Adderly, Beaver Harris, Frank Foster, McCoy Tyner, Sonny Stitt, Charlie Mingus, and the Duke Ellington orchestra under Mercer Ellington. A formidable group of names to drop, of places to have already been, for one so young.

Ricky also cites a few great names as his heaviest musical influences, even though he says he's been influenced "by the whole gamut of the industry." Like most of us, we're influenced to a certain extent by whoever we heard really doing it recently. But by the seventies

Sonny Rollins had become a major influence. And even though we can certainly hear that, we hear a whole lot else as well, a whole lot of Ricky Ford.

Sonny was also one of the first to bring Ricky to New York, to rehearse with his band, so impressed was Sonny with the young Ford.

In New York, Ricky also was turned on by another master, long, tall Dexter Gordon. But interestingly enough, the player who really first made Ricky want to play was Rahsaan Roland Kirk, whom he met through friends. "When I heard Rahsaan I knew I had to play."

By the early seventies Ricky was writing music and even beginning to feel he had matured as a composer. Studying at the New England Conservatory, he met people like Ran Blake, George Russell, Gunther Schuller, and Bill Saxton.

His first professional gig was with Ran Blake as a duo, working at the Gardiner Museum in Boston. Blake introduced him to the music of Miles Davis, Sonny Rollins, and Coleman Hawkins.

Future Gold, in a sense, sums up the direction and promise of Ricky Ford. We are exposed to both his free-blowing swing as well as to his compositions and interpretations of "standards" and jazz classics.

As a soloist, Ricky Ford seems always to be surging ahead, with notes tumbling every which way, like a young athlete flying along on instinct.

The open swinging he does on the album's title tune is, right now, his trademark. The line swings and moves like the player loves freedom, even while still in the act of defining it for himself.

Ricky's rhythm section is just right for the kind of music he wants to make. Jimmy Cobb has played with the classic Miles Davis's groups and was Sarah Vaughan's rhythmic anchor for a while. He is always "on it."

Ray Drummond's work with Pharaoh Sanders has distinguished him, and Albert Dailey is slowly gaining the reputation he deserves as one of the swingingest of the "younger" pianists.

Larry Coryell's reputation is based largely on his "fusion" playing, but Ricky has Coryell in another, more basic and (to my mind) more swinging context.

Ricky discussed his current work with "Extended Song Forms." The "Samba de Caribe," one of the most impressive of the pieces on the album, is fascinating evidence of the productivity of Ford's attention to these forms. In fact, except for "A Flat Now," a bluesy infectiously cooking tune, all Ford's pieces on the album show his experimentation with the extended song form.

Not coincidentally, this puts one in mind of Rollins's focus on "extended thematic improvisation," as one critic called it back in the sixties when Sonny made the monumental *Freedom Suite*.

Ricky's attention to Carribean and Latin rhythms also evokes memories of some of Sonny Rollins's most dynamic works, e.g., *St. Thomas,* etc. Ricky Ford has drunk from those life-giving Sonny waters, but listen, and you will hear where else he's taken that inspiration.

Ford also traces his roots back eight or nine documented generations in Barbados. Another side of the family hails from Jamaica, so there is an organic and personal link to these rhythms; and the fascinating "Samba de Caribe" and the other slow-rolling samba, "Hindsight and Necessity," show us how hiply Ford has harnessed those indigenous West Indian and Afro-Latino stomps.

The ballad, "You Don't Know What Love Is," I suppose one of everybody's favorites is given a really fresh reading by Ricky Ford. But here we are delivered the work via the broad lushness of sound that puts one in mind of a "Bean" or "Frog" (Coleman Hawkins, Ben Webster). It is yet another important aspect of a young player growing to maturity before our ears.

"Goodbye, Pork Pie Hat" is a jazz classic from Chaz Mingus's pen. Ford is a Mingus alumnus (and Mingus's jazz workshops, like Blakey's Messengers, were/are universities of Jazz Studies). The sweet irony is that Mingus is gone now and in his work he was summoning the spirit of an earlier departed jazz great. He of the porkpie hat, Pres, Lester Young.

So it is good to hear Ricky Ford evoke the spirit of Charles Mingus evoking the spirit of Lester Young. It is a celebration of the spirit of the music itself and the musical traditions of America and of the African-American people. It would be wonderful if our younger musicians would celebrate the jazz classics, by playing and mastering them and by so doing raise the standards of the music contemporarily.

Ford says of his piece, "Knowledge," that it embodies his desire to "push knowledge and education." Ricky experiments here with beginning on an upbeat, thereby, in his words, putting together "a new walking rhythm" with a "different sound" and changed intervalic relationships.

"Centenarian" is about Eubie Blake, who died this year (1983), not long after his one-hundredth birthday. To Ricky Ford, Blake "represents a force in music instrumental in a lot of social changes for musicians in later generations. For instance, the whole struggle against segregation." By influence Ford means "the striving for goals that reach beyond music—in the world community."

"Centenarian" is not only in 3/4, i.e., waltz time, but an extended form as well. Ricky says he is intrigued by 3/4 time. Such fascination was passed on to him by two masters, Mingus and Hampton. Both of whom played and composed quite often in 3/4.

Ford says Mingus's admiration of 3/4 was passed on to him from Hamp who, Ricky says, "is always involved with triplets or playing twelve-eighths on four-fourths or quarter-note triplets."

Since Ricky has played with both Mingus and Hamp, he cannot only pick up on the jazz-waltz legacy, but has even analyzed how much of the waltz form Mingus picked up from Hamp.

Ricky Ford is still growing, but he's already big enough to appreciate and project some ideas about his future. What is important about Ford is that he springs from *recent* jazz tradition, yet he is already willing and able to take the music in still newer directions.

Jazz Writing: Survival in the Eighties

When I began to publish writing about the music it was the late fifties moving into the sixties, and there was an explosive trend at work and perceptible in the society. What would be obvious as the civil rights movement began to lose its nonviolent black bourgeois trappings and erupt into the more popularly oriented Black Liberation movement.

My writing, after the first few pieces to appear in the *Jazz Review,* began to take on the same dynamic as the overall movement; bluntly in search of democracy, and seeing targets—i.e., obstructers to democracy and free expression—in all directions.

But even the fact of a black writer on African-American music at the time was part of the trend of intensifying democratic struggles. There had not been many black writers writing regularly on black music; slavery and national oppression had seen to that. So that the very act of an African-American trying to be self-consciously analytical and critical of the music was in part a demand for democracy and self-determination.

One of the first major articles I wrote, in the defunct *Metronome,* was called "Jazz and the White Critic," in which I tried to come to terms with why there were so many white critics of an essentially black music. One thing that was important to me in discussing this phenomenon was that many of these white critics, since they came from a different class life in America than the musicians and the essence of their music, all too often imposed a critical standard on the music that was opposed to the standards the music itself carried with it and described.

Years have passed, decades filled with struggle and some transformation; but after the high-water marks of mass insurgency against this exploitive and oppressive white racist monopoly capitalist society, the cooling out of that mass movement, by means of murder, imprisonment, behavior modification, exile, bribery, has meant that there has been a cooling out, decline, retreat in many other areas, such as the arts and critical writing, that take their impetus, like it or not, from the flow and motion of social movement.

So that today, the fact that the far-right-wing reactionary pseudo-populist Ronald Reagan is the president of the United States should also alert us that not only is this society hippety hopping rapidly toward the grim abyss of a fascism as American as apple pie, but that we have come to a point where satire and reality are neck and neck, almost indistinguishable, if for one moment we merely contemplate what kind of novel someone could write in which a stupid talentless American cinema mannequin could become an all-American Führer.

Or for that matter, let us contemplate where we have already come to, if one of my main men, Nat Hentoff, one of the jazz critics I respected most, has got to be an apologist for imperialist Israel, assuring us that Menachem Begin, though problematical, reminds him of his old irascible uncle. Therefore one must presume that even those piles of dead bodies of Palestinians massacred in Lebanon are vaguely excusable since we know his old uncle was *meshuga*.

Let us look over this panel, for instance, and see that but for the moderator and myself there are no blacks up here, defining and categorizing. Certainly, if we check the various magazines, newspapers, and media props we will see a few more black faces, but in the main most of the steady, paying jobs writing about the music are still held by whites. Though, for certain, there is a much more glib cover-apparatus involved with the jargon of these quasi-colleagues, since they are much more "hip" and knowledgeable on the surface than their counterparts a few decades back, just as the men I met in the late fifties and sixties were "hipper," verbally, than their predecessors.

Except for Stanley Crouch, a very knowledgeable analyst on the *Voice*, there are no regular black writers on the music, even in this town (but we should add the very rococo gee-whizology of Gregory Tate); but even so, at the *Voice*, Gary Giddins gets the real play; he is the constant factor of jazz definition at that burnt-out ex-liberal rag.

We could draw from this that there has been no real movement since those thrilling days of yesteryear I mentioned. But that is not quite the case.

In reality, the jazz scene has been affected just about the way the rest of the real world has, in strictly social terms. Since the eruptive democratic struggles of the sixties and seventies there has actually been a march, in some ways, straight to the rear. *The Jazz Review and Metronome* were very much more progressive ideologically and engaging intellectually than *down beat,* and more integrated. The *down beat* of that period was much more interesting a publication than today's slick sheet and did not have the reams of print dedicated to commercial rock and shallow fusion.

Many of the white critics of the period, like Martin Williams, Larry Gushee, Frank Kofsky, Nat Hentoff, Frank Driggs, Ross Russell, were ready and able to go beyond surface interviews, gee-whiz-ism, and commercial puff pieces, to deal with intriguing aspects of the music technically, historically, aesthetically, and socially. *The Jazz Review* had a great deal of input from the musicians themselves. *Metronome*

Dexter Digs In, monoprint by Vincent D. Smith   *Alex King, Jr.*

I'd Like to Holler But the Town's Too Small, monoprint by Vincent D. Smith   *Alex King, Jr.*

A Moment Supreme, etching by Vincent D. Smith *Alex King, Jr.*

257

Blues Singer, watercolor by Vincent D. Smith   *Alex King, Jr.*

took up some of the burning social questions related to the music and its principal players. And there were quite a few black writers who left their mark on the development of an all-around American critical standard, such as Larry Neal, A. B. Spellman, James T. Stewart, and, a little later, Ron Welburn and Holly West.

There were at least two important black-edited jazz publications, *The Cricket* (after Buddy Bolden's New Orleans sheet—edited by Larry Neal, A. B. Spellman, and me), and *The Grackle* (edited by Ron Welburn).

For one thing, even though there was the not quite legendary, but really quite typical, battle between the modernists and the moldy figs, both schools did assume that the music, principally, was an African-American expression. There did not seem to be nearly as much apology for the fact that the principal players of the music were (and still are) black. Just as one would not be shocked by the fact that the principal composers and performers of European concert music were Europeans. Despite André Watts and Leontyne Price.

This was true even though after each new wave of black innovation, i.e., New Orleans, big band, bebop, rhythm and blues, hard bop, new music, there was a commercial cooptation of the original music and an attempt to replace it with corporate dilution which mainly featured white players and was mainly intended for a white middle-class audience. But today, the corporate thrust is even much more aggressive (and carries a much sharper attack on democracy). Since it is the stance of the music *business* and its apologists, conscious and otherwise, that the corporate commercial music not just *covers* for the original but that it *is* the original. It is not too far-fetched to speculate that in a few years, like tap dancing, Afro-American music will be defined as an imitative adjunct to the real stuff, i.e., the corporate, commercial, largely white middle-class sounds of whatever school. Certainly most of us by now have heard that rhythm and blues *influenced* rock and roll. Or if we read *down beat*, we saw the front cover that declared that Phil Woods was "Chief Altoist of the Jazz Tribe." Or in the *Illustrated Encyclopedia of Jazz* we learn that "Benny Goodman is the most technically accomplished clarinetist to make a living (primarily) from jazz." Hot spit! Or we might just be dopily perusing the pages of *The New Yorker* (September 20, 1982) and find out from old crock Whitney Bailliet's that the greatest female jazz singers were Bessie Smith, Billie Holiday, and Anita O'Day, that it was "Boot Whip," Ms. O'Day, who influenced most of today's women jazz singers, including Betty Carter. And no, Mr. Bailliet does not even mention Sarah Vaughan.

Maybe we might be stumbling through the pages of *The New York Times* and bump into Robert Palmer who will tell us, like the great

Solomon, that one can play hot without swinging. When all this time I thought that indeed hot was a product of swing, just as in the rest of the physical world.

But then if you can arrange for Linda Rondstadt to be the female love object singing "Baby, Baby" with Smokey Robinson or being sung to by Smokey, "The Tracks of My Tears," two of the great romantic ballads of the sixties, on the televised *Motown Celebration*— you can ostensibly get away with anything!

The point is that the Reagan era is a period of open and vicious chauvinism, where the sixties and early seventies had made such social ugliness at least duck its head for a minute. And while there is a new breath of life in the music given by a newer generation, which includes the likes of David Murray, his octet, big band, and string ensemble, Arthur Blythe, Threadgill's Sextet, World Saxophone Quartet, Olu Dara, Craig Harris, Steve McCall, and quite a few others, there is also, right in the middle of the music (as critic Crouch observed in this week's *Voice*) a tendency by one sector of musicians, many of whom are black, to take it on a tired old trip, deliberately trying to *declass* the music, transforming it into a secondary appendage of European concert music, rather than the heroic expression of the folk and classical music of the African-American majority as well as the spirit of a progressive and populist high art.

This tendency links up with the corporate motive, to lead the music into the suffocating arena of middle-class unseriousness, though masqueraded as ultra hyper serious, which secures for it, one day, a place in the academy, not *overtly* commercial but security conscious, as a product of university intelligence, kindly, respected by the right people, and dull as any other product of the Establishment's aesthetic.

But this demonstrates, as well, that there is within the music, whether in its composition and performance or its appreciation, analysis, and critical writing, overt *class struggle*. So that even though there can be two players, both of whom are considered players, composers, etc., of "the new music," one, such as a David Murray, will be as far out as he might get, always in the act of redefining the social and spiritual aesthetic of a whole people. His music will carry with it the deepest aspirations, the oldest memories of a nation struggling for liberation. While at the same time, the opposing aspect of this contradictory definition of new music will be some player who merely wants to show us that he's heard Berg and Webern or Stockhausen. That is, his playing, for the most part, is showing white folks how intelligent he (they) is.

One violinist, from this *Tail Europe* school, is quoted in *Coda* as saying, ". . . Great Black Music has run the gamut of the human body from the feet, which would indicate that in its earliest stages it was appreciated more by the masses—a commercial music—and now it has run its gamut to the head and is purely cerebral." And if you hear his music you knows what he means!

Such class struggle relates to the overall confrontation and struggle in the larger society and in capsule shows the battle between those of us who want to transform this society and those who have come up with the newer-sounding ways of supporting the status quo of racism and exploitation.

There is a great deal more in this area that could be discussed, but we'll leave that until a later time. But one critical point that should be made is that the "survival" of quality writing on the music must be linked up to the survival of the highest levels of expression of the music itself. And both these must be connected to the survival of a general *liberating intelligence,* which must be about working and struggling to see that civilization itself survives. We must not forget that most of the lost and vanished civilizations died by their own hand or were destroyed by other human beings. Not by Martians, Gods, or Devils.

One positive thrust I would see that is part of the larger picture must be the reestablishment of progressive nonsectarian intellectual journals that deal with the music, in its many aspects, in probing, scholarly, scientific, socially rewarding ways. So that even the various controversies and disagreements would be given airing and our entire understanding of the music and indeed of art and society in general would be elevated.

It is time for the progressive and serious sectors of the intellectual and artistic community to stop U.S. critical and artistic journalism from being the laughing- (and crying) stock of the civilized world. It seems to me this is one important part of our overall responsibility, fighting for humanity, civilization, and their mutual advance. If this were a political gathering I might end by saying DEATH TO IGNORANCE!!!

Blues, Poetry, and the New Music

I begin with blues because it is the basic national voice of the African-American people. It is the fundamental verse form (speech, dance, verse/song) and musical form of the African/American slave going through successive transformations encountering various influences not only English but French, Spanish, Portuguese, and Native American. Blues is African-American. The verse forms of African-American culture and language. It persists musically in various forms, and there is always an updated and contemporary form.

The verse form has also undergone a variety of modifications, while retaining its essential freshness and flexibility. The modern rap form is much like the traditional rhymed couplets that characterize the "Signifying Monkey," "Shine," "Stagger Lee," etc. The complete form is meant to be *spoken,* with or without musical background. But its connection to the blues culture and spirit is clear.

The blues is so basic because it is black speech at its earliest complete articulation as a New World speech. The speech of black people native to the Western world!

The high poetry of the spirituals shares much of the same language/culture matrix. But there is still a heightened syntax that lifts them away from everyday speech. The blues is the actual secular day-to-day language given the grace of poetry.

As the blues developed in the nineteenth century, it is in the same wave of growing expression that characterizes the general development of an authentic written African-American literature. The folk forums, the various unwritten tales, ditties, rhymed-couplet stories, harangues, dozens, poems are accompanied now, in the nineteenth century, by the appearance of a legitimately mass-oriented black literature, an African-American literature, owing its form and content to the social, cultural, and political context of African slaves and freed persons in slave North America.

The slave narratives are not the oppressor-sanctioned, oppression-imitating polite house slave writing of the Wheatleys and Hammonds; they are the authentic mass cry of a people in slavery.

The stirring, agitational, completely functional form and content of the narratives are complemented by the pulpit-rocking speeches of the freed black abolitionists of the north.

But at the same time as the Fred Douglasses and David Walkers appear there is a largely unwritten lyric verse form that is reaching an expressive high point, black country blues.

The blues as verse form is always accompanied by a music expressive of the particular period and socio-cultural realities of its creation. So the country blues expresses the level of productive forces generally found as the property of the developing black majority. So a lone singer unaccompanied or with the African banjo or guitar or mouth harp is certainly materially humble in the face of a hundred-piece orchestra playing the *1812 Overture*. But we are witnessing two social groups in parallel though certainly unequal development. And those cannons roaring at the end of the *1812* are also used to keep such inequality persistent.

Just as the slave narratives and the black abolitionist-inspired rhetoric represent another higher level of social development than country blues, there are successive and continuing forms and levels of development of the blues form itself as a musical expression. In the book *Blues People,* I tried to show the motion from country blues to city blues to classic blues to rhythm and blues and some of their infinite variations.

Near the end of the nineteenth century, the blues impulse with its rhythmic insides reexpressed as its own ideal accompaniment as African drums (which had been banned because of their *political* use, and drums are still the most political of instruments!) were combined with European instruments found in marching bands, and a new level of social and aesthetic expression emerged (named after an African derived slang term jasm for sexual intercourse)—*jazz.*

New Orleans became famous because it was the city where the blues country impulse could remix with open African expression (Congo Square drum sessions) and come in contact as well with the urbane, even international flavor of French, Spanish, English, and Native American influences. Jazz is essentially a city music, a music sophisticated in its inclusion of broad urban influences that are international in depth. It is populist in its open expression of mass language and progressive by that fact and its openness. It could not begin in the conservatories and concert halls. It was banned from these. It was the music of slaves, newly "freed" and newly reenslaved under different terminology!

Jazz incorporates blues, not just as a specific form, but as a cultural insistence, a feeling-matrix, a tonal memory. Blues is the national consciousness of jazz—its truthfulness in a lie world, its insistence that it is itself, its identification as the life expression of a specific people, the African-American nation. So that at its strongest and most intense and indeed most advanced, jazz expresses the highest consciousness of that people itself, combining its own history, as folk form and expression, with its more highly developed industrial environment, North America.

Without blues, as interior animation, jazz has no history, no memory. The *funkiness* is the people's lives in North America as slaves, as an oppressed nation, as workers and artists of a particular nationality!

To think, as one critic has argued, that blues is merely a particular twelve-bar form is to think dancing is those footprints in the Fred Astaire newspaper advertisement! This same critic told me, and he has a prestigious position as curator of African-American music in a D.C. institution, that Billie Holiday wasn't a blues singer. So much for formalism!

The most important jazz players have always been great blues artists—Louis Armstrong, Duke Ellington, Billie Holiday, Coleman Hawkins, Lester Young, Charlie Parker, Sarah Vaughan, Thelonius Monk, Clifford Brown, John Coltrane. The most important players in African-American music are blues people.

See "More Trane Than Art," earlier.

The critical significance of this fact today is that as usual the music, like the people who created it, is under attack. On one hand most serious listeners of jazz know that as soon as a new jazz form reaches a certain point of development it is duplicated by corporations, diluted, commercially bowdlerized for the sake of max profit. Since the music is largely created by a people still kept forcibly at the bottom of society and just the fact of their being creators of such influential and profound a cultural resource as jazz would tend to reorient large numbers of people intellectually and politically by attacking black national stereotypes, the corporations must either *cover* the music (as records by everyone from Pat Boone to Linda Ronstadt are created to *cover* the real creators) or the music must be wrestled away from its originators and its creation ascribed to others. Elvis Presley is at once a cover and a fake originator. Rock 'n' roll is "influenced" by R&B because at first it *was* R&B only sung by white singers as covers for corporate profit and continuing racial segregation!

Traditional jazz had its *Dixieland;* Big-band jazz its *Swing;* BeBop its *Cool;* R&B its *Rock;* and Contemporary black music its *Fusion,* all of which, in the main, were corporate creations aimed at a white middle-class audience with mainly white performers. What this does is help keep black players and artists and the black nation itself at the bottom of society unable even to fully benefit from the creations of their own culture. Maximum profits, racial segregation, and discrimination, black national oppression maintained.

African-American music, to retain its freshness, its originality, its specific expression of its own history and contemporary reality in each generation, creates a "new music," an avant-garde. Why? Because the music literally is *separate,* in the same way that U.S. society itself is separate and divided. Jazz to a certain extent is an American music created by people who are not allowed to be Americans, hence its *outside* quality, its "foreignness" to the North American mainstream! The irony is that it speaks of an American reality that frightens and distresses many Americans. If Mr. Watts cannot take the Beach Boys, what can he do with Stevie Wonder or David Murray?

The players create a new music instinctively because they not only are expressing new perceptions and accreted wisdom, but they know the dilutions, the corporate cooptations, are not them or their fathers and mothers!

Even the calculated attempt at "weirdness" by the Boppers were realistic efforts to put distance between themselves and the mindless gibberish of "square"; i.e., commercial maximum-profit minimum-consciousness values that run the United States. It was socio-aesthetic activism.

See "Bang Bang/Outishly," earlier.

Today, attempts by the racist corporate mentality not only to continue to exploit the majority of U.S. workers but to superexploit and oppress the African-American people have been intensified. So that now not only are black musicians super-exploited but the racists even want to claim to have created and been the main innovators of African-American music as well. So that one bizarre chauvinist can put out a book, *Great Jazz Pianists,* and feature neither Duke Ellington, Thelonius Monk, nor Bud Powell but go on at length about Dave Brubeck, George Shearing.

There would be no panic, except in the offices of civil rights organizations sponsored by large white corporations, if we said the great innovators and creators of European concert music were Europeans (despite André Watts, Leontyne Price, and Yo Yo Ma).

The only reason there would be reluctance to understand that the great creators and innovators of African-American music have been and are African-Americans is white chauvinism which is the ideological tool of black national oppression. So that the status quo is maintained.

The other side of this exploitative and oppressive coin of white racism and monopoly capitalism is the pathology that such oppression produces among the oppressed, as Frantz Fanon, Amilcar Cabral, E. Franklin Frazier, and Malcolm X, among others, have told us.

The sixties and seventies civil rights and Black Liberation Movement produced quite a bit of social movement among the Black Nation. But such social mobility was obviously more pronounced and lasting among the black petty bourgeois, the middle class. On the negative side, dialectically, this motion also produced a much larger black petty bourgeois whose social development could occur *outside* the black ghettos; more suburban negroes, ivy league negroes, more sons and daughters of a black bureaucratic elite hoisted into affluence and power paved by the struggles of the black masses.

Many times this petty bourgeois, once they have risen into prominence by means of the blood and struggle of the people, then disconnect themselves from the people, becoming messengers of the people's enemies rather than the people's representatives. (The Gibsons in Newark and the Bradleys in Los Angeles are but two grim examples!)

A parallel of this political truth is the socio-philosophical and aesthetic alienation of some of these petty bourgeois blacks who became artists. There is, for instance, the *Tail Europe* school of negro musicians who, while presumably playing jazz, really seek to make African-American music a banal appendage of European concert music! Their entire musical mission seems to be to prove to white people that they have heard Webern, Berg, or John Cage. As one violinist of this school said, "Old black music was for the feet, the music I make is for the head." Does this sad person know anything about Duke Ellington? The Hot Five is not only an emotional experience, there are areas of the brain that can only be stimulated by new feelings, feelings not *expressed* by the formally intellectual (though they may be pointed to!). Does this person believe that Louis Armstrong's playing is not an intellectual process? Is he like the school of racists who believe Louis just came into the world playing them hot licks in his crib? A particular culture facilitates a particular kind of expression, but its high artistic articulation still must be learned!

Objectively, the *Tail Europe* school trumpets white supremacy and legitimizes black national oppression.

See "Reggae or Not": [Class Struggle 1 & 2, earlier].

The New Music that is really new is that music which reflects with the most precision new understanding.

The new music is always rooted in historical certainty, no matter how disconnected from history it might sound to the casual or neophyte listener. But it *uses* history, it is not paralyzed by it!

So that the truly new expresses where we are or will be. It after lets us know that what we feel or think *will be,* often *already* is! The new music, as any new expression, tries to impress us with motion, its constant; and with change, its persistence!

Each generation adds to and is a witness to extended human experience. If it is honest it must say something new. But in a society that glorifies formalism, i.e., form over content, because content rooted in realistic understanding of that society must minimally be critical of it— the legitimately truthfully new is despised. Surfaces are shuffled, dresses are lengthened or shortened, hair is green or blond, but real change is opposed. The law keeps the order and the order is exploitive and oppressive!

The new music reinforces the most valuable memories of a people but at the same time creates new forms, new modes of expression, to more precisely reflect contemporary experience! The most impressive new music in jazz—David Murray's various groups, Henry Threadgill's sextet, the WSQ, Arthur Blythe's groups, The Art Ensemble, Craig Harris, Olu Dara—are the latest wave of avants continuing the tradition of the new in the sixties, the direct inheritors of a still-living contemporary tradition—Trane.

The Phenomenon of *Soul* in African-American Music

The concept and expression (of) *Soul* is one distinctive persona of African-American music. In fact, though "Soul" has a more or less specific meaning, even a historically legitimatized presence, its general connotation is of an ingredient so essential to African-American music that its absence would cause knowledgeable listeners to question the authenticity (as African-American music) of what they were hearing.

This is significant because historically, and as used sometimes contemporarily, the concept has a specifically religious meaning. But the fact that it can be applied to a mainly secular music with some usefulness shows that its fullest meaning not only incorporates both the religious and the secular, but has a broad resonance throughout the whole of African-American culture.

In the music called jazz the epithet Soul reemerged most strongly during the fifties, specifically indicating the influence of the black church. This was particularly significant because it was the African-American church that was *soulful* and its whole development, description and character rooted in the conceptual phenomenon of the existence, elevation, and salvation of the human soul. In a very distinctive and colorful manner.

Both metaphysical philosophy and religion have generally spoken of a human soul. The earliest African projection of this concept, which found later expression in the cultures of Upper and Lower Egypt, was that the soul (Ba) was but one aspect of the seven qualities of "God." The "human-headed soul" had originated from earliest human reflection on that quality of human being that expressed, as a fundamental requirement, life itself. So that soul was literally linked to *breath* and also to *Spirit*. The Latin *anima* (soul) is the root of *animate*. African religion traditionally saw all things as being *alive* (with humans being "more alive" than, say, animals or trees), hence their religion was called *Animist*.

It is breath, and its religious double, spirit, that are prerequisites for being alive. Ancient peoples thought the human shadow was an expression as well of the life force, and if one lost that shadow one also lost one's (breath) life.

The spirit was what animated one, but it was also an aspect of the divinity itself, the human body being but an outward manifestation of this spark of the Godhead.

African religion and African-American religion are, of course, directly related. The poorer and more humble the black church, the more closely and directly the African connection. Contrarily, the more imposing and grandiose the black church, the more thoroughly intertwined with the traditions of Europe and Euro-America.

So that the most obviously African black churches are the tiny storefront churches that dot the black ghetto landscape in dizzying profusion or the backwood country shouting houses of the rural southern black belt. Though certainly even in some of the big black urban churches the soul can get loosed!

Ultimately, all African-American music springs from African music, which was both religious and secular. African-American music, as it develops from African, then African with elements found in the diaspora, then African-American, develops as both religious and secular. And the secular obviously would be more ubiquitous. But the church was almost the only black institution allowed to develop in any depth early in black people's lives in the West, and that institution was a vehicle for the development and circulation of the religious music.

The work song was primarily secular, but there were always similar musical and emotional elements in both aspects of black musical culture. Plus there are deep references to a spiritual life in all of the music. The religious music might yearn for a crossing into a new life, a raising of this life onto "higher ground," an ultimate salvation of the person and their soul and *freedom* from this wearying slavery world.

The secular too would speak of a time when "the sun's gonna shine in my backdoor someday" or shout that things won't always be like this, meaning that there will be a time of more money, more love, more self-fulfillment—that such a time will surely come. There is a harsh critical realism, but also a final optimism. There were church shouts and field and juke-joint shouts and hollers and yells. But perhaps the church hollers were a little more intense, the shouters and screamers seeking literally to transport themselves away from here into that other world merely by the energy of their screamed belief.

Spirit Possession in the black church is not a variable; unless one is possessed by the spirit (at some time) one was not really there for serious business, and this goes back into the mists of the ancient past. One only had religion if one literally was possessed by it; one had to, as my grandmother said, "Get happy" or religion was mighty shallow. My wife's grandmother, a member of one of the small sanctified churches, told her that if people didn't get happy, "they didn't love God."

W.E.B. Du Bois, in *The Souls of Black Folk,* says of the black church, its music and its characteristic spirit possession, "The Music of Negro religion is that plaintive rhythmic melody, with its touching minor cadences, which, despite caricature and defilement, still remains the most original and beautiful expression of human life and longing yet born on American soil. Sprung from the African forests, where its counterpart can still be heard, it was adapted, changed, and intensified by the tragic soul-life of the slave, until, under the stress of law and whip, it became the only true expression of a people's sorrow, despair and hope.

Finally the Frenzy or "Shouting," when the Spirit of the Lord passed by, and, seizing the devotee, made him mad with supernatural joy, was the last essential of Negro religion and the one more devoutly believed in than all the rest. It varied in expression from the silent rapt countenance or the low murmur and moan to the mad abandon of physical fervor—stamping, shrieking, and shouting, the rushing to and fro and wild waving of arms, the weeping and laughing, the vision and the trance. All this is nothing new in the world, but old as religion, a Delphi and Endor. And so firm a hold did it have on the Negro, that many generations firmly believed that without this visible manifestation of the God there could be no true communion with the Invisible."

Although the *frenzy* or spirit possession was the most important aspect of black religion, Du Bois says that it was one of three elements, "Three things characterized this religion of the slave—the Preacher, the Music and the Frenzy."

In the black musician, even of a secular bent, all three of these aspects of the black church are combined! The form of much black music is even in the Call and Response structure of Preacher and Congregation, plus the response of the audience in nightclub or concert hall is much like that of the fervent congregation. There are "Yes, sirs!" and "Yeh's" and even some "Amen's" shouted back at the musician, not just the silent murmurs of the Western concertgoer.

The black religious form expands past religion and historically permeates the entire culture, whether manifested through the African-American nation's poets or its football running backs who, after scoring a touchdown, might do a Holy Roller wiggle and leap in the end zone to express their joy! Certainly in that vehement fervor we hear in black song there is the ancient spirit possession remanifesting itself, whether the singer is Aretha Franklin, Shirley Caesar, Little Jimmy Rushing, James Brown, Stevie Wonder, Joe Le Wilson, or Sarah Vaughan.

What brought the concept of *Soul* so forcefully into the present was its use in the fifties. The history of African-American music reflects the general lives and history of the African-American people. It is the music of a people suffering national oppression and racism, but its beauty exists despite this tragic fact. National oppression consists of robbery, denial of rights, and super-exploitation. These things are expressed in most facets of black life. So that in the music, for instance, as the black masses created their various styles, the chance to benefit materially by their own creations, whether individually or collectively, was (and is) severely limited.

Slavery itself was certainly the most extreme limitation a human could experience. The discrimination, segregation, the continuing racism that followed offered little better. African-American music was, and is, considered a "raw material" that could be ripped off and casually exploited by the North American oppressor nation with little or no compensation for its creators.

From its earliest appearance, and even today, the initial response of the larger society's social and aesthetic rulers was that the music, like black people themselves, was degraded, degenerate, and savage. But when one wants to reconstruct a portrait of this country at any time in the twentieth century, one must go to black music to express the North American environment.

The tendency to dismiss the music as "primitive," on one hand, and to imitate it and utilize it for profit, on the other, are the twin social relationships of the rulers' ethic. And at each stylistic plateau of African-American music, not only will we find much grand talk about how hopeless black music is, we will at the same time find a great deal of imitation, appropriation, and exploitation of it going on.

For the traditional music, there was the "Dixieland"; the big bands spawned by Fletcher Henderson and brought to perfection by Duke Ellington had a commercial counterpart called "Swing." For bebop there was an antidote put together called "cool." In all of these cases, what was being done was that once the black style had surfaced and become popular, corporate interests (the concentrated expression of all that is evil in the United States) would concoct a watered-down version of that style played mainly by white performers and aimed mainly at the white middle class. Such corporate music was largely emotionally antithetical to the black originals, mainly because it was created only with profit in mind, not expression and revelation!

The fifties was a period of marked reaction in the U.S. These were the years of McCarthyism and the insanity of its anticommunist witch hunts! It was the period of the Korean War, the Cold War, and President Eisenhower whom intellectuals thought of as quaintly retarded.

So that it was really a part of the whole character of the fifties that they should produce a music that would be used to "cover" the hot rebellious music of the forties. Fifties' "cool" was almost the exact opposite of the forties' innovative and provocative *BeBop*. The fact that in the fifties the regular rhythms and grinning American countenances of Dave Brubeck, Chet Baker, Shorty Rogers, Gerry Mulligan, etc. should be used to cover the harsh and jagged uncompromising sounds and alien black faces of Charlie Parker, Thelonius Monk, Bud Powell, Dizzy Gillespie is part of the whole period of American reaction which also saw Langston Hughes, W.E.B. Du Bois, Paul Robeson dragged before the House Un-American Activities Committee and threatened for being black and radical, while Richard Wright was driven from these shores to France in permanent exile! It was corporate domination of U.S. life again, in its harshest and most reactionary forms.

But at each threatened swallowing of the people and their music by the corporate villains, there is a resistance, an adjustment, a restating of the people's fundamental values. So that the Dixieland reaction only forced new expressions like the big band; and the anti-swing "Swing" bands produced small groups opposed to their dullness who produced the music called bebop!

The cool reaction brought a sharp countermotion from the creators of the people's music. Cool threatened to starch and flatten the life out of black music, to replace its organic *swing* and the *hotness* created therefrom with mechanical lifelessness in which blues was all but eliminated and improvisation, the lifeblood of the music, replaced by mediocre charts.

What breathed new life into the music in the fifties was the arrival (or re-arrival) of *Soul*! People like Horace Silver, Art Blakey and his Jazz Messengers, Max Roach and Clifford Brown and their classic groups, Sonny Rollins, and some others went back to the wellspring of black music, the African-American church. Particularly this was true of Silver and Blakey and the others in those groups that called forth the epithet *Funky* to describe their music as well as *Soul*. Which meant that what they had created was *basic, elemental,* and so strong it could be perceived in extra musical ways. As "funk" was once used to describe a heavy odor associated with sex.

The blues, added to the traditional spirituals, produced what was called gospel music; now the gospel tradition and even earlier churchy modes laid on the modern jazz sounds produced a *soul music*. An antidote for the antidote!

Musicians like Max Roach, Clifford Brown, and Sonny Rollins—who at one time during the fifties were the featured players in one of the most influential and important groups in the music, the Clifford Brown-Max Roach Quintet featuring Sonny Rollins—not only were aware of the influx of church-oriented rhythms à la Silver and Blakey but went to the immediate past and brought the bebop impulse into the new decade with all its fire and feeling. This music they made was called by critics *Hard Bop* and together with the soul-music influence revitalized black music in the fifties, uncovering it from under the suffocating "Cool."

What Soul also signified was the element of ethnicity that is the national consciousness of the black players. In the face of the watered-down "cool" which eradicated any African-American identity to the music, *Soul* and *Funk* meant also not just *feeling*, but a feeling connected most directly with the African-American experience!

Part of the exploitation of African-American music has always been to appropriate it as some anonymous expression in the world, and not as the creation, primarily, of the African-American people! How can a people be oppressed as "worthless" if they are actually *creators*? Which is why the fiction of black music's "anonymity" continues. So that the terms *Soul* and *Soulful* also refer to the music's origins as an African-American cultural projection, finally, no matter the players. Because what is being expressed in the music, in its original and most striking forms and content, is the existence of a particular people and their description of the world!

This element of national consciousness is also very apparent in the most sophisticated players and composers, whether Duke Ellington or in the fifties' Sonny Rollins's *Freedom Suite,* which proposes to make a social statement about liberation at the same time being a musical example of that liberation from hackneyed Tin Pan Alley forms of commercial music.

Max Roach's *We Insist: Freedom Now,* which included the voice of traditional musical Africa, as well as the voice and social statement of contemporary Africa and the link between the African freedom struggle and the African-American struggle, shows how high this national consciousness can be brought. So that what is soulful expresses not a metaphysical freedom as the *surfaces* of the old spirituals did, but speaks to the liberation of a living people (just as many of the old spirituals did, laying on more symbol as well).

What Max Roach, Clifford Brown, and Sonny Rollins were playing in the fifties points directly to what was called Avant-Garde in the sixties, given a special urgency by the key figure of the period, John Coltrane. Coltrane is so important because he was the musician who brought together a wide expression of musical influences, black church, rhythm and blues, big band, bebop, hard bop, to create the most evocative and influential sound and style of his time. Coltrane is the essence of the Soul-playing black jazz musician. His playing is about and induces *spirit possession* in a way as fundamental as the church. Later, he even pointed directly to the forms of spirit possession older than the African-American church; he pointed to Africa and the East, and to the ancient divinities that still inhabit the consciousness of humanity.

Trane also spoke to black national consciousness, not only as a soulful player, but by the very forms he used which opposed commercial music in the extreme and spoke of African and African-American spiritual and cultural reality. Frequently, in fact, Trane is linked to the black leader, Malcolm X, not only because they were contemporaries, but the fire and vision and rage heard in Trane's music seemed to complement the violent truths of the great Malcolm!

And that is another element not included in the perception of what is soulful: that it be an expression of truth and the fullest expression of that truth in all its naked blinding beauty and power! Malcolm told it like it was, and Trane played it like it was—hot and illuminating!

Many of the players influenced by Trane and the earlier boppers, who were called the Avant-Garde, e.g., Ornette Coleman, Albert Ayler, Eric Dolphy, Cecil Taylor, created a "new music" that was also, at its most expressive, a soul music, i.e., a music of deep emotion and widening consciousness, a music that seemed as essential as life itself. But by the late seventies the corporate hosts had descended again to counterfeit feeling and fill their pockets.

This time there were two aspects to their *desouling* process. On one hand they created a music much like fifties "cool" but that utilized the bass rhythms associated with rhythm and blues, with a cool top or melodic line and instrumentation, so that what was arrived at was called "Fusion." In the late seventies and early eighties this was a commercial music that was all but ubiquitous even in many of the places one might look for legitimate and soulful jazz. Fusion, in the main had no soul, because it smelled of commercial dilution and money tricks.

The other "anti-soul" music was the "Tail Europe" school, as I have called it, which seeks to make African-American music an appendage of European concert music. This has been particularly evident because of the emergence of a somewhat larger black middle class since the sixties, a substantial number of whom seem quite committed to proving as conspicuously as possible that, yes, they have heard Berg, Webern, Cage, et al. But as Stanley the Crouch has said, Duke Ellington showed long ago that he knew what uses were to be made of European concert music, in ways that enhanced the expressiveness and emotional registration of African-American music.

But this "Tail Europe" phenomenon has always been one aspect of the pathology that arises out of national oppression or colonialism, where one small sector of the oppressed people feels that the surest method of ending its oppression is to become the oppressor, or at least to abandon all forms of its own national culture and take on totally the cultural forms and content of those in power.

One violinist from this "Tail Europe" school is quoted in *Coda* saying, ". . . Great Black Music has run the gamut of the human body from the feet, which would indicate that in its earliest stages it was appreciated more by the masses—a commercial music—and now it has run its gamut to the head and is purely cerebral." This should indicate the degree of pathology extant in the T.E. school, couched in an attitude that is clearly elitist and anti-popular, the antithesis of what is *soulful*!

This last kind of "anti-soul" music is not as overtly commercial as, say, Fusion, but it is aimed at academic institutionalization, which offers a form of security and even prestige that few jazz musicians know.

But whatever the attacks or attempts to dilute or "cover" African-American music or replace its authentic soulfulness for the sake of commerce or racism, the music will abide and develop as long as the African-American people do.

It must be recognized, however, that what makes black music soulful is that it is an authentic reflection of those people who created it, and an organic expression of their lives. If we spoke of Russian Music or Spanish Music or Gypsy Music or French Music or German Music, etc., people would have less problem understanding that one aspect of those musics would be a quality that expressed with some precision real-life elements of those musics' originators. Beethoven is certainly a universal genius, but one clear identification of his creation is as *German* Music. There is a cultural, historic, and social reference in the music that is quite German. But that is the music's particularity, and nothing can be universal unless it also expresses the particular. "The universal is a collection of *all* the particulars!"

In the most authentic African-American music, the quality of soulfulness comes from the elements Du Bois mentioned that characterized the black church, but these elements go back much further than even the existence of an African-American people, back into the mists of the African past. First there is the Preacher quality, or the direct *communication* with the audience (congregation) and its necessary response. Second, the intense emotionalism (the shouting or "getting happy" element) in the music, and as a result of the communication, in the listener. And then there is the conceptualizing of the music as an ultimate concern, as in the religion. As black musicians say "The Music" with a seriousness that is as reverent as any religious focus.

With these "religious" qualities there is also a more generalized commitment to *feeling*, like the intense emotionalism or frenzy of the church. There is also that commitment and will to *be* the *truth*, as well as to express it. And with that, the national consciousness of the most sophisticated musicians that they are African-Americans as are their creations, and this can be taken as expression, definition, or in many cases in so twisted a world, *defense*! But hopefully, also, development.

To be soulful is to be in touch with the truth and to be able to express it, openly and naturally and without the shallow artifice of commerce. And finally, it is the truth of a particular national experience that, in its most important expressions, is clearly international and accessible as art and revelation to the world.

A Tribute to Bird

Why do we commemorate and celebrate Charlie Parker? Because he helped create the contemporary language we still speak. As part of the yet developing African-American music called Jazz, really *Orgasm;* called that because it was a form of heat-transfer medium, the dancing coming from it, suggested that, the sudden ecstasy, the *Jism,* from the African *Jasm,* to mean a total epiphany, body-communicated revelation and psychological liberation. Come-Music!

But also in terms of our employment, like in New Orleans, it was music to Jazz By. HoHouse New Orleans was where all the cycles of culture had linked up, sweeping out the countryside from the plantations, the Native American villages, settlements of English, French, Spanish (Jelly Roll's Spanish tinge), Italian, Portuguese, all the various cultures, and the African base, African-American collective whatever-you-got-I-need-logic. In the city, the culture, and its art, was an urban, more elegant, slicker expression, still with the fire of Congo Square—and those sorrow songs express American tragedy, blind slavery, industrial savagery, the dawn of the twentieth century, and what was to come.

The early part of the twentieth century in the U.S. was called the Jazz Age, because by that time (the twenties) the music had come up-river as the people came, beat down by fake emancipation, destroyed reconstruction, black codes, boll weevils, the Klan, Republican betrayal.

Our modernism, the Harlem Renaissance, is contemporary with what's called the Age of Modernism. Langston Hughes went to Europe too, but came back, him and McKay. Zora Neale Hurston, Jean Toomer, along with the transformer of American music, Duke Ellington, the master American composer, who took the root and branch of African, African-American, peasant, city blue-black culture and raised it up to a sophistication that turned Europe on its ear. The most important composer in Europe by the thirties was Duke Ellington—or haven't you heard Stravinsky, Ravel? But the music had got to the Europeans befo dat—you haven't heard Debussy?

So that when the Eliots and Pounds, Hemingways, Carlos Williams, and Picassos and Ives were strutting what they were—the African-American Renaissance created a Jazz Age, for the whole world!

277

Bird took it upstairs another increment. Like Lenin said, Capitalism is the age of steam, socialism electricity, and as the nuclear age dawns, if we are not too primitive to harness it without destroying all life, communism is the nuclear age.

Bird blew a Nagasaki speed-up for us. He took it from the quarter note, as the main tongue, to the eighth note. As the new conversational form. The point being to make sense at higher and higher speeds! So then Trane came on the scene to make sense in long fabrics of sixteenth notes. Faster yet. Faster. Listen to the difference between earlier r&b and post-Stevie, you notice first the *speed*.

If you could speak the language of *Anthropology*, Confirmation, *Bloomdido, Klacktoveedesteen, Billies Bounce,* etc. you had entered the nuclear age, about the same time the Squares in their use of the same principle were destroying human life at Hiroshima. You see the different classes' directly opposite use of the same elements? Bird is nuclear, atomic; Trane, hydrogen. Duke was modern warfare, period.

Bird, Charles Parker, Bird, that name has been a spiritual symbol since before ancient Egypt. The hieroglyphic, bird, means *Spirit.* We used that symbol in Newark to indicate Spirit House. Ba. Bird. Soul. Ba. Bird's soaring lines, hip air calligraphy, the elegant sweeping dazzle of his line, the incredible speed. So he is also, this bird, the symbol of artist. The spirit catcher—spirit transferrer. From where he got it on over to us.

And his tragic death also must instruct us, that spirit can only be manifest through material life. That sensitivity and beauty can be destroyed easily by the gross thuggery of a primitive world. Record companies got big off Charlie Parker's wings—and thighs—and giblets, etc. Col. Sanders is smiling to let you know, you just a raw material, my man and sweet lady. Just a raw material. Until the bird consciousness also has its self-conscious entity of survival and self-determination.

Beauty without a self-created means of survival and development is what we mean by a chicken box! "A couple of them chicken boxes to go, please?" We celebrate Bird's life because of his music, but also because of our own lives, and our own collective music, and because of our own determination to prevail! And still be hip and beautiful!

Afro Pop

The concept of *Afro Pop* raises a stream of questions, dissociations, and other need-to-be-answered queries. First, we have to understand and make a distinction between popular and "pop." Popular obviously relates to appreciation by many people. Not to be confused with *commercial*. What is popular is often not "commercial," since the forces that determine what commerce is in U.S. society are not popular forces but those with enough power to manipulate the market.

Something popular could be commercially profitable to be sure, but what we mean when we say something is "commercial" is that its principal and often only focus is making money. Internationalism is more popular than nationalism, but at this point nationalism is more commercial. Freedom is more popular than different forms of slavery—but obviously slavery is more commercially viable to the traders in human flesh.

Popular, what is celebrated by the populace. The most popular African-American music has been and remains various forms of blues. In the United States, however, when we say "popular music" we mean those lifeless products of the corporations, commercial ditties of small consequence and less vitality. (In New York City think of WNEW and WPAT.) These hopeless artifacts are literally mashed on the U.S. populace as "popular" when they are commercial, and exist only as a result of corporate intention.

Really, as M. Rap Brown said, these people could sell dogshit if they wanted to. They already sell it, and make millions.

On the real side, the "popular" new commercial American music is a kind of slightly washed-out white Rock full of "youthful" narcissism and subjectivism. The really popular roots of this are Blues and Country and Western, but their commercialized homogenization barely resembles either. The straight-out C&W you are likely to hear more than Blues, for obvious reasons, but you'd be surprised at how often not even C&W is allowed to blast out true because in its deepest memory it also complains about a world it never made and wants desperately to change. Ultimately, this is not good for business or businessmen.

But the term "Pop" is something a little else, again. Pop is a term that summons white appropriations of black rhythms and blues to mind. But we need to understand a deeper entrance into the concept intended. The U.S. cultural etc. "Establishment" terms the music made by Americans, in general, "pop." Just as if you read *The Star Ledger* and the listing says in one box "Music" (European concert music, obcoats) and then another separate but equal box says "Jazz and Pop." Get it! (*The New Yorker,* being much slicker, segregates the two as "Music" and "Night Life."

To speak of *Serious* music, according to the eighteenth-century colonial roots of U.S. bourgeois traditionalism, is still to pay homage to *Europe.* There is no such thing as American culture—English departments still outweigh American Studies departments. That's why Henry James is celebrated, in academia, above Melville or T. S. Eliot over William Carlos Williams, because they still trumpet Europe!

The bourgeoisie must always point *backward,* and in this case, always away from the United States when speaking of art or culture, because to speak of *American Culture,* to admit that "G. Washington won the war," is to start to describe an independent and new culture, which at one very fundamental level of its aggregation is African, i.e., African-American, and Latino, Native American, Asian, and working-class! These elements combined with the Anglo, French, Spanish, and waves of immigrant European strains provide another measure, another essence. If you speak of *Serious* American music you cannot leave out African-American music, neither Worksongs, nor Spirituals, nor Blues, nor Ragtime, nor Boogie Woogie, nor Swing, nor Bop, nor noncommercial Cool, nor Hardbop, nor the New Music.

You cannot speak of *Serious* American music and not mention King Oliver, Louie Armstrong, Jelly Roll Morton, Fletcher Henderson, Bessie Smith, Ma Rainey, Duke Ellington, Count Basie, Coleman Hawkins, Billie Holiday, Lester Young, Sarah Vaughan, Charlie Parker, Miles Davis, Max Roach, Dizzy Gillespie, Thelonius Monk, John Coltrane, Ornette Coleman, and literally *hundreds* more!

There is no American culture without African-American culture! And whatever aspect of American culture you want to investigate, you will find, as Bruce Franklin says in his important book, *The Victim as Criminal and Artist* (Oxford), African-American "culture has, for more than a century, been central to American culture in general. Only in the academy, the last bastion of European colonialism in the United States, is it possible to pretend that our culture for over a century has not been primarily an expression of the interaction between two groups of peoples, one of European the other of African descent."

Whether one investigates speech, manners, cuisine, literature, music, dance, one will find a generous reference to African-American expression there at the core of whatever aspect of American culture is being investigated!

So "pop" is meant to de-serious American culture because according to colonial bourgeois ideology only European (literally) culture and art can be profound. The term is meant to exclude American culture from consideration as "serious," which is why Reagan's jingoism might sound fresh to someone who maybe balked at the idea that intellectualism was European or like NET a sterile retread of the Harvard humanities survey.

African-American popular music is one form of blues or another—whether country, city, classic, big band, R&B, or contemporary. It can be covered, electrified, instrumentally augmented, hooked up with strings, discoed, rapped, "converted" to anything else for the sake of commercial mischief, yet fundamentally its existence as the expression of the African-American people is its hold on them and whoever else has become enrapt by it. It has many legitimate incarnations as well—Rag, Boogie, Jazz, and the most moving and historically significant of these are always the most closely related to the parent music, and with that, the African-American historical and cultural development.

So there is a *blues continuum* that is one aspect of the culture and history of black Americans—it is the basic musical construct of black music and the basic verse form (word to music, rhythm word) construct expressive of that culture. *Blues is both word and music.* It is a song form and a verse form. It is also a state of consciousness, both the description of . . . and the emotion itself. This last is important because there have been observers, various formalists, who, for instance, say that Billie Holiday didn't sing the blues because they don't count twelve bars! This is when you have completely disrespected or missed the ultimate primacy of content over form. Because finally there is a *feeling* that is *blue* even without being the form Blues.

There are also various forms of African-American music that use blues as the basic given, whether formally, connotatively, evocatively, etc., but which, like Jazz, want to reach out to include a broader experience. Broader musically, emotionally, intellectually, socially. Jazz, at its most expressive, does this and for this reason is clearly an international expression albeit the product largely of African-American sensibility. (Though the presence of white British and Australian blues-derived music points out the international capacity of the parent strain itself!)

What is also clear is that the further a music like Jazz moves away from the deep emotional commitment of blues the less moving and significant that music becomes. Usually it has become some middle-class form exploiting black music on the way to some watered-down expression of the arrogance of the petty bourgeoisie (sterile "cool," "Third Stream," "Progressive," "Fusion," for example).

One sector of the "New Music" (seventies and eighties avant) has conspicuously moved away from the emotional roots of black mass or popular music and is the intellectual mood music for a younger petty bourgeoisie—many college-trained and sometimes even living in mid-dle-class enclaves away from the teeming ghettos holding the black majority. It is a music that celebrates the intellectual stewardship Eu-ropean concert music represents, indeed bourgeois European ideas represent, for this "newest negro" petty bourgeoisie.

"Fusion," because of its obvious but usually tepid reliance on the R&B Blues roots of black popular music, seems "warmer" than the *unblue* sector of the avant-garde, but it is also, for the most part, fur-niture music.

Both are contemporary examples of the debilitating effects of bour-geois ideas (white supremacy in the first case, commercial prostitution in the second) that make both of these by-products of African-Amer-ican popular music future "curiosities" of little intrinsic value or histor-ical endurance.

A great deal of "white rock" and disco has the same likelihood of survival, save as historical curiosities, for many of the same reasons. Since the fifties emergence of white contemporary blues-derived ex-pressions like Rock & Roll (as a separate category of music, not just *covers,* or white versions of black songs), the existence of white su-premacy has meant that many very poor examples of this genre could get raised up the flagpole of public exposure largely by virtue of the players' nationality. For this reason the field is dominated by commer-cial garbage, since it is the moguls of the corporate world who throw endless sad-sack white rock groups of varying styles out in the market, hoping to get rich quick. This lowers and demeans the entire genre, and too often defines it. This music becomes a more animated mood music of still another middle class masquerading (literally) as anything. The final irony of now being able to call many such players and fellow travelers PUNKS, to their general approbation, and to cite some quasi-established genre of artistic and cultural activity (in addition to the one previously connoted in history) *is* sweetly ironic.

Disco, as Max Roach said, is someone trying to "orchestrate your ideology." It is also largely about commerce. It exploits the rhythm of the blues for profit, not feeling. It intends to deprecate intelligence— and by hooking up the sides in an unending chain, with no breaks, it even abhors simple speech, much less exposition. Disco is a *surface* music, the exploitation of the rhythm, like rhyme without reason.

Compare the popular music of the sixties, issuing out of mass and intellectually extended expression of black mass music, with disco and fusion. The Impressions, Aretha Franklin, The Temptations, Martha and the Vandellas, Marvin Gaye, Smokey and the Miracles, James Brown sang and danced a music of incredible beauty and power and many times striking social relevance. *Keep On Pushin, People Get Ready, Dancin in the Street, Black and Proud, Message from a Black Man, What's Goin' On, Repect,* and the rest spoke to and of a people in motion, of personal and public struggle.

The same is true for the more intellectually presumptive music of the period produced by Miles, Rollins, Max, Monk, Mingus, Coltrane, Ornette Coleman, Dolphy, Sun Ra, Ayler, Cecil Taylor, Pharaoh Sanders, and the rest. Their cry was invariably, to one degree or another, *Freedom.* Free Music (e.g., *Freedom Now, Freedom Suite, Free Jazz,* etc., or what about *Let Freedom Swing*?)! Destroy the jail of the commercial song form, get away from endless deadly chords. The screams, cries—the actual confrontations about contracts, cabaret cards, artistic control, economics, production, the politics of music— were further reflections of the period and the people whom the music finally expressed (as a core of and part of a larger America as well . . . e.g., the Black Liberation Movement, rebellions). Black struggle *moves* U.S. society as a whole, and *reflects* it; as well as being the specific expression of black people; it is also a *class* expression, as the black majority are *workers* and their music expressed this class consciousness. (The white majority are workers as well, but the blacks are victims of white supremacy in addition, not its carriers and dupes, which functions bear with them a distortion of the perception and the consciousness and values of that class, and of course, is the root of the black majority's and white majority's continuing separation and estrangement.)

Although the popular expression of a people is a reflection, an exact portrait of them, people change from era to era in their interrelationship with the world. The sixties and early seventies were a period of upsurge; the music reflected it. The art of any social period reflects that period, and usually large art and cultural upsurges are the results of large social movements. So that, loosely, early Jazz does reflect the movement of blacks into the southern cities, New Orleans the most notable. Just as the Slave Narratives reflect the anti-slavery surge of the African-American people that we see culminate in the Civil War. The art of the Harlem Renaissance (its great Langstons and Dukes) obviously speaks of black movement at the beginning of the century into the sophisticated cities of the North as well as the emergence of fighting black organize resistance to white supremacy, such as Garvey's UNIA or the African Blood Brotherhood! And certainly we know that the Black Arts Movement and Free Jazz thrust of the sixties carry with them Martin Luther King, Malcolm X, the Black Panthers, i.e., the motion of the Civil Rights and Black Liberation movements themselves.

At the same time that the admonition "black writers fail because

THE MUSIC

they write too much about black people" can become a commonplace,
or new black writers can get published by putting down Richard
Wright (at the same time the FBI is driving him out of the country and
HUAC is attacking Robeson, Hughes, Du Bois), or official American
art is a dead formalism approved by the academic inquisition called
The New Criticism—sponsored largely by an outspoken group of white
southern conservatives such as Allen Tate, Ransome, Warren. When
in this same period (the 1950s) there is the Cold War, the Korean War,
McCarthyism, then we not only must understand the backwardness,
but should not be surprised to see emerge a commercial "cool" music
that pushed Chet Baker over Miles Davis or Dizzy Gillespie, and has
Brubeck take over for Bud and Monk and has Paul Desmond replace
Bird. The corporations have moved in and manufactured Swing as
noun to replace the verb or Shorty Rogers and his Giants or Spyro
Gyra. Until the Boppers show up to restore the primacy of African
rhythm, improvisation, and blues or later Horace gets nasty and brings
the church in it (helped out by Buhainia's *Messenger Univ* and Max-
Sonny-Clifford). Or until David Murray's octet comes full out to blow
both Spyro and Gyra plus a bunch of the other disco confusion back
into corporate nightmare.

The music, art, reflects the social life of the people themselves. The
popular music, the popular masses. What is going on in the music is
going on in the street. So when we look up rat nah and see Ronald
Reagan or the restoration of the death penalty, the resurgence of the
Klan, the elimination of social programs in order to buy more and
more weapons that may ultimately destroy human society, then we
know we're in another very backward period and a great deal of even
what passes for popular culture is going to reflect that backwardness.
Survey the wash of disco lyrics telling us to die, o.d., or become some
kind of sex freak, and you can see just how backward a period it is.
Yet, even in this freeze of reaction, there are voices carrying the same
message from may back, reflecting the nonreducible core of our lives,
history, and concerns. That core of democracy and socialism that is at
the center of every people's popular culture. Lenin said, that every
nation has two cultures, one of the rulers and the other of the ruled.
African-American Popular culture is the culture of the ruled, the
struggling, the seekers after the totally new, the worshipers of democracy ('cause they never experienced it), the demanders of the makers
of change. (And if the change gets coopted it gets changed—as music,
as movement . . .) The creation of an ageless identity yet unborn but
certain as history! Asked about the music Monk replied. "Jazz is Freedom"; to say anything else, he went on, gets complicated.

Billie*

Of all the singers I know there is only one can burn a hole in your heart and fill up your soul with deep blue-black history, a tragic poet of longing. Billie's voice was once light bouncy, a swing-band banner popping in the wind of syncopation. Life here changed that. As she lived it, grew heavy inside her a steel mystery murdering of feeling with feeling. By the end of her life Billie's songs were genuinely frightening. You not only hear the song but the pain. And it is lyric editorial that is so pointed as to the origins of its suffering . . .

Billie always changed the melody to suit her feeling for the language. She is fundamentally a blues poet, trapped in the bogus "sophistication" of the dead society pretending life.

The double dose of terror; being black and woman. She was a working woman, when she could get a card, that's a triple cruel and unusual punishment.

*This was the beginning of an introduction to a BBC documentary on Billie Holiday. The day I was to sign a contract was the day my murdered sister Kimako was to be buried. Because I couldn't show for the meeting, BBC nutted.

Miles Davis: "One of the Great Mother Fuckers"

P. J. Jones in conversation

In interviewing Miles, the fundamental question at the bottom of my questions was: How did you get from there to here? Meaning how did you get from being the sideman of Charlie Parker and playing that transcendental music to *Man with the Horn, Star People,* and the latest, *Decoy*?

To me, if I could hear that path and motion, that change of priorities, I could say something useful about Miles's journey and perhaps we could all learn something.

This was not idle academic analysis. For many years of my life Miles Davis was my ultimate culture hero. Artist, cool man, bad dude, hipster (old meaning), clear as daylight, and funky as revelation.

The prospect of finally doing a piece on Miles, of having to interview him, to meet him up close, was very important to me. I remembered one night when I was a little boy trying to be a jazz critic. I had gone without benefit of a sponsor to the Village Vanguard where Miles was playing.

I don't remember the exact group Miles had with him then. But Trane was gone, and Hank Mobley, one of my roadies of the period, who I'd met in Newark, was with Miles.

When I went into the back room which still passes as a dressing room, the musicians were spread around casually rapping, Miles all the way to the rear like a point.

I remember Hank was there, and none of the others. Only a vicious sycophant, a male jazz groupie, called Freddie Freeloader. Miles even recorded a tune with the same name on *Kind of Blue.*

Miles waved off my rather timid request for an interview, mumbling something, I guess, about how he didn't want to be bothered.

With that youthful mixture of rejection dregs and crackpot daring I spat back, "I bet you'd do it if I was Nat Hentoff!"

I can't remember Miles's reaction, because suddenly Freeloader was forward and talking loud, "Hey, goddamnit, the man say he don't want to be bothered."

"I wasn't talking to you."

"Hey, man, I'll throw your ass out."

"Shit," the thing had gotten completely out, but I certainly couldn't back down. It looked like I was gonna have to bash this negro up side his empty knot. But at that moment Hank intervened, telling Freddie to cool it, wrapping his arms around my shoulders, telling the assembled audience I was his homeboy.

I never got that interview. Ironically, musician rumor has it that a few years later Miles got incensed at one of Freddie's freeloads and tossed him down a flight of stairs. The last time I saw him he was limping terminally, making the rumor seem very real.

So the prospect of the present interview raised the spoor of that history. It also made me smile a little. And now, coming into the well-appointed, mirror-sparkling bar at the United Nations Plaza Hotel where we met, I wondered would he ever remember the incident. But I never raised it directly.

I was sitting for a short period, meditating on some Courvoisier, when a bright and bouncy brown-skinned woman appeared, all energy and business, the waiter steering her toward the table. It was Sandra Da Costa, CBS's publicist, whom *The New York Times* people turned me on to in order to reach Miles. We talked to Miles for a few minutes, and after a while I heard some arrival and attention sounds, not much on such a low-key weekday afternoon, but someone more than the many had shown.

When I turned, my very first impression looking at the beautiful black man moving gracefully yet walking with a cane and talking to various of the waiters he seemed to know was that Miles Davis looked like a star, a real celebrity.

The way he dressed, first, obviously set all the rest of himself off— probably as he meant it to. Miles Davis's deep black-brown skin is still a marvel of the African aesthetic. There is no doubt he is a black man. At once the old soubriquet he carried comes back, *The Black Prince.* The gold-topped cane he handles like a casual guidon of elegance. The bone condition that makes it necessary, the prosthetic hip that he later told me had slipped out of place, is not what the cane makes us focus on. It is something Miles digs, we are convinced, not staring too directly as he glides into the slick Upper East Side bar booth.

We old-time Miles worshipers have always dug Miles's "vines," whether the cap pulled down around his ears on the hot fifties *Dig* or the green button-down shirt, sleeves rolled up, the impenetrable shades of Milestones. Miles was always "clean." Though, and this is instructive as to our perception of the whole aesthetic, that as he seemed to get more into what was later termed "fusion," Miles looked from various flicks as if he had also begun to hook up in some Sly and the Family Stone-type wild threads we old-time neo Ivy intellectuals thought of as frankly "out to lunch" and then some.

But what you get from Miles in conversation and from his manner is a Man always, as Richard Wright said the intellectual and artist must be, "at the top of his times." Aware of who he is and the nature of his time, his art therefore "the state of" that doing, which his superior knowing and feeling has made possible.

Dizzy Gillespie told me recently, at the Blue Note the night they celebrated Dizzy's and the club's birthday, that Miles "was like a man who had made a pact with himself . . . to never repeat himself." It is like a "curse," Miles said elsewhere, to constantly change.

But it is his deep sensitivity, the artist's throbbing antennae of consciousness—forever impressed with the real, and the real, for any latecomers, is in constant motion.

Miles, this day, wore some unbelievably hip fisherman's or truck driver's (depending on where you've been) cap, made of what looked like black raffia. A military-type jacket, appropriately matched ballooning black pants, and black clogs, Dutch wooden shoe lookalikes.

It all went together because he placed them on himself together. Along with the cane and some extremely expensive-looking sunglasses.

The introductions were going round as Miles sat. We shook hands, he said, "The mystery man!" Me, a mystery man—you never know how people perceive each other across the cloud of time and distance. What they look like to each other, from wherever. What they mean to each other.

I had said to Da Costa over the phone that I only needed an hour of interview. I guess because I know most people don't like drawn-out interviews—I know I don't. Plus, I thought I knew so much over the years about Miles.

But being there with him, the herd of questions just his presence occasioned, was actually embarrassing. I knew I couldn't ask most of them. I could not really be an interviewer in a certain sense. To probe in a cold way someone who had in one sense actually given you consciousness. Nothing happening.

Yet there was this basic interrogative in my present feeling for Miles and his music. How did you get to here, to playing *The Man with the Horn* and *Star People,* albums I did not care very much for? What brought you from the sublime heights of "Now's the Time" or "Ornithology" and "Venus De Milo" or "Move" or "Walkin" or *Milestones* or *Kind of Blue* or the myriad other anthems of the deep hip, the smooth know, the coolly funky expository? Here to an over-heavy back beat blocking the light whirring metal ideas and now less than there, and not quite sound.

But it was not only in the asking and the telling that something changed for me. The new album *Decoy** (particularly the title tune) is a clear return to a much hipper level of performance for Miles, more competent technically, more emotionally rewarding aesthetically.

What it was is that from the conversation I had with "The Prince of Darkness," the *reasons* behind his development became clearer to me. It sent me back to his music to test and confirm the understanding his words compelled me toward. The "interview," a later presence at his most recent recording session and the many musicians I talked to about Miles, allowed me to penetrate and perhaps elaborate for myself a deeper rationale in reflection of a long career that has been (and is), by any knowledgeable measure, amazingly productive and destined, in all its phases, to be called classic and emulated until the planet itself "books."

The interview in truth was not much of an interview. But it was much more than that and much much longer than an hour. By liquid measure, it was a four-cognac interview. Not question and answer, but a conversation that did give me the substance I wanted but also closer access than I had ever had to a superbly creative mind. One of the most consistently dazzling creators of our time. A fact that will only be more clearly ascertained as the society itself reaches higher and higher levels of democracy and the genius of black artists is finally dealt with in critical and institutional processes free of chauvinist distortion or commercial segregation.

Miles's influence and effect on the music called Jazz and its players is predictable to the knowledgeable but still somewhat astonishing. He has been at the center of one stream of African-American music and its various variations and performers for forty years. Since the time he first arrived in New York City (1944) from East St. Louis, Illinois, to look for "Bird" (alto genius Charlie Parker) and enroll at Juilliard.

But like the music itself, Miles's influence has not been limited to jazz musicians. Black music has touched and influenced profoundly every wave of music coming out of America and Europe, and points in every which direction, from Debussy to Hawaiian guitar players. So too "Dewey," as some of the cognoscenti used to call Miles, letting you know they knew his middle name, is almost as well known by contemporary European and Euro-American classical composers and followers of that tradition worldwide, as Jazz players.

Blues people, Rock folk, Reggae runners, Gospel chanters, serial structuralists, chance champions, neo-classical or neo-romantic revelers, and on out know Miles, his music, and the most sensitive have even been directly changed by it.

Miles Davis's music, like African-American culture generally, origi-

You're Under Arrest is even heavier!

nates as a specific reflection of African-American life and perception in the still mostly segregated black communities of the society, but it, like Miles, reaches in all directions within the whole of that society and transforms them. So that African-American culture (and indeed to varying degrees all the other minority cultures within the society) touches and changes and "darkens" any "objectively" American culture.

There is virtually no "American Music" that exists untouched and unshaped by black music of one kind or another. So it would seem that there could be almost no "pop" music in the United States untouched by the Milesian perspective.

"What can you say about Miles?" Dizzy went on. "He's always changing—you never know what he's going to do next. Plus he's got . . . a kind of—"

Another younger musician broke in, "An aura."

"Naw," said Dizzy, "I don't know about that, it sounds too much like some other word."

"Mystique," the younger man rejoined.

"Yeh," said Diz, "that's it. A mystique. Miles got a mystique about him. Plus he's at the top of his profession." Diz began his hoarse laughter. "And he's got way, way, way, way, way, way more money."

Diz could sum it up as only the Diz could do. Miles Davis constantly changing, possessor of a mystique, a presence that sometimes even threatened to obscure his music—but created in part by the deepness of that music, as well as by his legendary personality. Miles, now at the top of his profession, and even reputed to have snatched a few coins in tribute to his topness (and his longevity).

And Miles is perceived by a wide cross section of artists, in all disciplines, as a creative artist of the highest and most intense level. There are few artists of my generation, whether writers, painters, dancers, who do not know his work, and who are not influenced in some ways by his work. Who have not, for instance, sculpted or painted while *Kind of Blue* intoned its modal hipness. Who have not used some of his pieces, whether from *Sketches of Spain* or *Round About Midnight,* to create their dances. Who have not stayed up all night whacking away at the typewriter while *Walkin* or *Steamin* or *Cookin* made the darkness give up its lonely aesthetic to art.

We could write a whole essay on what modern American painting or writing or dance owe to Miles Davis. Or perhaps the influence of Miles Davis on the personalities and creativity of American Artists and Intellectuals. Don't worry, it'll be somebody's thesis before long.

The music has always had that single vulnerable feeling, like a lone person beautiful and solitary, moving gracefully, sometimes arrogantly, through the night. Now, I was asking what he thought of his own music, from those first records and residence with Charlie Parker, and his later changes.

"Later on, when I was playing [with Bird] we were always playing way up there [referring to the tempi]. It was all so fast, nobody knew what we was playing. Blam. It was over. I thought people needed a bottom. Something to refer to."

He was referring to the 1945–1949 tenure with Bird around Fifty-second Street where the revolutionary music of BeBop and the hottest of the Swing players congregated downtown after the initial uptown experimental developments. He also probably meant the recordings of the period that helped define the reconstruction and renovation of advanced black music in the forties after the corporations and racist commercialism had tried to transform swing from a Dukish and Countly verb into a hundred bands with identical commercial arrangements.

Miles Davis was a young middle-class intellectual seeking high art. Cross-referenced between the hottest new innovations in Western music and the conservatism of the small landowners and professional class from which he was spawned. He could study at Juilliard by day and hang out with the artistically brilliant but socially incorrigible Bird the rest of the time. He and Bird are reputed to have lived for a hot minute on a weekly allowance sent by Miles's dentist father.

"I thought everybody in New York was hip. I came to New York City expecting everybody was sounding like Dizzy!"

Miles began to draw it back through his mind, amused at his own youthful naïveté, which made me think of my own, in similar context.

"I played with John Kirby," called the Biggest Little Band in the Land. "The first records I was on was with the Savoy Sultans. I was on a Keynote record with Pres and Nat King Cole." He mused rapidly, "Ya know, Bud comps like Nat Cole." I thought of Miles's later championing of Ahmad Jamal and Red Garland, Wynton Kelly, Bill Evans, Herbie Hancock, Chick Corea, Keith Jarrett, all of whom owe at least a spill of grog on the floor in tribute to His Majesty the box-cooker. He was mentioning Ellington and Tatum as piano masters. "I found out you could get scores from the library. Couldn't do that in St. Louis."

The photographs of Miles during that period show a young blood swimming in New York drape suits, his hair gassed, running the hip thing, standing next to Bird, in the eye of the hurricane.

Miles's "flubs" and cracked notes from the period are legendary but also, alongside the awesomely articulate Parker, soaring through the musical way-gonesphere. Davis, in striking contrast, anxious, young, archly lyrical, his sprouting musical voice as much a question as a statement.

Those records, and that time, place Miles among the disciples and

291

prophets of the new music that appeared from the experimental sessions uptown in the temples of Out, Mintons, Monroe's Uptown. Miles, though younger, is forever linked to the ancient classicists of the Weird, the Frantic, the Groovy, to Bird and Diz and Monk and Klook and Max.

Miles went through the stretched-out social ostracism of heroin, in deference to Bird's poisoning. For a minute, he even got a little greasy. But he came out on the other side, now a well-known sideman to genius and himself touched by the magic as well.

Those early efforts would make Miles immortal by themselves. There is enough music in them and enough mystique surrounding them to provide for a world's lifetime. But a few minutes later Miles had hooked up with Gil Evans and Gerry Mulligan, and some of the young white players drawn by Evans's arranging and guidance to the Claude Thornhill orchestra.

These cool lush harmonies that Evans gave to Thornhill, and even the innovative use of brass and Dukish (reeds, winds) scoring had a heavy effect on Miles. A number of his major successes commercially and artistically make use of this orchestral approach and Evans's arrangements—*Miles Ahead, Sketches of Spain, Porgy and Bess,* even *Kind of Blue* to a certain extent, and others.

The nine sides that the album later put together as *The Birth of Cool* are the first important result of this collaboration. These records brought a kind of "symphonic" orchestra to the music even with a small group concept. For me, "Venus De Milo," "Move," "God Child," "Budo," "Darn that Dream" were the highest art I had ever contemplated. They are still estimable road signs of mastery.

I had asked Miles how he got to the Cool from the very hot. This music was a prototype and example that set a whole musical, social, and commercial movement in motion. Though what the corporations finally came up with as "Cool" used the understated surfaces of Miles's sound to suggest that Bop could become mood music just as Swing had been distorted previously.

They even got a Baker (Chet) to cover Miles. I remember being pissed off constantly by media critics constantly suggesting that Baker was Milesier than Dewey himself.

But this is the predictable devaluing of a black art form for reasons of profit and chauvinism that still go on. Sidney Finkelstein in *Jazz: A People's Music* agreed that within the African-American expression, even as art, is the fundamental cry for democracy. The music speaks for a people outside the city demanding entrance, while yet there are inside the walls struggling with the "double consciousness" Du Bois spoke of, how to be black and an American at the same time.

The corporations water the music down so that it can be merchandized more easily, but the essence of this "modification" is to cool out what is too hot to handle. To flatten the offending rhythms that speak of an earlier freedom, to "whiten" the blues, as if it was just a mood or at worst the profitable whisper of some middle-class alienation.

Miles's own view was that he was creating a "bottom." He said he was drawn to Thornhill's music because there was "something to relate to." Not just the flying fury of Bird's aerial wizardry. Aside from the reemphasized Africa of new Bop rhythms, the reassertion of the primacy of blues and improvisation in African-American music. Miles wanted a music with more melodic access and a "cushion" of harmonies that made his own simple voice an elegant, somewhat detached "personality" effortlessly perceiving and expressing.

It is this harmonic cushion or bottom, the Evans/Thornhill (quasi-Dukish) music parallels; the "something to relate to" that Miles described that speaks to the kind of *lush* sensibility Miles has, essentially melodic floating in relief above shaded chromatic harmonies.

There is an element of pure "mood music" in Miles, and even when he is cracking at his hottest or coolest, this aspect of his sensibility provides a *distance,* actually, making his voice apparently more clearly perceived, but actually creating an aesthetic distance, a sensuous alienation, that makes us think we can circumscribe all of the player/composer with our feelings.

Miles's "coolness," for instance, is in his need to balance the Hot Bird with the implications of *warmth* (love, affection, sensuality), not just the blue-white Bop *fire.*

It is this melodic and harmonic insistence that makes us dig Miles as *Cool.* He does not step as gracefully as the hot Bird tracks, even in those collaborations, so well as he comments and indicates and implies and defines by contrast.

Miles is the filler, so to speak, the pointillistic "other" gorgeousness, which in one sense is just a "series" of *holes* in Bird's soaring design.

What seems *subdued* in Miles, as say his middle-register light-vibrato tone would seem to confirm, shows up elsewhere however as *tension.* There is a tension in Miles that is *dramatic* and musically (rhythmically) very funky.

Miles's *downness* is that there is that undercurrent of tension, as funk comes with the smallest sound of his horn. He can wail like craziness with one or two notes placed, dropped, fired, drawled, sung, whispered, as light, reason, sweetness, regard, elation, because it does come. His solos are extensions of the rhythm, yet divide it, as time can be divided, even seemingly obliterated, but be as it is, as abstract and as unpredictable as our hearts.

The coolness in Miles is social and aesthetic. Art was a path to self-realization that ultimately could not be stopped even by the police. The mocking intellectual can see the foulest and most repressive circumstances, and the workings of his mind, never mind its content, itself is a verification of his "superiority." The young black intellectuals and artists of the forties and fifties treasured the irony of their self-understood superiority (intellectually, even morally) to the square US of A. It was an attitude they walked with. Later on this attitude would spill out of the personal and hook up with the mass assertion, which, a few minutes later, was the Civil Rights Movement!

I suggest that the coolness of Miles is the "dignified," even quietest, stance of the black intellectual of the period. Yet even that coolness is a-broil with not so hidden heat, and tension, because face it, finally, even the black bourgeoisie "are" niggers!

Miles and Ms. Da Costa speak of a date coming up where he will record his version, much acclaimed in concert, of punk queen Cyndi Lauper's "Time After Time." Miles pulls out a small tape recorder, on it a cassette of a live date with Bob Berg on tenor, Newport Sunday. Both Lauper and Berg are white. Recently Miles has received some criticism from certain black circles for hiring so many white musicians, thereby depriving some black musicians of some well-paying prestigious gig. In the present band, the one featured on the newest record *Decoy,* saxophonist Bill Evans and guitarist John Scofield are white. In fact, in each of the recording and concert groups Miles has put together since he made his "comeback" in 1981, each group has gotten successively whiter (though certainly the music has not).

But interracial bands are nothing new to Miles. So talk of Miles's eye to the buck as being the principal reason for using white musicians doesn't really wash. Though it is my own feeling that Miles knows always almost exactly what he is doing around the music—form and content, image and substance.

There is something in the mix that Miles *wants* to hear. It might be commercial, to some extent, but it is also social and aesthetic.

The Birth of the Cool sides featured many outstanding white musicians, Mulligan, Konitz, plus important arrangements.

Much of the most celebrated and popular of Miles's recording work has been in collaboration with Gil Evans and featured Evans's *distinctive* arrangements *(Miles Ahead,* 1957; *Porgy and Bess,* 1958; *Sketches of Spain,* 1959).

Pianist Bill Evans was featured on some of the key classics Miles has made, e.g., *Kind of Blue.* In a recent videotaped interview Miles spoke on the subject with his usual personal clarity and understated hilarity. He was explaining that what he wants to play is "today music" and how he has to tell many of the young musicians who have played with him over the years, "Don't play what you know but what you hear.

"White musicians are overtrained and black musicians are under-trained. You got to mix the two. A black musician has his own sound, but if you want it played straight, mix in a white musician and the piece will still be straight, only you'll get feeling and texture—up, down, around, silly, wrong, slow, fast—you got more to work with. There's funky white musicians. But after classical training you have to learn to play social music. You have to learn to underplay. I tell 'em, 'Don't practice all the time or you'll sound like that.'"

After the Cool sides Miles was a fairly well-known musician, but still his fame according to American white pop standards was modest. And he made no real money. Actually, this was the end of the second stage of Miles's career, but the growing recognition could not provide the life cushion Miles needed. He went off into drugs, and stayed hooked four or five years.

It is said that during his romance with the killer, scag, that Miles was backed into the worst kind of almost marginal ghetto existence.

At the same time he had become a popular sideman whose horn was much in demand. He was recording with Prestige records and some of the classic names in the music. It was the early fifties and Miles was at the center again, as the music was changing.

A refreshing neo-boppian style was emerging, as almost the anti-dote to the commercially watered down "Cool," which made stars of mostly white musicians. It was the so-called West Coast Jazz that gave us Chet Baker, Shorty Rogers, Bud Shank. Dave Brubeck rode in on that wave, and a new popularity was achieved by estimable musicians like Gerry Mulligan, Lee Konitz, Lennie Tristano, who were first-rate jazz soloists and composers in their own right; whose cool was stylistic, not commercial.

During this next period Miles did make another important record with Konitz (1951), including George Russell's jaggedly hip *Ezzthetic*. But his main thrust was the classic "hard bop" recordings with J. J. Johnson, Walter Bishop, Curly Russell, Art Blakey; a new record with Bird and Max, plus fantastic dates with Sonny Rollins, Bennie Green, Percy Heath, Roy Haynes, ("Morpheus," "Down," "Blue Room"); with Tommy Potter, Kenny Drew ("Half Nelson," "Tempus Fugit," "Move") and later Philly Joe Jones, Horace Silver ("Weirdo," "It Never Entered My Mind").

Lucky Thompson and Rollins were on the historic *Walkin* session, combining the Pres tradition (Lucky) as well as the Hawkins tradition (Rollins). A contrast that spells out the musical symmetry of Miles's playing and composition. The melodic elaboration as well as the use of time/space as statement.

295

Miles's debt to Pres, Lester Young, must be acknowledged, laying back off the rhythm, commenting on it as well as riding or floating above it.

Walkin was so marvelous, and a conceptual predecessor to the *Kind of Blue* music, e.g., "So What," because it used bop accents to make exciting a very cool, insinuating, even subdued melodic/rhythmic line. It carried a lyrical tension—as if we did go strolling up or across town, for instance, digging everything we could.

This was *urbane* music, precisely sophisticated. The coolness of the early fifties was giving way to a stomping sound, people marching; the assertion of gospel music and Africa expanded the music stylistically. These developments in the music coincided with a rising national consciousness among the African-American people characterized by the Civil Rights Movement.

Miles thinks this music, more so than the Bird-Gillespie style, is more a New York style. What we think of as the classic forties BeBop, Miles says he thinks is a transported Oklahoma style. He mentions Ben Webster and Ben Pruitt, who "played like Monk. There was a St. Louis trumpet player [Little Dips?]. I used to emulate Buddy [Anderson] in B's [Billy Eckstine] band, not just the Kansas City style. I used to dig Stoggie Gibson on trumpet. He had a round and fat sound, but fat alone won't do it."

Horace Silver introduced contemporary gospel into post-bop jazz. Its national identity called *Soulful*! DuBois pointed out in *Souls of Black Folk* the centrality of music to black worship, *Christian or Animist*.

The *funk,* smell, essence, slavery, segregation, and the dream of freedom! The real actual lowdown world. Roots, these are. The reestablishment of the primacy of the Blues, the feelings and lifestyle of black people! Africa, syncopation, Saints and Devils. The reemergence of the black vocal sound, the scream, the honk, the sound of abrasive reality. Consciousness in a black sector of the world.

Horace along with younger protegés like Bobby Timmons, plus the Max Roach-Clifford Brown-Sonny Rollins quintet; Art Blakey and the Jazz Messengers, the reemergence of Thelonius Monk. "Hippy," "The Preacher," "Moanin," "Dat Dere," the simple bebop-gospel mixture. Plus the sophisticated music that Miles made "Take Off" and "It Never Entered My Mind," "Blue Haze," "Solar," "Airegin," "Oleo," "Doxy," "But Not For Me," "Blue and Boogie," "Bags Grove" with Milt Jackson, Monk, Bemsha Swing. These are the Philly/New York players, Brown from Delaware, the northeastern ghetto blues. The Black Experience was raised as a principal and unique social, historical, and aesthetic experience, which is where "Funky" comes from.

It was a quick funky music, with a sharper eye on arrangement, in response to the "cool," but there is a free screaming, rhythmic emphasis to this music, even whispered! Miles became its most sophisticated master.

Miles's life and times combined to enable him to reassert his genius at a higher level. He was now a leader, not just a sideman. As well as an innovator and creator of a distinct trumpet and musical style. Whatever the context, his own voice was strengthening, growing more authoritative and self-referencing.

Miles here develops a new black post-bop, post-cool ensemble and solo style. He's laid back yet hot. Reserved yet funky. Melodic yet tense and searching.

It is his ability to balance in aesthetic "perfection" the contrast, contradiction, struggle, and unity of the Pres/Cool/ever-lush harmonic bottom aspect of his music and the Bird-shaped dazzling aggressive fire and rhythmic dominance that makes the next few years of Miles's work a measure of *all* the music of that period!

The appearance of Red Garland, Philly Joe Jones, and most importantly, John Coltrane, shaped the heaviest elements of "The New Miles Davis Quintet," formed in 1955, the same year Bird died.

In this period of rising black political consciousness, *soul* (blackness, negritude, etc.) and its expression *funk* (the heat, "odeur," of basic blues, and like jass also connected with *sex*) emerges. Jass (Jassm and Jism) is literally ejaculation music. "Funk" is the "smell" that goes with it, a piano drawling with blues reclaims its ancient "frenzy," the hard bopper (funky bopper, i.e., new and blue, and reemphasizing the rhythm almost at times to a back beat—you could dance with a tambourine to it) is the Preacher, driving the music and the congregation with the music into a mutual frenzy.

Blakey's Messengers were and remain a university of funk through which some of the hottest and bluesiest young musicians have passed. Especially people like Horace Silver, Bobby Timmons, Hank Mobley, Lee Morgan, Wayne Shorter. They were major influences. The incredible Brown-Rollins-Roach groups were perhaps the most sophisticated and heatedly lyrical of the bringers of the harder sound. This is a period of Rollins developing his long orderly logical extended improvisations and West Indian influences.

Miles's view that Hard Bop was the real New York music, the classic early Bop a southwestern style identifies the Caribbean, West Indian, Latino contributions, and the gospel inflection as part of an authentic New York style that emerged with Rollins, Blakey, Roach, and the rest.

Rollins's magnificent *Freedom Suite* reflected the stylistic and philosophical content of the times. Plus Max Roach's *Freedom Now Suite* with Abby and Max cooking at white-heat intensity and celebrating the intensifying African Liberation struggles. Mingus's *Fables of Faubus* took dead journalistic aim at real stuff as the times themselves spoke to the struggle against American apartheid. By '54 *Brown* v. *Topeka Board of Education* supposedly ended 1897's "separate but equal," and by 1957 a new hero named Martin Luther King had transformed Rosa Parks's personal resistance to Montgomery bus segregation into a national democratic movement!

Monk's *Brilliant Corners,* with Monk in the red wagon behind the shades, drew together the earlier, more experimental BeBop with the funky later music (Trane and Hawkins on the same sides).

Miles mentions the fantastic groups he worked with during the period. One particular stretch he worked with Trane and Rollins. "We did a concert uptown for Paul Robeson. Doug Turner Ward [founder of Negro Ensemble] helped put it together.

"I used to tell them, the bass got the tonic. Don't play in the same register as the sax, lay out. Don't play."

These seem very appropriate stylistic caveats for the group that Miles put together now that took the finger-poppin' urban funk blues of the hard bop era and combined it with a harmonic placement conditioned by Miles's need for a cushion, plus his gorgeous melodic invention. It was called simply *The New Miles Davis Quintet.* It caused a sensation among jazz people.

It was funky and sophisticated, swung hard, at the same time being wispily lyrical. During the fifties years, Miles in a bop or hard-bop context, and finally in his symmetrically exquisite quintets and sextets with Trane, later with Trane and Cannonball ('57–'59), and in the fresh and lyrical Gil Evans collaborations created music at a level very few people ever approach, anywhere, anytime.

It is this music, from the raw funky and exhilarant sides like "Dig" or the interracial experimentation of "Ezzthetic" or the street-hip "Dr. Jackle" to the exciting maturity of "Straight No Chaser" or "Bye Bye Blackbird," to the moody symphonic lyricism of *Porgy and Bess,* or the new music minimalism of *Kind of Blue,* Miles created at a level and on a scale that needs a Duke or Billie or Armstrong or Monk to equal for aesthetic influence, length, and consistency.

This is also a period that Miles's own mystique gets somewhat reshaped. In the post-cool period Miles had begun to live hard in the ghetto, a condition particularly depressing because he also addicted to heroin.

From the drape-suited, gas-haired "cat," the Harlem music, particularly "Dig" and "Walkin" and "Dr. Jackle," complete with Miles in pulled-down "black boy" hat and better-fitting Italian and Ivy threads, gives Miles the "down" quality of the time. *Down,* the current parallel word for hip. Like Robert Thompson has said of Kongo culture, it prizes "getting down," bending the knees and elbows. It also favors "cool" as subtle fire.

But now, too, the political sweep of the times meant one had to be down with the people, to be in touch with one's roots. The gospels and the blues were part of these roots. The music of this period is superbly funky and bluesy.

Miles even had the unfortunate but spiritually "in tune" experience of being jumped on by racist policemen outside Birdland when he tried to take a "breather" in between sets. Black newspapers called it a "Georgia head whippin," placing it squarely (1957) shoulder to shoulder with the beatings black civil rights marchers were receiving marching against segregation and "Jim Crow."

In a sense Miles embodied a black attitude that had grown steadily more ubiquitous in the fifties—defiance, a redefined, contemporary function of the culturally traditional *resistance* of blacks to slavery and then national oppression.

I stopped drummer Steve McCall, one of the elder statesmen of the new music, a few days after I'd talked to Miles. "What's Miles make you think of?" I asked.

"When I think of his influence, I think he's had a positive influence on black people in general. He transcended the slave mentality. I remember when he was setting all kinds of styles. The artist. He had class. Good taste. His music had a density."

So Miles was not only the cool hipster of our BeBop youth, but now we felt he embodied the social fire of the times. All the musician-hippy stories about Miles told us he was "bad," that people, including the pó-lice, didn't mess with Miles.

We knew Miles went to the gym all the time and boxed. We had even been close enough a couple of times when the Quintet opened at the Bohemia in the Village, to hear the hipster fog-horn bass that was his voice. That was the way Miles was supposed to sound. It was hip—somewhat mysterious with a touch of street toughness.

John Coltrane's tenure with Miles Davis helped produce some of the finest music played by anyone. Just the torrid classic *Cookin, Relaxin, Steamin, Workin* sides and the amazing and beautiful *Round About Midnight*—all these albums done in one year (October '55–October '56)—reveal Miles as a confident master having assembled a musical organization that was, during that period, without peers.

Trane, a rough-toned saxophonist from North Carolina, grew up,

299

especially musically, in Philadelphia. The son of a tailor-musician, Trane later worked in Philadelphia factories and learned BeBop in a Navy band. He had a background not only of spirituals and musical religious frenzy, but a more recent history of honking rhythm and blues, often while walking the bartops of Philly. He had played with Big Maybell, 3 Bips and Bop, and later Jimmy Smith and the Dizzy Gillespie big band. There is a fantastic flick of Bird and Miles on the stage at Birdland, while in the background a very young and slightly nervous-looking John Coltrane.

Miles's darting blue flashes and sometimes limpid lyricism were now placed in tandem collaboration with the big densely powerful song of Coltrane. If Trane's early efforts seemed crude and not quite articulate to some, the feelings and aesthetic bearing his playing carried caused quite a few hip people to pick up on Trane very early.

It was Philly Joe Jones who urged Trane on Miles as a replacement for Rollins. A vibes-playing roadie of mine in the early fifties had heard Trane somewhere and described him even pre-Miles as "a genius."

In some superficial ways Trane was similar to Rollins, except when Trane sounded most like Rollins he was just beginning to sound like his real musical self, which came a little later. Both possessed large dominating blues-filled honking tones, but Trane tore into the bulk of his sound to investigate ceaselessly the fundamental elements of timbre and harmony, combining complex rhythmic insistence with seemingly endless melodic and harmonic invention. John Coltrane was not just a great tenor saxophonist, he was an *innovator*.

That is the real secret of the classic Quintet and Sextet music of Miles Davis in the fifties and sixties—not only is there the Davis direction and innovation, but he carries with him as one part of his fantastic arsenal a "straight-out murderer," as we used to say, John Coltrane.

Trane gave Miles a balance that allowed his purple whispering lyricism to still touch the raw funky sidewalks. But Trane was not only "street," he was intense and searching. What Miles implied, the tension his silence and placement of notes created as an under feeling, Trane readily and openly proclaimed. Trane was a wailer—a throwback to Big Jay McNeely and Illinois Jacquet of the howling fifties. The sound of shouting and screaming, whooping and hollerin', crying and singing. Coon-hollers, yells, "Arwhoolies" were all in there, and low-down blues and gospel trembling. Plus, later, Trane carried it all back to its righteous source, the "East," Africa, the animist memory.

With the later addition of Cannonball Adderley, a Florida funk merchant in the keening tradition of a more simplified Charlie Parker. Along with Trane and Cannonball, Paul Chambers, bass, Red

Garland, piano, and Philly Joe Jones make up the rest of the immortals, a band as heavy as Louis's Hot Fire.

Miles, when I asked about that band, talked of Cannonball's coming with the group and reacting to the music, "This ain't no blues. Trane took Cannonball in the back and showed him what he was doin'. Trane be around there suckin' his teeth. I told Trane to show him and stop him from accenting the first beat.

"Bass got the tonic, don't play in the same register as the sax. Lay out. Don't play." The Milesian aesthetic for the group. Miles talked about people playing too many notes. He said when he listened to his own music, "I always listen to what I can leave out."

In one sense he is like Monk with his incisive blue pointillism, but Miles could not dig Monk's "comping" behind him for the same reasons. "Monk don't give you no support." No cushion or easily related-to pattern, for sure.

The quintet and sextet were the most popular jazz group of their time. With them they carried the sound and image of the contemporary urban American intellectual and artist, one that was *Kind of Blue*. The *MilesStones* and *Round About Midnight* albums were great social events as well as artistic triumphs. They confirmed the astuteness of the listener. *Straight No Chaser* was the state of (the) art—any art! *Kind of Blue* led us into new formal and intellectual vistas. (You remember "Green Dolphin St.?")

For me what the Trane-Cannonball groups represented and set up was the direction(s) the music has been moving for almost the last thirty years.

The two reed soloists each summed up certain stylistic tendencies in the music and revived these in more contemporary accents. The funky alto man had been a music teacher in Florida. And his expansive and rotund silhouette was the reason for his nickname.

Cannonball had the sky-highing piercing wail of Bird, but it was not the innovative rocket-sword "Yard" had. Ball's sound was stylistically like Bird, but not out of the deepest *understanding* of that aesthetic, it seemed to me, but a kind of appreciation.

It's what separates all the people who play "like" John Coltrane from really creating the emotional aura Trane did. They pick up the style, the form, but the philosophical and aesthetic mandates, which make that sound necessary, they often miss.

So that I thought much of what Ball played, certainly in contrast to Coltrane, seemed cruelly superficial. But at other times, Trane's thunder and lightning contrasted perfectly with the finally less complex but lilting melodic improvisation of Cannonball.

What is so heavy is that Trane and Cannonball, themselves the two opposing weights of saxophone balance in the classic Davis groups, are also two musical schools coming into being—first as key parts of the whole Davis vision, but later as musical (and philosophical) tendencies in the whole music!

From the Cannonball side of the Davis groups, one got the *pop* aspect of the funk/gospel hard-bop development. (A gospel *nightclub* opened briefly in New York during the same period!)

Ball's glibness and easy humor coupled with a kind of swinging formalism and miniaturism enabled him to create the kind of solos and compositions that would be commercially significant. (Although the *Something Else* album with Miles under Cannonball's leadership is one of the hippest albums released in the period. But it is Miles Davis-like music.)

Cannonball had several jazz hits with his own bands. He had a stylized glib gospel/funk kind of tune that really got over. "Jive Samba" (actually composed by brother Nat), Bobby Timmons's "Dis Heah" and "Dat Dere," Zawinul's "Mercy Mercy." What is seminal in this is that it is Cannonball and the characteristic music and musicians he developed that are the prototypes for the music later called *Fusion*! The combining of jazz lines with Rhythm & Blues rhythms, or tuneful melodies with R & B bottoms.

Joe Zawinul, the major domo of the most successful fusion group, Weather Report, was a Davis/Cannonball sideman—in fact, the majority of the key musicians who created the cool-top blues-bottom music called Fusion are alumni of one Davis group or another. Cannonball's bands were earlier practitioners of the form before it became a style.

The various funk miniatures Cannonball liked to play are one of the prototypes for which came to be known as Fusion, a largely commercial music. But it is Miles who is the real originator of the form. The cool-top/R & B bottom sound, commercial version, is obviously given inspiration by Miles's general approach, particularly as interpreted by Cannonball and his bands.

On the other side of the bandstand of that great band was the great John Coltrane. The music Trane made and wanted to make with Miles's band and after was almost the exact opposite of what Cannonball was doing.

Where Cannonball seemed to treasure the glib artifact, Trane seemed with Miles always in the middle of creativity, sometimes driving Miles buggy because of the drawn-out length of some of his solos. And in these solos Trane searched and thrashed and struggled, always it seemed, looking for higher and higher levels of understanding and expression. Trane was the ceaseless experimenter—Cannonball the pragmatic miniaturist, creator of funky ready-mades.

So that Miles had two guns at his disposal, Trane the expressionist and Cannonball the formalist. These two horns marked the breaking off of two schools of jazz conception. But so powerful and broadly expressive was this classic Miles group that it contained the elements for establishing or redefining two significant jazz styles that have dominated to one degree or another the music for the last thirty years!

Both these styles make use of the blues in very definite but very contrasting ways. Cannonball was bluesy as form, Trane bluesy as essence. Hence Cannon thinking, when he first got to Miles's band, that what the group was playing wasn't the blues. That is, he was looking for the standard twelve-bar *form.* Miles on the other hand, wanted the blues *expressed,* not just as form, but as feeling and color. It was in Miles's band that both players developed as much more mature and forceful soloists.

Miles talked about the two directions Trane and Cannonball represented. In 1959, they had done some eighteen concerts for Norman Grantz in Europe. It was there that Coltrane had picked up the soprano saxophone, his later use of which, beginning with the big hit "My Favorite Things," revived the instrument among jazz players all over the world.

The chordal experimentation and chromatic lyricism Trane began to be identified with, even before he left Miles and which revolutionized the music, Miles casually accepts credit for laying on John. "I showed Trane all that," Miles averred. "Cannonball just played funk. But he could interpret any feeling."

What is important is that Trane's direction and legacy was to redefine avant-garde, to spread the social upsurge in society of the time, which somehow affected *him,* into musical revolution.

Cannonball's direction and legacy was to take the *form* of the fifties bebop, now hard-bop explosion, to include the "new" *gospel* awareness as jazz soul music and new emphasis on funk, and to repeat the classic form of a blues somewhat gospelized. Yet the reason for the upsurge of the blues was as a flag for the popular *social* feeling of the time. Its redefinition, as of that day, had to yet identify the *meaning* of the blues, which is alive and still with us. The *being* of the people, their minds and condition. The awful calamitous circumstance of their real lives.

Cannon's direction is more commercial because it freezes blues as blues form. This is the Fusion phenomenon. Miles's "bottom" is a desired connection, with "America." It can be lush horns, strings, atmosphere, America will always dig *The Birth of the Cool, Miles Ahead, Porgy and Bess, Sketches of Spain,* and *Kind of Blue* (black people and most intellectuals too). But the music that speaks most directly of the black urban experience are the forties Bird sides, "Billie's Bounce," "Now's the Time," "Ornithology," "Anthropology,"

"Donna Lee," "Scrapple from the Apple," etc.; or the fifties hard-bop gems and classic funk/cushion balancing standards "Morpheus," "Down," "Bluing," "Dig," "Tempus Fugit," "Weirdo," "Well, You Needn't," "Walkin," "Airegin," "Oleo," "Bags Groove," "Green Haze," "Dr. Jackle," "Ah-leu-cha," "Bye Bye Blackbird," "Round Midnight," "It Never Entered My Mind," "If I Were a Bell," "Green Dolphin Street," "So What," "Straight No Chaser," and "Kind of Blue." But the hugely successful pieces with Evans are symphonic tone poems, to a certain extent summing up mid-century American concert music. *Miles Ahead* was the giant step, replaying yet extending even further the Evans/Thornhill *Birth of the Cool* concept.

Miles's special capacity and ability is to hold up and balance two musical (social) conceptions and express them as (two parts of) a single aesthetic. The "cushion" Miles speaks of is the luxury, ease, mood, of sensuous well-being this society sports—its lushness and pretension. (How does access to all that sound?) Sometimes Miles's horn alone holds out for this warmth in the midst of fire, e.g., with Bird or the hard boppers or the classic Coltrane/Cannonball sides. But by *Miles Ahead,* Miles understood enough about the entire American aesthetic so that he could make the *cool* statements on a level that was truly *popular* and which had the accents of African-America included not as contrasting anxiety or tension but as an equal sensuousness!

Sketches of Spain and *Porgy and Bess* are high American musical statements; their tension is between a functional impressionism, serious in its emotional detail, vs. mood without significance. It is the bluesiness of the Davis conception even submerged in all the lushness that gives these moods an intelligence and sensitivity. There is yet a searching quality in Miles's horn, above, beyond, below, inside, outside, within, locked out of the lushness, the lovely American bottom. It is a searching, a probing like a dowser, used for searching out beauty. Miles's horn itself is so beautiful, except there is a feeling in us that maybe all of this is a dream. A film. An invisible pageant of feeling. *Miles Ahead, Sketches,* and *Porgy* are great movie music. But add them as well to a native U.S. impressionism brought here on Duke's back that is linked as well to Debussy and Delius and Ravel.

Kind of Blue is the stripped-down recombining of the two musical tendencies in Miles (the American and the African-American) to where they feed each other like electric charges. Here the mood, the lush, the bottom is also *sketched.* Miles has discovered chords and the implied modal approach that link up object and background as the same phrase and note. *Blue* is not contrapuntal, it is pointillistic, yet its dots and its backgrounds are the same lines flowing together.

The harmonic bottom of Miles is sometimes translated as Eastern drone, what Trane later made even further use of. The drone here is that the chords link up, continue each other like a single modal insistence.

Miles's penchant for minimalism has gone back to his earliest music. It is the "fill-in" quality we remember with Bird. Only the essentials. Bird's ever-flowing elaboration must have consolidated in Miles the need to try to fill the "other" space (Bird did not fill). So that throughout Miles's playing days he has always cautioned his sidemen against playing "too much."

Miles says when he listens to his music he is listening for "what can be cut out."

Max Roach was as young as Miles during the BeBop revolution. He was another of the genius teenagers to hook up with Charlie Parker to help create the explosion of Bebop. Max's seriousness and integrity over the long haul are unquestionable. And while it was rumored back in the sixties that Max was critical of Miles, the master drummer responds directly and with no diversion, "Miles just shows several aspects of being creative. If you're being creative, you can't be like you were yesterday. Miles exemplifies it. The record industry keeps reading us out—but Miles will step out. Lester Young did that . . . always looking. It's the law of everything. Miles is that way . . . Ella and Miles breathed new life into the record companies. I think what Miles is doing is in keeping with our creative people today."

By 1960 Miles had created a body of music that could compare favorably with any in jazz. He had come in with BeBop, innovated with Cool, got down with Hard Bop, and put together his symphonic excursions into contemporary American music with *Sketches, Miles Ahead,* and especially *Porgy and Bess.*

It is fitting that *Kind of Blue* closed out those intensely creative years, because it sums up Miles's major musical tendencies as well as indicates what new roads exist not only for him, but for the music generally. Bass great Reggie Workman calls Miles, "an important figure. He contributed a lot to our music. More than just stylistic." Laughing, Reggie goes on, "a typical Gemini. He's got strong convictions. You can hear in his art forms. He's a great person. A real wonderful person."

Both Coltrane and Cannonball left the band at this point. In Trane's wake, inspired by him, a whole raging avant-garde arose. People like Eric Dolphy, Pharaoh Sanders, Ornette Coleman, Albert Aylcr, John Gilmore, and thousands more arrived all lit up by Trane's search for a new sound and a new direction. A search that went on openly in Miles's classic bands.

The musicians that followed Trane, Cannonball, Chambers, Jones, Garland with the band reveal exactly in what direction the band, and Miles, were moving. After a series of Trane "replacements" (e.g.,

305

George Coleman, Hank Mobley, Sam Rivers) Miles moved to the next more stable period with Wayne Shorter, Herbie Hancock, Ron Carter, Tony Williams and a music that while not at the overall level of the Trane-Cannonball-Philly Joe years is excellent music, the hip restatement of that classic period.

Just as Trane was identified with and inspired the screaming revolutionary players of the sixties and beyond, Cannonball's direction, as noted, was also significant and also a Miles by-product. Cannon put together a fairly stable quartet during the sixties and made some of the biggest commercial hits in the music—his "Sack of Woe" and "Jive Samba." Joe Zawinul (an Austrian pianist, who later went on to head up the most successful fusion band in the business, Weather Report) while with Cannon's band contributed "Mercy Mercy" again in the formal soul/funk vein. It was one of the best-selling jazz records ever!

The Cannon/Zawinul approach was to take the surface or formal lines of the hard-bop funk/soul renaissance and make popular miniatures out of them. To emphasize the ensemble-arranged aspect of the music while deemphasizing the free improvisation.

What is interesting is that the Shorter/Hancock etc. band that was first noted for its further statements of the Miles classic fifties groups, by the late sixties became the vehicle for Miles's increasing use of the pop/commercial aspect of his own mind. But Miles's "cushion" or "bottom," the "handle" that he speaks of, was always a way for the music to be more accessible to himself as well as the people.

Miles went to Juilliard. Miles's father was a medium-sized landowner and dentist. All that is in his life and to a certain general extent is in his art. But Miles is still tied to the blues, and that emotional aesthetic matrix.

Even in the American symphonic impressionism he created with Gil Evans there is always an echo of the blues. At times, Miles's version of Duke.

After Trane and Cannonball left Miles in '61, the best Miles bands were a restatement of that music. But Miles's classic small-group music of the fifties not only is the state of the art but a signpost of what is to come.

The late fifties civil rights era was marked not only by an increase of democratic struggle against American Apartheid but also with that, as a concommitant benefit of sharpened resistance to segregation and discrimination, there was a rise of black national consciousness, witnessed in one aspect by the attention to "soul" and "funk" (a spiritual confirmation of national identity).

Another aspect of the period's reflection of the people's lives was in its gradually more popular expression of rage (i.e., militance). Much of what later came to be called avant-garde meant particularly to express that rage.

The classic fifties Davis group expressed both the soul and the rage. The restatement Hancock-Shorter et al. does not carry the balance in the same way. Yet Miles says of this period that he was telling the younger musicians he worked with the same thing he had told others, telling them what not to play. What "not to do too much of." Miles in some cases did see the Hancock-Shorter band as a continuation of the classic groups. He says, "Philly Joe liked Tony [Williams] more than any of the other drummers I tried to use. Philly would scare the other drummers. He liked Tony."

Miles's music, by the end of the sixties, had begun to take on a somber (somewhat formal) tone. Expressing various linked moods, but no galloping in abandon. The music became more and more studied. There is some experimentation, but the mood is introspective, even in open-horned romps. Miles had begun the practice earlier of using the Harmon mute. But there was fire behind it. Albums like *Nefertiti,* with the title track droning and gray, gives an indication of a whole period of the sixties for Miles. *Sorcerer* is similar. Miles was still trying to move, as always. Trying to develop new forms, use different materials. There are more recently released albums from the period *Directions* ('68), *Circle in the Round* ('67) that do contain some swinging hip music. But there is also a "gray" quality, a kind of turning inside. At once creating the harmonic cushion new drone or modal form, the fusion-like music Miles has made since then.

But also in the late sixties Miles's music was undergoing still another change. Simply put, it was the gradual rise in "prominence" of the Milesian bottom and the use of electrified instruments once thought to be the exclusive property of rhythm and blues. Also the bottom, or harmonic cushion, at times becomes the dramatic focus of the music. Sometimes the melodic line is a mere doodle or fragment stretched somewhat abstractly over a vamp or repeated chords ostinato line.

The title piece "Circle in the Round" is a case in point. The album *Miles in the Sky* ('68) brings in the electric piano, played by Herbie Hancock (on "Stuff"), who had a Cannonball Adderly-like hit, *Watermelon Man.* Hancock went on, after Miles, to become one of the most consistent stars of fusion. As a matter of fact, all the players in that Davis group of the late sixties became fusion superstars. Another fusion headliner, guitarist turned vocalist George Benson was also on that album.

The new lighter, swifter, more pop-oriented R&B music had also risen to unprecedented popularity in the sixties. Motown's famous lineup, Smokey Robinson, The Supremes, The Tempts, Marvin Gaye et al. had to influence anyone in the period of any sensitivity.

By the time of *Filles de Kilimanjaro* ('68) Miles was moving to change his music and, one would suppose, himself, once more. He was also changing the personnel in the band. White musicians now became more ubiquitous within the Davis lineup; not just for the more or less one-shot recordings Miles had done earlier but as regular personnel within the band. Pianist Chick Corea and English bassist Dave Hollard replace Hancock and Carter on some of the recorded music of the period. Joe Zawinul, now leader of the hugely successful fusion group Weather Report (of which Wayne Shorts is also a member), appears now, and soon guitarist John McLaughlin, who after his stint with Miles put together another well-known fusion group, The Mahavishnu Orchestra. Corea also went on to become leader of another commercially successful fusion group, Return to Forever. At one point all these groups, plus Hancock's group with which he made *Headhunters,* were all making more money than Miles. The albums Miles made when he returned from "retirement" in 1980 (*Man With the Horn, Star People,* and his latest *Decoy*) changed all that! Actually most of the music Miles has made from the seventies has had a growing commercial success.

The album in *In a Silent Way* is in my own mind the beginning of the elaboration of what came to be known as fusion. It is the sound, the approach, the instruments. Miles has come up with a new direction, neither more of what had become "mainstream," i.e., the restatement of the classic fifties' hard bop, but also not the screaming energy music Trane had become the patron saint of.

The music was all rhythm and (harmonic) texture. Fragments of melody drawn out and abstracted over repeated rhythmic figures. In one sense it is mood music, but one cannot quite fathom the mood. It is contradictory, subdued yet bright. Now the cushion has become both drone and soloist—background and foreground seemingly exchange places constantly.

The same year, Miles brought out *Bitches Brew,* which demonstrated not only that his music had changed, but that he was ready to elaborate on the changes. By now even the slowest folks were aware that Miles had made fundamental changes in the music. He had taken the cushion and begun to make it less shifting and diaphanous. The rhythm implications now are clearly R&B-derived.

The music was, like they say, controversial. Since it was no longer an isolated piece or passage in a larger work, but the center focus. What we had glimpsed or speculated about in *Miles in the Sky, In a Silent Way,* and to a certain extent in parts of *Filles de Kilimanjaro* becomes open and aggressive in *Bitches Brew.* That Miles Davis was using straight-out R&B rhythms, a clear back beat, and growingly electrified instruments.

The long passage of the sixties had worked its magic on Miles. In one sense, he was of course moving forward, absorbing, being changed, changing. The Trane-Cannonball band was a kind of starting point as well as a culmination. Trane's fire spoke of revolution, but one other aspect of it led to a kind of black cultural nationalism, atavism, mysticism.

The straightforward rock songs Cannonball made money from signified another aspect of the sixties equation. Their "soulfulness" was their claim to and expression of the popular mood. It was almost like Miles had had a southern SCLC preacher at one saxophone (Cannonball) and a Dashiki-wearing consciousness-raising revolutionary (Trane) at the other.

But the mystic "ooomism" that characterized some of Trane's last efforts could not represent a real direction to the hip Miles. Just as it could not to the majority of political forces of the black movement.

Miles, throughout the sixties and seventies, repeatedly does make homage to Africa. But he is always firmly Black American in his approach. When Miles came out of his conservative neo-Ivy threads in the seventies, it was not for an *Agbada* or *Bubba,* it was for the leather-fringed jacket that the Panther, hippy, flower child might wear. When Trane had given way (dying in 1967) to Pharaoh Sanders as the carrier of the big screaming saxophone tradition, we used to see the music Pharaoh was making as the antithesis of say, someone like Jimi Hendrix (even though Hendrix was an innovator, too.). But the white or "integrated" media-ubiquitous rebellion Hendrix represented was the other side of the social and musical equation. Miles was friendly with Hendrix, but given Miles's background and general experience, it was predictable, perhaps, that he could identify more completely with what finally is the more secular, integrated, and ultimately more popular and commercial consciousness of R&B or Rock or fusion that led him even to the music he is making today.

Miles was rebelling in the late sixties too—his penchant for change predicts it anyway. Any group of pungent Miles Davis quotes will show a deep and constantly expressed Afro-American patriotism. But if Trane & Company were closer, by implication, to the Malcolm X, Nation of Islam, cultural nationalist aspect of the movement, Miles's new changes placed him much closer to the Black Panther Party, in terms of a social metaphor his new aesthetic reveals.

Even the "new" infusion of white musicians on a "permanent" basis in Miles's bands in the early seventies was akin to the coalition politics of the Panthers rather than the isolating nationalism of the cultural nationalists.

English bassist Dave Holland remembers most about Miles and his music "the dignity, self-determination . . . the economy of the music" and Miles's "direct dealing with the musicians."

Keith Jarrett played in the band. Steve Grossman replaced Wayne Shorter. John McLaughlin and Joe Zawinul helped shape Miles's music during the period in a serious way. Despite growing criticism about this stance, for instance bitter criticism of saxist Dave Liebman (as well as of Grossman and McLaughlin), Miles works and records with them as well as with other fusion luminaries like Lonnie Liston Smith, Airto Moreira, and jazz crossovers like Garry Bartz and Jack DeJohnette.

What is clear even now, though, is that Miles carried these players and many many others in *his* direction. The music called fusion that had its high holy commercial success in the seventies is in the main Miles Davis's *creation*. The personnel of his bands during the late sixties and early seventies is a who's who of fusion—i.e., the combining of R&B rhythms (bottom) with a "cool," even languid, top (melody line and timbre).

Interestingly, Miles raised *cool* in the fifties as an expression of his concepts (class) and personality. It was carried to extraordinary commercial lengths by the corporations. In the late sixties and seventies, Miles created *fusion*, a style that also becomes highly arranged and ultra-commercial music in the hands of those same corporations. But that style, as well, seems one natural expression of certain of Miles's own personal and conceptual predilections.

Miles was a very young Turk in the BeBop revolution; he was a consistently amazing master in the Hard Bop reexpression of those musical ideas.

The late sixties–early seventies change that brought fusion and the "jazz-rock" of the eighties was occasioned by Miles's feeling that new stones needed to be turned, that he had reached the end of one road. And that all around him people were doing the same thing; speaking in the same language, a language that Miles helped to perfect. But now that language had a host of diluters, and a myriad of maddening clichés. Miles's need for both a "cushion" and a "handle" in the music, plus a stance made understandable by sixties black populism, produced both Miles's fusion and the music he is making today. What should also not be left out is the fact that Miles was not only excited musically by the impulse to make such changes, but there is a social element that made the inclusion of the soi-disant soul, R&B, funk, rock elements seem like a way of finding access to a much larger black audience! At least as far as Miles was concerned, one should not gloss over the idea that Miles could also dig there were probably ways to paraphrase Diz, more money to be made in that direction as well.

But by 1975 Miles had dropped out of sight, neither recording nor touring. By the time of his "cooling out," which lasted from 1975 until 1981, Miles had made still more personnel changes—now adding a permanent electric bass and guitars with the music, like Mike Henderson, Pete Cosey, Reggie Lucas, Larry Coryell, and some of the young players like drummer Al Foster, who is still with him, or percussionist Mtume, who went from black cultural nationalism to blue movie top forties funk (e.g., see song titles in Miles's 1974 *Get Up With It:* "Dark Magus," "Moja Wile Tatu Nne," i.e., titles using Swahili numbers or names "Mysha"—or in *Big Fun* titles like "Red China Blues," "Calypso Frelimo," "Zimbabwe"). But musically these sides seem less than dynamic or striking—it's like Miles had got to one of those places in his life and head where he was ready to change up again.

He stayed off the scene because he was recuperating physically (even though he still has some health problems) and because, to paraphrase Miles, he just didn't feel like doing much musically. In reflection, Miles moves smoothly from one period to another in his life and music. Commenting on this personality, that music, various incidents, some with social, some with aesthetic implications. But there is a sense that Miles has thought about it all, his own motion and even stature in the music many times. And that he is constantly evaluating and summing up.

A quiet, soft-spoken, even gentle man with a bright and quick sense of humor, Miles does not appear to be the overbearingly hip ogre some have made him out to be.

He banters with the various waiters at the United Nations Plaza Hotel, all who seem to know him well. One has been promoted to afternoon maître d' and he glows proudly, saluting Miles for having predicted his ascension.

Miles is eating poached salmon and drinking Perrier. Wherever one goes in the jazz world or the art world, one knows Miles. One could not be a contemporary intellectual and not.

Drummer Billy Higgins: "I'm glad to see him."

Pianist John Hicks: "Miles always been an inspiration. I heard him when I was in St. Louis. He always had strength as an instrumentalist. He can be churchy, but he's a lyricist."

Ahmed Abdullah and Butch Morris, two young trumpet players, are sitting with Hicks at the Village's Sweet Basil: "Brilliant—a perfectionist," smiles Ahmed. "Unique," agrees Butch Morris. No young trumpet player could escape Miles's reach.

New star trumpeter, Olu Dara tried to sum up Miles's concept and contributions. "Miles bridged the gap to both Americas. He's hip to the whole culture here. He is playing it in his music. Miles was dealing with all that America had to say. He makes you a true American. He's off the Mississippi River [a reference to Miles's birthplace, Alton, Illinois, near East St. Louis]. He's like the center of the pendulum. He goes where the history is—east, west, north, south. He's a consummate musical scientist.''

Miles is talking about concerts he's played and how "You can't b.s. a black audience. You got to play the blues. I heard this black woman sitting in the first row saying, 'When is he gonna play the blues?'''

There is a sense to Miles both in print and in person of a person not only anxious to be appreciated and celebrated by blacks but sensitive to the tragedy of race in America, particularly as it relates to his musical and social life. His various run-ins with police, his bouts with the critics, mostly white, particularly their opinions over the years about his playing. (The music magazine, *down beat* once had to rewrite their reviews of the Bird-Miles records because the original reviews were uniformly negative, therefore idiotic.)

Yet, in his approach to his own life-music, Miles is not nationalistic, though fiercely in search of democracy: "I don't pay no attention to these white critics about my music. Be like somebody from Europe coming criticizing Chinese music. They don't know about that. I've lived what I play.

"How come they don't let you write reviews about the music?" he was saying to me, musing about the social-aesthetic contradictions of American life. He was offering me a small tape deck with a recent performance at Newport with saxophonist, Bob Berg. We talked some four hours at the United Nations Plaza Hotel.

Driving Miles to his midtown-west destination, he spoke to my wife Amina and me about Cicely Tyson, the well-known black actress (perhaps the best-known black actress in the United States), who is also Miles's wife. Cicely was at their spot in California. Miles moves as easily back and forth across the country as he does through the years in his conversation.

Miles and Cicely go back a ways, as friends and confidants. Though their marriage is more recent. "We were talking about Cicely doing more scripts by black writers and people like James Baldwin." Though her presentation of Earnest Gaines's *Miss Jane Pittman* was extraordinarily popular in its TV production. "She looks at a lot of scripts. She gets a lot of scripts." Miles described a recent long-distance phone conversation with Cicely. One could hear an open funny relationship formed on the basis of deep feeling and respect—one could imagine their words, hot and cool, sliding back and forth across the country. Miles himself was leaving for the coast in a few days.

A week or so later I looked at a tape of Miles's new video, *Decoy*, and a TV interview. Both gave aspects of Miles's abiding passions and his most recent pursuits. "I'm doing a video because I can," he said at one point on the tape. The video of *Decoy* was Miles as he is when playing, somewhat exaggerated in his gestures, his tongue pushing out the way he does after playing sometimes; it seemed he was being whirled slowly in place with computer graphics much like his own spare drawings, bouncing out of his horn.

Miles's own original concept for the video had been more theatrical and dramatic. "I wanted to show what a Decoy really was." But a simple and probably less expensive company-suggested video was put together. "It's OK," said Miles.

The TV interview was sparkling and funny. Miles talked about the difference between white and black musicians. How he "went with his feelings" in playing. How much he loved music. "I always play the blues . . . my body's full of rhythm. I like broken melody—strong melody—smooth voicings on the piano. Chords—I use the synthesizer DX 7—whole other attitude. It's like sketching." And the camera showed us Miles pursuing another of his passions, drawing and painting. When we spoke earlier he mentioned how much he liked Anthony Quinn's work. Now Quinn wanted one of Miles's strange colored stick figures—examples on the cover of *Star People* and on the inside jacket of *Decoy*.

Miles spoke of playing "today music" and elsewhere of requiring his young musicians, no matter "their training, to learn to play 'social music.'" Miles's *Bitches Brew* and *Live/Evil* made clear that that social music was related in Miles's mind to blues, specifically rhythm and blues, and even rock (i.e., the white adaptations of R&B).

What is interesting is that Miles came into prominence just as the music was being "separated," as the musicians say. The big jazz bands of the twenties and thirties always had blues singers. The KC blues shouters like Jimmy Rushing were identified with big bands, like Joe Williams with Count Basie. Even when Mr. B, Billy Eckstein, had his hippest bebop-oriented big band, he would belt out blues anthems like "Jelly Jelly." But the bop era saw blues, like rhythm and blues, go one way and the jazz groups, though the best must always be blues-oriented, use blues in the music rather than being "blues bands."

One reason for the seeming compartmentalization of African-American music was that now there were more people playing the music, middle-class blacks, whites, etc., who did not necessarily grasp the essential continuum and coat of many colors that the *whole* of the music is. Jazz *is* impossible without blues. Jazz is blues' child, Langston Hughes told us.

But commerce "freezes" life into marketable categories. And an artificial separation is concretized by the demands of corporate marketing as well as the sharpening class divisions among the African-American people.

Miles has been trying of late to reconnect jazz, the most advanced

313

black musical form, with its most popular and commercial forms, blues and rhythm and blues. There has been a great deal of outcry from people who dug classical Miles, saying the music Miles has been making since *Bitches Brew* has been "sell-out" commercialism. There is no doubt Miles does want to make a popular music. He is concerned that his music reach and be appreciated by black people. He has said quite a few times in print that this is the only way it will last.

But one thing the most astute observers can see or hear is that Miles is not himself changed in essence. Reggie Workman pointed out that Miles is doing the same thing, he's just using the electronics to reach people. "Miles's music is what he's always been playing. He's surrounded himself with electronics as a mediator between himself and today's market."

Miles says of *Man with the Horn* and *Star People,* two of the albums released after his "unretirement" in 1981, "They're just records." But it's clear that *Decoy* represents something else again. What's also clear to many Miles watchers is that *Decoy* is so much better than those earlier versions of his most recent "social music" because Miles is getting his "chops" back.

The trumpet is a notoriously taxing instrument. As "pretty" as Miles is, he still has the characteristic big knot on his lip from years of wailing. One cannot lay off that horn and then just pop up crackling. *Decoy* is so much hipper than the first two albums because Miles is playing stronger, and the quality that Reggie Workman spoke of is piercing through the electronic environment more tellingly—i.e., Miles "himself."

"What can you say about Miles?" Rouse added. "He's doing what he wants to do."

New bone man Craig Harris put it this way, "Miles survived. He kept his mind open. He understands business and he's doing what he wants to do. Miles don't care who agrees or disagrees with him. Miles says, 'This is what I'm gonna do.' And he sticks by his guns. And everybody follows Miles."

Miles and his Columbia publicist had talked about the fantastic response audiences had been giving Miles's playing of rock queen Cyndi Lauper's "Time After Time." A few days later, I went to a recording session in which Miles was to put the final touches on the piece. The one tune will comprise the whole album.

Listening to Miles's version of Lauper's tune, there was no way I could connect it with the dizzy-looking punk girl I was looking at on the cover of *New York* magazine.

But jazz has always been able to do just that. Take any kind of anything and transform it via the jazz concept and performances. So we can get a "My Favorite Things" from John Coltrane and never think of Julie Andrews. Miles's "Time" had mostly ditched Lauper as well.

Miles is overdubbing his solo against a tape of the rest of the band. He experiments with the mute, then with open horn. A playback, and he winces at the fluffs and off intonations. The band tape is played once more with an "eternal" kind of "patness." Again Miles addresses it with his horn and the wizardry of technology.

When there is a short break Miles, in cap and dark glasses, whacking on gum, "Stop it when I start fucking up . . . OK."

Open horn . . . sounds good . . . but . . . Miles's hand is raised. "Sounds sharp . . . Go where we left off." Miles fits right into the taped rhythm. His hand goes up again. "Go back." A few runs. Miles calls to the engineer, "Bob . . . you hear when I doubled the melody?" The engineer answers in the affirmative. "It's nice," Miles responds. "I'll keep it."

Miles in suede-skin "Guinea slippers," silk-mixture pants, the gold-headed cane Jimmy Baldwin says Miles handles like an accoutrement of his cool, with not the slightest reference to his *needing* it to walk. "Miles is a very beautiful person," Jimmy added, "all the way deep down—no pretension."

Miles is waving his cane and gesturing now, listening to a playback with some of his younger musicians who are in the studio. It is a sweet melody, this version of "Time After Time," repeated as a vamp (suggests a modal ostinato flavor) with Miles's classic song quality. It definitely puts me in mind of a kind of hip "mood music," but now I can hear underneath a reggae beat. "Ohhhhhhhhhhhhh, shit," Miles drawls, at a fluff. "Go to the tag."

Young electric bassist Darrell Jones is called on to dub in a stronger reggae flavor. Miles didn't think the tracks had enough of the reggae, so he gets Jones to boot it up a little as they had done live. Lauper's "Time" was a simple ballad; Miles has created a Milesian funk-ballad with a sly insinuating reggae float to it. There's no doubt in this listener's mind that the side will be a killer commercially, and it is very lovely music.

George Butler explains to us that the record will be out in maybe ten days. Columbia is letting no moss grow on the concept.

Miles is standing in front of the young brother on bass with his cane, gesticulating, a bouncing conductor, demonstrating he wants still more reggae, a *sharper* reggae feeling as the music is dubbed. He bends deep, at the waist, to indicate the level of reggae funk he wants. When it's over, he slaps the bassist's hand. Real joy dominates Miles's finely sculptured black face.

As Miles's chops get stronger his "rock" becomes more "legitimized," because he sounds more like himself and the background, any background, simply a contemporary "cushion" to show off M.D.

Miles is pacing. He comes into the booth with Jones to listen to the playback and simulate the mix they will use on the record. But finally he decides to do another take. Miles is playing a black trumpet. He also has a blue trumpet at the ready. "Try not to stop him, Bob," Miles calls to the engineer. The other track had been recorded three weeks ago. But whatever, listening again to the soft reggae, soft rock blues ballad, it is the music Miles has always made.

As master drummer Art Blakey said to me, "Even if he was with Okiedoke and the Salt Shakers, Miles can play. He doesn't have to prove anything, he's already proved it."

Like Craig Harris said, "Miles is gonna do what Miles wants to do. And everybody else can follow, if they feel like it."

I talked to another giant of the music about Miles, Philly Joe Jones, a stalwart of the classic small band of the fifties who echoed most of the other musicians, but like Philly J's own personality, his answer was more emphatic: "Miles," Philly said. "Oh man, Miles is one of the great motherfuckers. One of the geniuses. I know what he's doing regardless of what he seems like he's doing." Philly Joe went on illuminating recent Miles, but actually, for me, Philly Joe had summed it up aptly and succinctly, "one of the great mother fuckers."

When Miles left the record session, my wife and I drove him midtown west where he was staying. He talked to us on the sidewalk for a few minutes. "Go listen to the music," he was saying as he turned to split. "Yeh, check out the music."

Class Struggle in Music

Class struggle in music is class struggle in the society, where the music is coming from anyway.

The creators (of the music) are/have been in the main the Afro-American workers and small farmers (particularly early blues). There has always been a sizable sector of the black middle class contributing to the creation of the overall treasure chest of black music. But the mainstream has obviously been produced by the black majority.

This has been the case traditionally, historically. What has changed? (1) The wider class divisions that came into the Afro-American community with the greater wealth that came into that community with World War II and again in the sixties—two periods of sharp black "upward social mobility" catalyzed by the struggle of the black majority; (2) the impact the creations of the black middle class have had since the 1940s on black music and inside United States culture generally.

Both aspects of this changed condition of black society (in the relationship of the black nation to the larger society) result from economic changes that create social motion. The dialectic of this situation, though, will show that World War II itself, on one level a struggle between imperialists, was also an anti-fascist war. The mobilization by U.S. imperialism involved employing black people at higher levels in the job market. (This happened also as World War I approached. It was this political/economic catalyst that helped move millions of African-Americans out of the South and into the North; and moved those same millions from farms and small towns to factories and big cities—the Harlem Renaissance is another result.)

The forties and sixties are more germane to this discussion of recent developments in the music, but part of the same general social (etc.) motion. By the end of the sixties what was clear is that there was a whole sector of black petty bourgeoisie who had grown to maturity increasingly disconnected from the main part of the African-American community.

Even today some 89 percent of the African-American people live in black communities. The number that live as minorities in white and other communities is still very small. (96 percent of African-American people are workers, about 3 percent petty bourgeois). Slavery created segregation; its continuation, after slavery supposedly ended, created ghettos.

It was this wider separation that developed between one sector of the black middle class and the majority of blacks that caused the clear and significant emergence of what I call the "Tail Europe" school of black music.

There are now more and more blacks who live outside the middle-class mainstream of the black community. (Even though almost 90 percent of the blacks live in mainly black communities, mostly ghettos.)

This means there are more and more African-Americans for whom "being black" is an *abstraction* that they can relate to or not! A philosophical category they can "adopt" or reject, rather than the normal reality of their lives.

This is especially important if one understands that what has kept the African-Americans out of melting-pot America has been slavery and the segregation that it has projected even into this past part of the twentieth century. Blacks have been *separated* from America as an "untouchable" group, despite liberal hype and official lies.

The general negativity and oppression of this segregation we know, but it is this "nixed from America" reality that has made black music American yet *outside* it, at the same time.

Sidney Finklestein points out in *Jazz: A People's Music* that the "cost" of integration into that mainstream by the Irish, Italians, and Jews, among other European immigrants, was to give up their own cultures for the sake of their hard-won "Americanism." No such melt-down has happened with the African-American people except for a small sector of the petty bourgeoisie. This is what we "see" now with the "Tail Europeans."

Much of what goes advertised as "avant-garde" is simply a regurgitation of contemporary European concert music. It is not *hot*. It does not *swing*. Its references, though sometimes couched in or purporting to raise up African, African-American life, culture, mythology, etc., musically make more consistent references in their own structure and actual musical content, to Europe and its aesthetic.

The fact that someone might be "biologically" African-American means *less* today socially in terms of who they will be in the world. Environment, and finally class identification, define who we are and what we want and will most likely do.

So that in the newest of the "new music" we see a struggle, made operative by the relationship the record companies, club owners, media star makers take toward the various kinds of music and musicians. There is no "equality of dispensation" to the musicians or their music, but rather varying support for this player or style, more for this, less for that, based on the aesthetic of the money owners.

Any personal aesthetic is a reflection, in a general sense, of where one is in society. It is a verification of that place. A signature or abstraction, even made real, of the actual social and philosophical structure of society—ultimately of the economic and political structure and content.

Black music is the music the slaves created, and their children. It is "low down" literally in society. Its players have, from day to day, the *actual* blues—it is not merely "a style."

For the "Tail Europeans," jazz or blues is usually a style, an exotic covering or reference. Their lives are other, and the essence and feeling *in* their music squeals about this.

"White" blues and jazz, as a single admittedly somewhat abstract categorization, is distinguishable in general because it is based on an appreciation or adaptation of the jazz aesthetic. (This is not to say that white players in the appropriate context are not impressive. It is just to insist that just as we can distinguish between German music and French music, we can also distinguish between African-American music and white styles—in the main because they reflect a different aesthetic, reflective of a different *place* [and perception, rationale, experience, etc.] in society.)

So too the "Tail Europeans" reflect a sector of the black middle class (a white sector too) that needs Europe as their ultimate legitimizer and judge of their creative efforts. The official bourgeois culture of the United States still, for instance, must pay homage to Europe in a fashion that raises eighteenth-century colonialism. As if George Washington and them didn't win that war! English departments still larger, in the main, than American Studies.

It is not that we are proselytizing for some "black purity" in the music. Cultural "purity" in anything sounds like backward cultural nationalism of one sort or another. But black music is an actual genre, whose most impressive styles and works have not only been created by the African-American people, but more importantly carry an aesthetic that is generally identifiable. For instance, it *swings* (is syncopated), it is *hot* (intense, rhythmic) even if it is presidentially insouciant. It is blues or bluesy or makes reference to blues (as life tone and cultural matrix, not just as *form,* Martin Williams!) It is improvised, and even its most Ducal arrangements and compositions provide room or allow for improvisation.

But also its sound, its total art face, carries the lives, history, tradition, pain, and hope, in the main, of the African-American people, not accidentally or as a formal sterile hat tipping, but as a *result,* one significant result of all those categories. The music is one part of black life that identifies it as what it is, African-American.

The music, like the culture, has gathered everything it has moved through, past, or over. It has borrowed and stolen like all cultures and art, specifically from French, English (Irish), Spanish, Native American cultures, all resting on the African, the slave, the freedperson, the segregated and discriminated against.

But its main reference is itself. It is African-American expression, which is historic (i.e., historically accredited) in order to be "deep." As the African-American nation came into being, between 1619 and the beginning of the nineteenth century, coming into existence as the collective product of people who have been (as Stalin points out) "historically constituted" with common language, land, economic life, and psychological development; i.e., common culture.

The Tail Europeans and white players like them want to make black music's principal reference Europe: as its "art flair," its cutting edge. That's why such music generally is not bluesy, does not swing, is not hot, etc. It is, moreover, less funky than Beethoven!

At best this Tail Europe school (e.g., quickly, Braxton, Leo Smith, etc., Anthony Davis, alas, even some of the Art Ensemble and their clones, all of whom would do well to at least give some deference to Sun Ra) is a kind of interesting neo-European concert music. Many of the players suffer from bourgeois elitism that thinks that what they are doing is isolated, for instance, from black folks because it is too "heavy." Right on!

They think if blacks knew what was happening they would dig it. (See reference to *coda* interview with the violinist.) But all middle-class elites think that. However, there is an even colder portrait of some bloods for whom intellectual heaviness must be European. Wow! It is simply one mark of our national oppression.

Of course, such music gets pushed by the pushers (media, corporations, etc.) as what's happening. People like Anthony Davis think those of us who dig JAZZ (dig that) are trying to keep him, them, etc., from including *all* they know—but that's not the case—my own problem is that they seem not to know *enough*. At least on the black side (at least not enough to make it *swing*!).

"All is permitted," to quote Raskolnikov, but what it is is what it is, not necessarily what you *say* it is! What is created can be understood and traced like anything that communicates!

Like we said, way before, most times you get the mood music of an emerging middle class.

Now as this Tail Europe avant appears and gets touted (as "3rd stream" and "Progressive Jazz" or "Cool" before this), its existence predicts or is predicted by the reemerging voice of an authentic hot jazz avant. Just as Bop called forth Cool, and Cool in turn by its attempt at aesthetic (and social, etc.) revisionism caused Hard Bop to appear as its antidote in the fifties, so today as the TE's reached their pinnacle of promotion and prominence the so-called "Avant Gut Bucket," or vice versa, jumped out.

It would seem that young players like David Murray, Arthur Blythe are the spearheads. Ironically, David Murray has been related to the TE's to a certain extent, but his playing and compositions re much hotter dan any of dat.

The group WSQ (World Saxophone Quartet) seems a perfect example of the class struggle going on in the music. In a sense, at its best, this group carries the two aspects of this contradiction and at some point the tension between, say, the funk (i.e., David Murray and Hamiet Bluiett) and the more TE-oriented Julius Hemphill and Oliver Lake.

But often the arch cerebral writtenness of Hemphill's vision caused WSQ to sound more like the typical "TE" group* than was heatful. Murray's octet and big band (and even his string groups) give him the vehicles he needs to begin to fully explore what state-of-the-art absolutely contemporary *hot music* should sound like. His dates at Sweet Basil in New York City confirm this. (Also get *Murray's Steps, Home,* etc.)

Blythe's more "experimental" band with tubas and cellos finally left heat for posture and formalism, but his quartets with John Hicks absolutely smoke.

Henry Threadgill, the de facto leader of Air, is a complex personality, and Air was a very interesting and often exciting and engaging group—but many times it was in the chamber.

But that group also boasted two of the finest instrumentalists of our time, Fred Hopkins, bass, and Steve McCall, drums. The breakup of Air, after some ten years, showed something about the class struggle as well as its resolution on higher levels.

Threadgill's sextet, which has been his main vehicle recently, is a much superior group, hotter and more swinging. The band is obviously influenced by Murray's big band and octets, but it is a positive influence for sure.

It is equally positive to see Threadgill's sextet add to the ranks of the hot, and led by David Murray's groups weight the class struggle to the side of hot jazz. Musicians like Pharaoh Sanders' wildly liberating groups, including John Hicks, Idris Muhammad, Eddie Blackwell; the "new" Sun Ra who now plays anthologies of the classics—Fletcher Henderson, Duke Ellington, Count Basie, Charlie Parker—have as-

*Though by 1986 the group WSQ had grown overall much hotter.

sumed the role already of the great bridge of music history, swinging hotter than ever. John Gilmore and Marshall Allen continue to be amazing players on any scene. These musicians help bulk up the re-emergence of the hot.

Not so strangely many of the TE's when they want to swing, swing over to a Fusion that sounds veddy "white." Earth, Wind, and Fire wipe any of that!

Many of the players in Murray's groups play in Threadgill's sextet, and quite a few of these young players have hard swinging groups of their own. Trumpeter Olu Dara's various Okra orchestras definitely uphold the hot—likewise trombonist Craig Harris (see notes for *Aboriginal Affairs*).

But even so, the legion of anti-jazz publicists will try to raise up the vapid and the tepid, the ersatz and the imitation, just as they always do, pushing the non-hot mood music of a new wave of petty bourgeois TE's. They will also push so-called fusion which is 1980s cool—more ersatz anti-consciousness music, which seeks not only to divert us from the actual, but coopt popular funk on the way in.

The commercial and media prominence of rock (a white appropria-tion of black rhythm and blues) is yet another manifestation of the class struggle. Racism, most obviously, will always see that white musi-cal styles, even those in direct imitation of black styles, are pushed by the official pushers. These are called in the music business, "Covers." (Remember they even tried to keep Michael Jackson off of MTV.)

But there is another aspect to this we should not miss; viz, that because of the separation of people in a racist society, much of the white rock is more commercial by virtue of the fact that the ideas it pushes are less progressive, less injurious to the status quo. There are even many leading punk and heavy-metal groups, in particular, that could be KKK marching bands. (Compare, for instance, the general philosophy of Rap, I should say now, black Rap, not only to white appropriations of the genre but to the general level of ideas in white rock.)

Black rap, a popular child of the hot sixties black revolutionary poetry scene (e.g., Spirit House Movers, Lost Poets—both the original and the later better-known version; Gylan Kain, Yusef Rahman), still carries elements of black democratic struggle.

But commercial carriers must oppose the heaviest rappers for the same reason Mikey Smith said reggae was opposed by the American-controlled stations even in Jamaica itself! In 1984, when *Black Nation* interviewed Mikey Smith, he made the following comments:

Why is it important to have an international perspective?

People live all over the place and different people are feeling different hardship and you suppose to be aware of that so the system does not have you in total ignorance; because then you become passive and reserved and you won't take no action.

So you have to know how to define yourself in this here Babylon. For the final confrontation you have to know who your enemies are.

What are the common issues that face Black people internationally?

Cultural imperialism and political imperialism, that's what face them internationally. Stagnation of our young people so we are reduced to a state of powerlessness. What we must be determined to say is that they not going to destroy I, make I give up, for our life got a sense of purpose.

What path can a black youth embark on who is confused but wants to find their sense of purpose?

Check for history and check for your culture. You have to know where you are coming from to know where you are going, and until you find out that you will always be confused.

Spiritually, what is our greatest dilemma as a people?

Spiritually, the system have we morally bankrupt. We have to redefine ourselves ourself and we can't allow ourself to be governed from their perspective of things. We have to define ourself and our sense of purpose from our own cultural, political and historical perspective. Not by the perspective them hand down because their history is bias. They are liars, they are thieves. They tell us that Christopher Columbus was a great, great man and Burning Spear say Christopher Columbus is a damn blasted liar. So if we continue to read the history books that they write with their biases and continually believe that what them say is so—well we goin' to get fucked!

Poetry book is not the ultimate success of any artist. What the artist should be striving for is to try and create work that is of substantial value to his community. Then, if him find out as he go along to put it down in book form, then it is so. I never particularly think about putting it down in book form because I always think that it's better to hear me than to read me.

323

THE MUSIC

Who inspires you as a poet?

My mother. Then I was inspired by some Black American writers like Langston Hughes. Marcus Garvey played a very important part in my life and Rastafari. Marxism had some effect on me too.

Do you use patois as a political weapon?

No man, is not no patois. It's a Jamaican language. It is the majority language. When you go to Jamaica you don't go and talk English. The people in the street don't talk English but the dominant language that is pushed in the schools is the English language, which is the language of the status quo. The national language is not patois, that sounds derogatory.

What are your plans as a poet/artist?

I am going to put out an LP which I've been dodging for a long time, and a book . . . When I first started to "read" my primary objective was to try and spread the message as far as possible in Jamaica . . . the next is documentation stage and reach a wider international community on issues that affect the oppressed and dispossessed whether they be in London, New York or JamDown.

Is there anything I haven't asked you that you think people should be aware of?

Right now, Rasta man in Jamaica facing a cultural threat. But them (the oppressor) can't win, they can't get us out. The Americans are coming into the country and they want their culture to dominate the indigenous culture. When you listen to the radio station you hear more disco music than reggae music, and that is fuckry . . . you can't have that. But when you come to London you hear a whole heap of Rockers . . . you can't hear that in JamDown, something wrong. So it show you that the establishment have not fully understood . . . or they have understood but are afraid of the consequences that the music can have.

The music will build up people's consciousness because it is talking about the particular social and political happenings in the country and its relationship to black people. So if you don't play certain music on the radio people will never know and will be locked in a certain cultural bind. Now if you put certain music on the radio, people's head-space will open up

and they'll start to see. So if you keep people blind and ignorant it will serve the interests of the oppressor.

Like American music, for example. When you listen to
some of the contents it's love and love and love and boogie-
down and shake-down and more boogie-down. And you don't
hear what's happening in terms of the (racist) "moral majority" in the music. You never hear about what is happening
with the Ku Klux Klan. There are artist who talk about the
"moral majority" and the Ku Klux Klan but you don't hear
them on the airwave. So it can be used a divisive method so
that people just think that it's pure party and shake-down and
boogie-down and everything's all right and everything's great
and have a senselessness as such that reduce people to nothing, naught, zero.

What do you see in the future for Black people in Jamaica?

There is a new movement happening right now in Black people. In the sixties black people have taken a beating and there
was a retreat. But the oppressor has confused the retreat and
think it was a defeat. Now black people voices are coming
back. Black people are getting their energies back together,
and they are talking and saying this thing can't go on no longer
(this is happening in Jamaica now) . . . and very soon there
you are going to hear a tremendous shout. And it is not going
to be just one person but thousands and millions of people
all over the world who will shout out, "Yea, we want to be
free . . ." from your political slogans and all kind of rhetoric,
and your mock ritual of poverty that the politicians issue out at
appropriate times.

Even within the precincts of black popular music (which is always a
form of blues) we can observe class struggle and even the use now of
black "covers" for works or artists the corporations don't want to
push.

The recent surge to mind-boggling celebrity of Michael Jackson was
a carefully orchestrated cover to obscure the great Stevie Wonder, because Wonder had offended the owners by using his art so Won-
der/fully in the African-American struggle for democracy. Particularly
around the battle for Dr. King's holiday!

You could see this coming way down the pike. Not only did Michael Jackson cop Stevie's style (with the production Svengali-ism of
Quincy Jones, part of the *Mod Squad*) but with the injection of new-
wave Rock effects and Michael's complete change of appearance into

an androgynous lama-loving non-threatening wind-up toy for the teeny boppers of all ages, he could be used not only to cover Stevie but revitalize the pop industry which had the bottom drop out of it earlier because they were pushing too many covers and not enough substance. (Three white boys of any description, with no known talent, as long as they dressed or looked funny or had some other gimmick, could get a record asap—but ultimately *Gresham's law* went into effect and the covers just sat.) But Michael Jackson *is* a *great* performer and he can dance his ass off!

Michael Jackson not only sold 49 million copies of *Thriller*—7 platinum records. *Off the Wall,* earlier, had 3 platinums, raising Columbia Records off the floor. He could be used on the fly to try to pump life—figuratively speaking—into Brooke Shields's fortunes.

The sweet irony is that when Michael tried to get a black producer (Don King*) for the Victory tour with his family, not only did the biggies stop this and impose themselves within the profit-making apparatus of that tour, bad-mouthing the tour right up until they could get their paws in, but now they've since tried to pump up the bilious-looking suburbanite, Prince as, dig it, Michael's challenge to the almighty top spot. *A cover for a cover?!*

(Prince, an androgynous colored porno p-rock crossover person with no family or religious restrictions on his merriment, has already had a movie, *Purple Rain,* and loads of ink. But that ain't the mainstream. Plus, like I tolt ya, M.J. can dance his ass off. Prince is clumsy.)

But all this to point out how class struggle, war between classes and their interests, the struggle of ideas, rages within the music world. And, as usual, it is the people versus the bourgeoisie. The *owners* of the music business and their middle managers and scribblers are the people's enemies.

Unfortunately, we do not have the journals and publications and venues (clubs, concert series, cultural and artistic organizations) we need to adequately intensify our struggle against the owners. They shoot their lies and distortions and covers at us from all directions. (Notice how quickly; e.g., music videos, noxious reactionary chauvinist—racial and sexual—non-entertainments.)

The owners know what Confucius meant when he said that the people must not be permitted to hear the wrong music or the empire will fall. The ideas in the mainstream of black music are democratic and revolutionary. They reflect the history and lives of the African-American people. What else, in the main, could they be?

The class struggle in music is a manifestation of our fight for de-

* Indicted since this writing for tax evasion!

326

mocracy opposed by the racist owners of society. Let the work songs and spirituals or Louis or Leadbelly or Bessie Smith or Duke or Lady Day, Bird, or Monk or Trane or Stevie or Sassy play in our schools every day. Let the children hear our history, our traditions, the history of revolutionary democratic struggle—whether black, brown, or beige, or "God Bless the Child" or "Impressions," and watch the radical change. There are progressive ideas in that music. Ideas the keepers of the status quo cannot allow to be spread through society at large, especially not to the people on the bottom, the African-Americans.

That's why the most advanced music in society, African-American improvised music, can only be played very sparsely and selectively and even the R&B stations are winnowed down to a minimum and the music on them pointed mainly at the "non-disruptive" top forties funk-pablum.

A people struggling for liberation even sing about that process. They sing and play that stuff all the time. The opposition to this is what creates class struggle. Dig it!

327

The Great Music Robbery

"Reality/For You/Is Minstrelsy"
—Wise

Although I have talked often about the "cover" and "cooptation" relationship of the bourgeoisie to black music and to black culture in
general, the recent trend in these classic oppressor/oppressed relationships is alarming in much the same way as is the "steady deadly"
move to the right in this country (and in capitalist societies internationally).

Earlier, historically, traditionally, the capitalist relations prevailing
throughout the sixteenth through early twentieth centuries enforced,
first, straight-out "people theft" (i.e., European slave trade and chattel
slavery). The relations in the superstructure would amount to these as
well (reflecting the production relations). Whatever Africans, then African-Americans, did or had, including themselves, could be coldly and
bestially *taken*. But the "contributions" of the black folk were generally denigrated, mostly said not to exist. Niggers were animals—with
neither past nor future—existential genies, beasts of burden, *property*.

By the time the Africans no longer thought of Africa as home and
had become African-Americans, the culture of the United States itself
was *brownish*.

By the end of the nineteenth century, Du Bois documents (see *The
Souls of Black Folks*), there were two centuries of African-American
influence on Western music as well as black creation of an African-
American music (e.g., the work, secular, and "sorrow songs").

Minstrelsy was not a form limited to the nineteenth and early twentieth centuries, it is an *ongoing* form of bourgeois appropriation of
black culture. The irony of the "existential" black being imitated by
the oppressor is both "flattery" and denigration. But the *other ness* of
the black, outside the normative social relations of the order, yet
whose labor, even being, can be appropriated, means that the ridicule
and dehumanization of the minstrel portrait is a put-down but also a
kind of distorted admiration. (All this continues even today, somewhat
altered by modernization.)

Bourgeois thinkers (no matter what class or nationality) see black
life as a caricature of the "norm." When blacks created the Cakewalk

they were caricaturing bourgeois white life (the Cakewalkers are not white workers!). This is because the blacks saw/see bourgeois life as stiff, overelaborated, and pompous.

The white minstrel caricatures black life as ignorant, slow, animalistic, and bizarre—and always funny as hell. Oh, the side-splitting life of the Coon!

"They wild—loose? No morals—morals? Ha. Wild, Loud, Carefree" (a carefree slave?—oh, irony).

"They work all day—fuck all night—dance till the sky lose all moon/light."

It is this distorted legitimization of slavery that the oppressor "imitates." That is, they imitate their own mind! Hey, the cakewalk is a *black* dance!

The significant change in minstrelsy is that it more and more purports to be *real* white life! That is, the half-hip white, certainly as the twentieth century has unrolled, appropriates black style as an *attribute*—the denigration being an automatic function of the social system both existing as different classes (or if in the same class, of different *castes*—since black national oppression means that even the white and black workers are not equally exploited—the working class is segregated vertically, blacks on the bottom and the darker you is the worser off you is!).

So that the former put-down of all that is black, even as one used black labor, has been mitigated to the extent that such social reduction is no longer as openly the case though, of course, the use of black labor and black life is as thorough. But now the minstrel caricature is no longer acknowledged as making fun of the Darkies. This caricature, to various degrees, is suggested as a kind of white lifestyle! (And profitable as a Muh' Fuh'.)

This is legitimate in the sense that U.S. culture is brown (drop a little chocolate bonbon in *yo leche* and check it). It is illegitimate to the degree that national oppression still exists in the U.S. and to the extent that any black anything can be appropriated without exact reciprocal social compensation!

The point being that gradually the strict open condemnation of black life as "inferior" has retreated. We can use the formal mitigation of the legal and juridically based segregation and discrimination as a somewhat parallel indicator of the other changing superstructural condemnation. (The laws once openly stated blacks inferior. Now it is the relationships these laws uphold that maintain the de facto oppression ["inferiority"]).

Just as black music was once loudly proclaimed inferior, derivative, etc., this is no longer so directly stated. Though even now that affirmation can be easily gleaned from the resources and prestige, etc., available to bourgeois European concert music or pop music in contrast to black music. Or merely by casually reading music and art criticism.

So, too, any focus on the state of the African-American people in the United States will quickly confirm to all but the mentally infirm or racists blacks' negative (inferior) position in the society. But such lower status than the mainstream is more de facto now than de jure. (Though R. R. moves inexorably toward restoring the straight-out legal restrictions to black life; e.g., with his Supreme Court racism.)

The more subtle functioning of black national oppression carries with it many not so delicious ironies. For instance, now that the music and the culture are no longer termed inferior or primitive as articles of faith, the notion in the last few years has been simply to *claim* it! The racist line more and more now holds white players, etc., responsible for the high points of the music. The corporations through their media and bourgeois scribblers not only continually push and emphasize the greatness of white musicians, orchestras, arrangements, approach to the music, etc., but more and more each year lay claim to the music's very creation! And, of course, as responsible for most of its excellence.

For instance, Len Lyons in his dizzy white-chauvinist tome *The Great Jazz Pianists* names Joe Zawinul, Jimmy Rowles, Keith Jarrett, Paul Bley, Dave Brubeck, Marian McPartland, George Shearing, Steve Kuhn, Chick Corea, Ran Blake as great jazz pianists! But Tatum, Waller, Bud Powell, and Monk are left out—not to mention Duke Ellington, Willie the Lion, James P. Johnson, etc.

The idea of this is so infuriating because these are not just the opinions a drunken racist at a party might give out. William Morrow published this garbage.

Lyons also wrote another piece of *merde* of late, *100 Greatest Jazz Albums,* full of the same racism in which he lists more records by Chick Corea (three) than Bud Powell (one), one of the innovators of the music. In fact, Corea and Monk have three apiece, Bill Evans has two, John McLaughlin, one, and Benny Carter, zero, ditto Ben Webster! (See "The State of Jazz Writing" or my review of Jack Chambers' book on Miles Davis.)

Recently I watched an WNET program ("Education in Racism") on the Swing Era in which not one black group or musician was featured, although the great Frank Wess sat anonymously as a side man!

We are now told magnanimously that R&B *influenced* Rock & Roll. Whew! My friends, Rock & Roll *is* Rhythm & Blues! We realize Fats Domino, Chuck Berry, etc., could never get as rich and famous as Elvis Presley and company who are written about as if they had actually *originated* something rather than copied.

Europe's genuine regard very early for African-American music (e.g., see Ernest Ansermet on Sidney Bechet or understand the profound influence of the music on Debussy or Duke's specific influence on Ravel, Stravinsky, etc., or the general regard of serious European critics and musicologists for black music back when most U.S. critics said there was no such thing—only the crude attempts of niggers to imitate the good shit).

The consistent, though often otherwise distorted, attitude of the Europeans that the music was important, in fact one of the most important projections of the American culture in general, was an undermining element for U.S. racists' dismissal of black music. It showed such comment as the shallow national chauvinism it was. Delaunay, Dance, Berendt, Panassie, etc., always insisted on the seriousness of the music, although their chauvinism came out in various other obvious ways; e.g., insisting that they could stand as some kind of ultimate aesthetic arbiters and judges of what made African-American culture valuable and when it was not. The dismissal of post-New Orleans style as "fake" by some—the rejection of post-swing, BeBop, and later forms as "non-jazz" or "anti-jazz" was particularly odious. As if black art did not undergo the same stylistic formal or content innovations in different periods as all other art and culture. Though such backward thinking exists in general bourgeois criticism of European or Euro-American art as well. But with European critics of black music (and American white critics as well) it seemed like an attitude linked to colonialism and slavery.

So the Great Music Robbery is, boldly, attempts by the bourgeoisie to claim and coopt, in a growingly more obvious way, black music as the creation of whites. Another irony: Certainly African-American music is, as more and more commentators say, "American music." "American classical music" they say happily. But behind this assertion is no warm welcome of blacks finally as full citizens into the American mainstream (complete with democracy and forty acres and a mule).

No, this late mumbling is another attempt to deny the peoplehood and the lives and history of black Americans. A rip-off from the "left," just as the segregated disregard was a rip-off from the right.

There can be no inclusion as "Americans" without full equality, and no legitimate disappearance of black music into the covering sobriquet "American," without consistent recognition of the history, tradition, and current needs of the black majority, its culture, and its creations.

But this entails a national democratic revolution which in this society is only part of a single upward stroke to socialism. Black music cannot be just "American music" until all Americans have equality and democracy. Otherwise such a term is just more racism.

What makes the Great Music Robbery and rip-off so increasingly effective is that the bourgeoisie now has the means to steal and coopt

331

THE MUSIC

so quickly and feign integration and democracy where mainly segregation and racism still exist.

They can constantly revise the history of this country (and the world) to their own needs. Not only do they retell with lies the history of black music and black people, they mostly hide them. They create starts, movements, pump up certain personalities, debilitate and *cover* others.

The black arts poetry movement of the sixties with its emphasis on the declamatory oral tradition can quickly become "Performance Poetry," with "Performance Poets," dominated by whites.

A guy was introduced to me as a "Body Percussionist," no shit, when what he was was a white dude doing the *Hambone*!

Blondie "raps," there are TV programs and films where only white folks "break-dance." Reggae was thought up by The Police and we know "The Greatest Rock & Roll Band in the World" is spastic Mick Jagger and The Stones.

Black forms are shot back at us with the social stance "fixed," spaded. There are ten break dance movies coming out, and in the totality of their projection black participation will be "movied" into invisibility. Like films and TV generally.

It is the lack of democracy that makes all this criminal. Labor is still being stolen, resources vandalized, and the colored still ain't got nothin' but bad reputations.

From black art alone the African-American people should be as wealthy (literally) as anyone in the United States. What makes the art and music so attractive is its core of democratic longing; inside that music is a cry for equality and liberation, and it is part of its historic beauty and emotional impact.

"Free Jazz" was a battle cry as specific as the civil rights movement. Black musicians struggling to free themselves from the prison house of Tin Pan Alley bars and oppressive, emotionally deadening chords. The parallel in general society should be obvious.

So it has become more and more necessary for the society to fake democracy and equality since U.S. apartheid formally ended. And the hippest of the fakers are in need of democracy themselves! (As a style.)